BACK TO FREUD'S TEXTS

BACK TO FREUD'S TEXTS

Making Silent Documents Speak

ILSE GRUBRICH-SIMITIS

Translated by Philip Slotkin

Yale University Press   New Haven and London

Originally published as *Zurück zu Freuds Texten*,
© 1993 S. Fischer Verlag GmbH, Frankfurt am Main.

The publication of this book has been subsidized by
Inter Nationes, Bonn.
Thanks are due to the Freud Literary Heritage
Foundation (Philadelphia) and the Köhler-Stiftung
(Darmstadt) for substantial contributions to the
cost of translation.

The previously unpublished Freud texts and the
facsimiles are reproduced by kind permission of
Sigmund Freud Copyrights, Colchester.

Library of Congress Cataloging-in-Publication Data
Grubrich-Simitis, Ilse.
　　[Zurück zu Freuds Texten. English]
　　Back to Freud's texts : making silent documents
　speak / Ilse Grubrich-Simitis ; translated by Philip
Slotkin.
　　　　p.　　cm.
　　Includes bibliographical references (p.　　)
and indexes.
　　ISBN 0-300-06631-7 (alk. paper)
　　1. Freud, Sigmund, 1856–1939—Manu-
scripts.　2. Criticism, Textual.　I. Title.
BF109.F74G7813　1996
150.19′52′092—dc20　　96-8117
　　　　　　　　　CIP

A catalogue record for this book is available from
the British Library.

The paper in this book meets the guidelines for
permanence and durability of the Committee on
Production Guidelines for Book Longevity of the
Council on Library Resources.

10　9　8　7　6　5　4　3　2　1

Our prime concern must therefore be to guarantee the maximum of presence and independence for the object of our study [that is, the text to be interpreted], so that its own existence is consolidated and it can offer itself to us with all the hallmarks of autonomy. It must be able to assert its difference and maintain its distance. The object of my attention is not within myself; it lies before me, and I would do well not to appropriate it from the aspect which my desire confers upon it (in which case I should be the prisoner of my own whim), but to allow it to deploy all its properties and particular determinations. So-called objective methods, not yet constituting genuine dialogue, strengthen and augment the material aspects of the object, causing it to stand out in bolder relief, with a sharper outline, and anchoring it to contiguous objects in space and time. A great text will always be surrounded by a plethora of documentation, which, however external or inessential it may sometimes appear, combines with everything which endows that text from within with a distinct personality. After all, if we truly wish to gain a thorough knowledge of the object, we must begin by aiding and abetting it in its ability to resist us.

—Jean Starobinski
"Le texte et l'interprète"

For Spiros

CONTENTS

ILLUSTRATIONS

Thanks are due to Sigmund Freud Copyrights, Colchester, for permission to
reproduce the facsimiles.

Acknowledgments

I should like to express my thanks, first of all, to K. R. Eissler (New York), the cofounder and for many years the secretary of the Sigmund Freud Archives, established in New York at the beginning of the 1950s, who assisted me in my work on Freud from the beginning. Without his decades of ingenious collecting activity, not a few of the documents I present to the reader in the following chapters might well have remained dispersed or even been totally lost. At a time when neither Freud biography nor the historiography of psychoanalysis was on the agenda, it was essentially to his indefatigable and selfless efforts that we owe the preservation of the treasures that will remain the lifeblood of Freud research for decades to come and that will one day also serve the editors of a new large-scale critical edition of Freud as the basis for their work. We all bear him a debt of thanks.

My close collaboration with Ingeborg Meyer-Palmedo (Murnau), which has extended over the more than two decades covering the period of our work on the Freud editions issued by S. Fischer Verlag, bore particularly fine fruit with this book. While it was still in preparation, again and again she helped me with the deciphering of Freud's handwriting and checked my transcriptions. She read the entire original manuscript critically and made countless valuable suggestions. She also compiled the bibliography and the list of Freud titles. For all these labors I am filled with a deep sense of gratitude. I am grateful, too, to her sister, Marion Palmedo (New York), who facilitated my work by undertaking some earlier Freud transcriptions.

Thanks are also due to Mark Paterson, of Sigmund Freud Copyrights (Colchester). Without his generous permission to quote unpublished texts from Sigmund Freud's manuscripts and letters as well as from the correspondences of Anna Freud and to reproduce some facsimiles, this book, with its particular documentary character, could not have appeared. By their kindness, furthermore, Mark Paterson and his archivist, Thomas Roberts, helped to ensure that the most productive use possible could be made of the limited time at my disposal on my various study trips to the Library of Congress.

The same applies to James H. Hutson (Washington), chief of the Manuscript Division of the Library of Congress, where the Sigmund Freud Collection—the body of documents assembled essentially on the initiative of the Sigmund Freud Archives—has found its permanent home. My thanks to him are also extended to his expert colleagues Ronald S. Wilkinson, Allan Teichroew, and Marvin W. Kranz as well as to the helpful staff of the reading room, especially Fred Bauman and Mire Kline.

I wish to thank the following for their help and kind cooperation in specific matters: Heinz L. Ansbacher (Burlington) for providing information about Alfred Adler; Anneliese Arendt and Herbert Bareuther (both Frankfurt) for bibliographic searches; Gottfried Bermann Fischer (Camaiore) for his account of early contacts between S. Fischer Verlag and the Freud family and for permission to quote from one of his unpublished letters to Sigmund Freud; Harold P. Blum (New York), the present director of the Sigmund Freud Archives, for facilitation of my work at the Library of Congress; Erica Davies and Michael Molnar (both London) for supplying copies from the archives of the Freud Museum; Judith Dupont (Paris) for permission to quote from letters of Sándor Ferenczi; Peter Gay (New Haven) for some copies of documents from his abundant research on Freud; Eva Laible (Vienna) for knowledgeable investigations so to speak on the spot; Donald S. Lamm, chairman and president of W. W. Norton (New York), for his help with the attempt to clarify the purpose of the unpublished "Postscript to *The Question of Lay Analysis*"; Veronica Mächtlinger (Berlin) for casting a friendly and critical eye over some passages of my manuscript; William McGuire (Princeton) for promptly forwarding the original text of a letter from Freud to Smith Ely Jelliffe; Margarete Mitscherlich-Nielsen (Frankfurt) for allowing me to quote from letters of Alexander Mitscherlich; Paul Roazen (Toronto) for drawing my attention to reports by Sándor Radó and Theodor Reik on Freud's writing habits; Joan Rodker (London) and Dominique Tiry (Paris) for their contributions to the reconstruction of biographical data on John Rodker; Alfonsa Schmitt and the Alexander-Mitscherlich-Archiv (Stadt- und Universitätsbibliothek Frankfurt) for assistance with my research there; Michael Schröter (Berlin) for information based on his knowledge of the Freud-Eitingon correspondence; Mark Solms (London) for some details from his research on Freud's early neuroscientific writings; and Othmar Spachinger (Vienna) for documentation on the history of the publishing house of Franz Deuticke.

With regard to the present English-language edition, I wish to thank first of all Philip Slotkin (London). I consider it a stroke of good fortune that I was able to secure his services for the exacting task of translating this book. After all, most of the chapters are concerned with subtle nuances of Freud's prose at the various stages of its genesis, and I had initially thought that not a few passages might be virtually untranslatable. In following the progress of Philip Slotkin's work and observing how he took infinite pains to find one convincing and often ingenious English equivalent after another, I learned a great deal about the potential of the English language and the art of translating. I feel immensely grateful to him.

G. W. Pigman III (Pasadena) kindly advised us on the translation of specialized terms in the fields of linguistics and editorial theory.

I should like to express my thanks to Gladys Topkis, senior editor at Yale University Press, for her keen interest in my work and for her determination to publish the English edition of the book on her renowned psychoanalytic list. I am also grateful to Tina C. Weiner, associate director of Yale University Press, for her inspiring support, and to Lawrence Kenney for his expert copyediting.

Last but not least, I owe a debt of gratitude to the Freud Literary Heritage Foundation (Philadelphia), Inter Nationes (Bonn), and the Köhler-Stiftung (Darmstadt) for making the translation possible by their generous contributions to its funding.

Translator's Acknowledgments

I wish to thank the author, Ilse Grubrich-Simitis, for valuable lessons in translation, especially as regards accuracy and stylistic fidelity, not least through her challenging insistence that no iota of meaning be lost, for unflagging help with the subtleties of the German language, and for promptly acceding to all my requests for information; my wife, Brigitte Slotkin, for assistance with recalcitrant German expressions as well as for general support; Jill Duncan and Paula Lavis (Institute of Psycho-Analysis, London), for unstinting aid in locating hundreds of references and quotations; Lawrence Kenney, for resolving residual inconsistencies and eliminating some infelicities of style; and Margaret Keene, who burned much midnight oil in transferring the draft text of the translation from my dictation to the computer. I also acknowledge the help of Judith Dupont (Paris), F.-M. Gathelier (Frankfurt), Lisa Levinson (New Haven), and Mark Solms (London), all of whom supplied information.

thodical self-reflection"[17]—the prerequisite for the ongoing creative exploration of the unconscious—will continue to exist in the future. It may be that the extraordinary "deepening of apperception" which Walter Benjamin considered to have been brought about by psychoanalysis[18] will be lost in the foreseeable future and will be remembered only by historians as a noteworthy variant in the history of the transformations of human perception.

Second, it is surely no coincidence that the sudden upsurge in historicization or self-historicization commenced at about the time of Anna Freud's death. From this point of view, it would appear to be an expression of a melancholic assimilation, the consequence of an excessively personalized professional identification—as if the final severance of the family bonds were compelling the psychoanalysts, now effectively orphaned, to invest what they had lost with eternal life by a kind of mythologization, imagining themselves to be a part of a magnificent family saga.

Third, in Germany, the beginning of the intensification of interest in the history of psychoanalysis followed the preoccupation of the psychoanalytic community with the consequences of the crimes of the Nazis, a preoccupation delayed for many years, until the beginning of the 1980s.[19] It was as if the German analysts could only now dare to look back and appreciate the extent and worth of all that was irrevocably destroyed in those days. However, some ten years earlier, something had happened in the Federal Republic which, at first sight, appears in international terms to be a unique success story for the Freudian heritage: while still in the midst of their "ahistorical" phase, the German psychoanalysts had succeeded in having analytic treatment integrated into the public health insurance system, and this has undoubtedly benefited countless patients who could not have afforded to pay for their own treatment. But it has now become impossible to overlook the high longer-term cost of this advance: limitation of independence with regard to such central decision-making powers as determination of the setting of treatment, of conditions of access to training, and of guidelines for the curriculum. It is surely not inconceivable that dismay at the dawning of awareness of this dialectic, which may well constitute a threat to the future of psychoanalysis in Germany, represents an additional motive for the historicizing process—that is, bringing back to life a different psychoanalysis, the early psychoanalysis, which proudly asserted its outsider position.

---

[17]Habermas, 1987, p. 214.

[18]Benjamin, 1969 [1935/36], p. 235.

[19]Considering that the German edition of Alexander and Margarete Mitscherlich's pioneering work, *The Inability to Mourn*, was published as long ago as in 1967, this may at first sight appear surprising; however, the majority of their colleagues manifestly failed to complete their own confrontation with the past at that time.

Be that as it may, the person of Freud has certainly become much better known—or more notorious, as the case may be—through the effects of tempestuous historicization and *furor biographicus,* and there is no doubt that, as far as the mass media are concerned, he is now one of the most discussed figures in intellectual history and perhaps the one about whom the most impassioned arguments rage. Even the Austrian state has recently commended itself to our attention as Freud's country of origin, doing its best to attract tourists with the postmark "*Freudiana* You can see the original only in Vienna." However, Freud's texts are retreating more and more into the background and becoming less and less known, even granted that they have never been particularly familiar to the public at large because of their complexity. But their unfamiliarity seems to be on the increase. One need only consider all the assertions that are made about them without calling forth any contradiction, and how wickedly interpreters are allowed to ill-treat them without any fear of themselves being exposed. Yet we need only follow Starobinski: we should "go back to the text to discover the starting point of the projections, fantasies, and arbitrary manipulations" of the interpreter.

However, I chose the title *Back to Freud's Texts* not only in order to affirm those texts' right of perusal of what is said about them. *Back to Freud's Texts* is also intended as an appeal against concentration on the person. In the form of pure biographism, more or less detached from the work, we are apparently seeing a new kind of resistance to the revolutionary and profoundly disconcerting discoveries, thoughts, and writings of the founder of psychoanalysis—to that for which, after all, he is primarily memorable. *Back to Freud's Texts* is intended not least as a recommendation to psychoanalysts to sublimate, to identify not primarily with the person of Sigmund Freud but above all with the radical method of psychoanalysis, which is so difficult to learn and so deserving and needful of protection, as still the most effective instrument for the exploration of human subjectivity.

It is to be hoped that my advocacy of a return to the basic texts of psychoanalysis will not have the effect of further historicization, let alone dogmatization or canonization. On the contrary, direct acquaintance with the context of their genesis by making the documents speak for themselves allows a confrontation in the here and now with the nascent psychoanalytic method and with the logic of observation and research from which it was born as something new.[20] Again, what is simultaneously revealed to us as

---

[20]It was after all precisely in this sense that Freud himself ultimately recommended that his readers consider the history of his researches; in his view, insight into the stages of their genesis would afford a particularly graphic demonstration of the essence and fundamentals of the psychoanalytic method.

new is the strangeness, the seeming unnaturalness of Freudian thought, a reflection of the genuine strangeness of the unconscious inner world. To illustrate to Albert Einstein the extent to which psychoanalysis goes against the grain—this being its characteristic feature—Freud put the common-sense viewpoint to him in a telling contrast: "All our attention is directed to the outside, whence dangers threaten and satisfactions beckon. From the inside, we want only to be left in peace. So if someone tries to turn our awareness inward, in effect twisting its neck round, then our whole organization resists—just as, for example, the esophagus and the urethra resist any attempt to reverse their normal direction of passage."[21] The reason for going *back to Freud's texts* is therefore to aid and abet them precisely in their ability to resist us or to provoke resistance in us. All this retains intense present-day relevance, as is evident not least from the fact that, again and again, echoes of current reality impose themselves on our attention as we explore the landscape of the manuscripts.

Such biographical material as *is* included in this book almost exclusively presents the reader with Freud *at work*—Freud observing, listening, feeling surprised and stimulated, reading, learning, associating and fantasizing, concluding and conceiving, noting, drafting, rejecting, making fair copies, busying himself with his manuscripts, correcting proofs, editing, and publishing. "With regard to all the recent endeavors to disclose the secrets of Freud's life, the verdict must after all be that the investigation of Freud's working methods, whether as therapist or man of science, is the most urgent, if not the only appropriate, Freud disclosure that is a fitting object of our curiosity." Alfred Lorenzer[22] wrote this on the occasion of the publication of a draft manuscript[23] that came to light unexpectedly a few years ago; if disclosure it be, then my book is a Freud disclosure in his sense. It can also be read as a supplement, presenting concrete examples of his craft, to the studies of Freud as a writer or of Freud's prose,[24] because it reveals for the first time the traces of the creative process documented in the manuscripts.

The structure of the book reflects the chronology of its genesis. Part I presents the reconstruction of the history of the editions, in their Vienna, London, and Frankfurt phases, which was the starting point for my work.[25]

[21]In a letter dated 26 March 1929, in the Sigmund Freud Collection of the Library of Congress; cf. Grubrich-Simitis, 1995.

[22]Lorenzer, 1986, p. 1166.

[23]1985*a*.

[24]In particular, the fundamental studies of Muschg, 1975 [1930], Schönau, 1968, and Mahony, 1982, 1987.

[25]This part of the book is a thorough revision of the paper I published in 1989. I have omitted a considerable body of material that appeared dispensable in the context of the book, while adding a great deal of other material which accrued from subsequent research, takes

Freud appears here as a man of books, a single-minded publisher and pro-
moter of his own work. The reader will, in addition, get to know some of the
history of the literature produced in exile and finally also some of the history
of the publishing house of S. Fischer—publishing house history as the history of the impact of an oeuvre, and the history of the impact of an oeuvre as
publishing house history. The principal subject of this part is therefore
external reality, including political reality—that is, the macrocosm.

Part II, the book's center and its very heart, on the other hand, affords
access to the microcosm, the inner, private reality of Freud's creativity. It
begins with a description of the particular conditions and rhythms of his
process of writing, based predominantly on the evidence of his own statements. Information on how the material has come down to us is followed in
the subsequent chapters by the first ever guided tour of the landscape of the
manuscripts. On the level of primary rather than secondary literature, this
intimate, direct encounter with the texts in their original manuscript form,
brought vividly to life by numerous facsimiles, affords access to some hitherto unknown regions. The terra incognita includes: notes that show Freud
engaged in a scientific soliloquy, collecting the raw material for his oeuvre;
drafts, by the writing of which he felt his way toward the definitive versions; variants identifiable in the fair copies, which demonstrate the impact
of Freud's linguistic art like lessons from a writing school and open up vistas
onto the stages of development of psychoanalytic concepts as annual
growth rings, so to speak, in works which matured over prolonged periods,
betraying in the form of parapraxes intensified emotional involvement on
the part of the writer or bearing witness to third-party editorial intervention
after his death; as well as rejected first versions of two speculative works and
some material that was written down for publication but then remained
unpublished.

Part III, which concludes the book and, like Part I, is relatively short,
presents a sketch for a future critical edition of Freud; it contains the themes
and ideas I originally wanted to discuss in my planned second paper, albeit
substantially enriched and modified by my intervening work on the autographs. As in part I, the reader's attention is directed outward, this time to
the wider context of established editorial practice, to which any future
editors of Freud will have to conform whether they like it or not. A brief
comparison with the contrasting textures of some other authors of similar
rank throws into greater relief the particularities of the Freudian tradition,
which the editorial style would have to emulate. Some suggestions of the

---

account of more recent developments, or is conducive to the integration of the three parts of the
book.

principles that must underlie a new edition of Freud are discussed in the form of signposts, and conjectures are presented on the results we should be entitled to expect from this large-scale project, should it be implemented, as well as its impact, not least from the point of view of the future of psycho-analysis itself.

*   *   *

I should like to conclude this introduction with a few technical notes. In order as far as possible to relieve the text of bibliographic information that would obstruct its flow, the titles of Freud's works are often given in abbreviated form without the year of publication. The List of Freud Titles given in the appendix, which includes the abbreviated form of the titles as given in the text, contains all the information needed to identify the relevant work with full bibliographic details in the Bibliography. Notes comprising only a year followed by an italicized lowercase letter, without a name, refer to Freud titles that can also be readily found in the Bibliography under the relevant year and letter.

Where patients' names occur in Freud's hitherto unpublished manuscripts, I have disguised them; in the case of persons identifiable as people already coded in earlier Freud publications, I have used the established pseudonyms. Transcriptions of Freud's actual material follow the original spelling and punctuation; where the author has made subsequent corrections, I give the original wording only where this is relevant to the context of my argument. Additions made by me to facilitate understanding are printed in square brackets. Because the secondary literature on Freud has now expanded to such a point that no one can be aware of every single publication, I cannot absolutely rule out the possibility that a particular Freudian text which I am to the best of my knowledge publishing for the first time in this book may have already appeared elsewhere, perhaps without the permission of the copyright holders. At any rate, none of these texts is listed in the complete bibliography of Freud,[26] which undergoes constant careful updating, as having already been published.

The series designations and container numbers of the Sigmund Freud Collection in the Manuscript Division of the Library of Congress are still subject to changes due to the ongoing integration of hitherto restricted parts of the collection; for this reason, in order not to give misleading information, I do not as a rule state the precise location of the documents quoted below. However, the catalog of the Manuscript Division makes them not too difficult to find.

[26]Meyer-Palmedo and Fichtner, 1989.

PART ONE

History of the Editions

. . . without a publishing house

we should be powerless.

—Freud to Sándor Ferenczi,
24 January 1932

Discontents, and the *New Introductory Lectures on Psycho-Analysis.* After the foundation of the Internationaler Psychoanalytischer Verlag, whenever Freud had to write a contribution for another publisher, he tried to secure at least the reproduction rights for his own publishing house. For instance, in 1924 he originally wrote *An Autobiographical Study* for the collection *Die Medizin der Gegenwart in Selbstdarstellungen,* edited by L. R. Grote and published by Felix Meiner in Leipzig. The publication rights were transferred in 1934 to the Verlag, which produced a separate edition, to be followed in 1936, on the occasion of Freud's eightieth birthday, by an enlarged new edition.

However, the *individual editions* published by the Verlag comprised not only the titles mentioned, which were presented from the beginning as separate publications, but also texts that had first been offered to the public in the periodicals; for example, the following appeared individually in 1924: "A Seventeenth-Century Demonological Neurosis,"[36] "On Narcissism: An Introduction," "On the History of the Psycho-Analytic Movement," the case history of the "Wolf Man," "Thoughts for the Times on War and Death," and the three "Contributions to the Psychology of Love." With the evident aim of reaching different groups of readers, the individual editions were produced in a range of qualities and prices, usually both stitched and paperbound, and sometimes in half cloth or full cloth or both.

In addition to the periodicals and individual editions, Freud presented his works, as published by the Internationaler Psychoanalytischer Verlag, in theme-based *anthologies.* He began in 1924 with the compilation *Psychoanalytische Studien an Werken der Dichtung und Kunst* [Psychoanalytic Studies of Works of Literature and Art], which included the essays "Creative Writers and Day-Dreaming," "The Theme of the Three Caskets," "The Moses of Michelangelo," "The 'Uncanny,' " and other works. The same year also saw publication of the anthology *Zur Technik der Psychoanalyse und zur Metapsychologie* [On the Technique of Psychoanalysis and on Metapsychology]. Freud had resolved years earlier to dedicate a specific book to each of these two subject areas, one practical and the other theoretical, but had never been able to bring these plans to fruition. He assembled only elements of the two projects in the anthology.[37] *Kleine Beiträge zur*

---

[36]That is, only a year after its first publication in *Imago.* In 1928 there followed a bibliophile edition produced for the 1928 Congress of German Bibliophiles in Vienna, "on Dutch handmade paper," adorned with reproductions of the Mariazell Codex. Cf. the activity report of the Verlag in the *Internationale Zeitschrift für Psychoanalyse,* vol. 14 (1928), p. 573.

[37]The division into two parts is made clear by the repetition of the word "zur" [on] in the formulation of the title. The section on technique includes the fundamental papers on technique dating from 1911 to 1915 and that on metapsychology the five classical metapsychological texts of 1915.

Traumlehre [Short Contributions on the Theory of Dreams] were presented in 1925 in another anthology, followed in 1926 by a collection whose themes were loosely linked: *Studien zur Psychoanalyse der Neurosen aus den Jahren 1913–1925* [Studies on the Psychoanalysis of the Neuroses 1913–1925]. The three anthologies published in 1931 are arranged chronologically rather than strictly by subject; these are the *Schriften zur Neurosenlehre und zur psychoanalytischen Technik* [Papers on the Theory of the Neuroses and on Psychoanalytic Technique], *Kleine Schriften zur Sexualtheorie und zur Traumlehre* [Short Papers on the Theory of Sexuality and on the Theory of Dreams], and *Theoretische Schriften* [Theoretical Papers]; all three volumes, somewhat repetitively, contain reprints of papers already included in earlier anthologies. This is not true of the fine anthology *Vier psychoanalytische Krankengeschichten* [Four Psychoanalytic Case Histories], published in 1932, in which Freud put together the case studies of "Dora," "Little Hans," the "Rat Man," and Senatspräsident Schreber. In its advertisement for this collection in the *Almanach* for 1933, the Verlag quoted Freud's famous assertion from the *Studies on Hysteria* that it still struck him as strange that the case histories he wrote should "read like short stories."[38]

In 1923 the plan was forged to bring out Freud's oeuvre to date in the form of a *comprehensive edition of the works*, under the title *Gesammelte Schriften*.[39] Editorial cross-references throughout the edition again and again refer to it without qualification as the "Gesamtausgabe" [complete edition], a term Freud himself often used in his correspondence. The edition was initially intended to be confined to ten volumes, "arranged by themes, in order to allow the sale of single volumes and the photostatic reproduction of individual volumes in pocket size."[40] Volumes 4, 5, 7, 8, and 10 came onto the market in 1924, and volumes 1, 2, 3, 6, and 9 in the following year. An eleventh volume was issued in 1928, containing miscellaneous writings— newly written texts such as *An Autobiographical Study, The Question of Lay Analysis*, and *The Future of an Illusion*—as well as numerous forewords and commemorative articles. A twelfth and final volume followed in 1934, containing all the works dating from 1928 to 1933, including *Civili-*

---

[38]1895*d*, p. 160. It may also be mentioned that the fifth and last volume of the *Sammlung kleiner Schriften zur Neurosenlehre* was also published by the Internationaler Psychoanalytischer Verlag in 1922, after Deuticke had published the first three volumes in 1906, 1909, and 1913, respectively, and Hugo Heller the fourth in 1918. Heller subsequently transferred his rights to the Verlag.

[39]Cf. Jones, 1957, p. 102.

[40]A. Freud, 1952, p. v. Entire works were in fact set up in type that was used both for individual editions and for the *Gesammelte Schriften*.

zation and its Discontents and the *New Introductory Lectures on Psycho-Analysis* as well as "Supplements to Volumes I–XI" and other material.

The selection of material for those two supplementary volumes was inevitably somewhat arbitrary, given the circumstances of their production. However, the structuring of the ten volumes that were planned consistently and published in quick succession in 1924 and 1925 is also not entirely convincing.[41] The only volumes that seem to have been assembled in accordance with strict criteria are those numbered 1 (*Studies on Hysteria* and early papers on the theory of the neuroses), 2 (*The Interpretation of Dreams*), 3 (supplementary material and additional chapters for *The Interpretation of Dreams* as well as other papers on the theory of dreams), 7 (*Introductory Lectures on Psycho-Analysis*), and 8 (case histories).

Anna Freud and A. J. Storfer are named as the editors of volumes 1 to 11; volumes 4, 5, 7, 8, and 10 were coedited by Otto Rank. The twelfth volume was edited by Anna Freud and Robert Wälder, A. J. Storfer having meanwhile left the Verlag.[42] The reader will look in vain for a general introduction by the editors explaining the structure and principles of the edition. However, individual sections of the volumes are sometimes preceded by short editorial comments, stating, for example, that certain of Freud's texts are set out in the pages that follow, but usually without any attempt to justify the relevant editorial decisions. There are no scientific appendixes containing bibliographies and indexes. According to advertisements by the Verlag for the *Gesammelte Schriften,* the original intention was to furnish a bibliography and complete index in the eleventh volume.[43] As a rule, the reader is given only meager and unsystematic bibliographic information at the beginning of the relevant section or indi-

---

[41]To give just one example, in volume 5 the paper "Formulations on the Two Principles of Mental Functioning" is not included in the "Metapsychology" section but assigned to the "Papers on Sexual Life and the Theory of the Neuroses." However, the short editorial preliminary note on the "Metapsychology" section (p. 432) indicates the intention to group under this heading the texts that Freud had originally wanted to publish in book form under the title *Zur Vorbereitung einer Metapsychologie* [In Preparation for a Metapsychology]. It is indeed noteworthy that, on this occasion, not only the five metapsychological papers of 1915 (1915*c–e*, 1916–17*f* and *g*) were to be included, but also "A Note on the Unconscious in Psycho-Analysis," which dates from 1912.

[42]However, Anna Freud later reconstructed the responsibilities somewhat differently: "The first 'Gesammelte Schriften von Sigm. Freud' were published by the Internationaler Psychoanalytischer Verlag, Vienna, in 1924–1934, planned, compiled and edited by A. J. Storfer, the then director of the Verlag" (A. Freud, 1952, p. v).

[43]This never actually happened. Cf. the editor's comment on p. 306 of vol. 11, which states that, although the manuscript of the complete index to the eleven volumes had been compiled, it had not been printed but would be included in a later, additional volume of the edition. When this twelfth volume appeared some years later, the complete index was again omitted but without explanation.

vidual work. Editorial notes in the run of the text are mostly confined to cross-references—for example, the location in the *Gesammelte Schriften* of another of Freud's works which he mentions. These references are occasionally set in square brackets, thus flagging them as editorial additions; elsewhere, however, they appear in parentheses, so that they are not clearly distinguished from Freud's own text. On rare occasions, the interpolation "[addition . . .]:" appears in square brackets together with the relevant date, to draw the reader's attention to the fact that a given passage or note was added by Freud only in a later edition of the relevant work or specifically for the *Gesammelte Schriften*.[44]

The only complex and bold editorial decision—although once again no detailed reasons for it are given—concerns *The Interpretation of Dreams*. The second volume of the *Gesammelte Schriften* confronts the reader with the text of the *first* edition, as it were the primal dream book; the numerous and in some cases extensive "additions and supplementary passages, including material not yet contained in the last edition, will be contained in the next volume (vol. III)," according to an editorial note.[45] A letter from Freud to Ferenczi dated 13 September 1924 shows that he himself was the initiator of this new presentation of his magnum opus: "I intend to revise this book for the complete edition. The *first* edition is to be reprinted in one volume, to be followed by all later additions assembled into new chapters making up a second part."[46]

The twelfth and final volume occasionally contains somewhat fuller editorial prefaces, informing the reader about the circumstances in which some of the works reproduced were created; for example, the editors give an outline of the political background to Albert Einstein's letter to Freud in 1932 setting out the questions that Freud then answered in "Why War?" All the same, this volume cannot be said to have been provided with a critical apparatus either.

It must be concluded that, in the terminology of editorial theory,[47] the

---

[44]Cf., for example, the important note of 1924, identified as an addition, concerning the role of seduction in the etiology of the neuroses, which Freud added to the reprint of "Further Remarks on the Neuro-Psychoses of Defense" (1896*b*) in the *Gesammelte Schriften* (vol. 1, p. 369; *S.E.* 3, p. 168).

[45]Vol. 2, p. 2.

[46]In his "Editor's Introduction" to *The Interpretation of Dreams*, James Strachey made the following critical comment on this: "Unfortunately, however, the work was not carried out very systematically, for the additions themselves were not dated and thereby much of the advantage of the plan was sacrificed" (*S.E.* 4, p. xii).

[47]As described in detail in chapter 13, three types of edition are customarily distinguished, as follows: *Reading editions* are ones which simply present the text to the public, with little or no commentary. *Critical editions*, on the other hand, are intended as a basis for teaching and research. Scholarly introductions and appendixes as well as notes reconstruct the history of the

edly against "the soul-destroying glorification of the instinctual life, for the nobility of the human soul";[58] this marked the beginning of the violent political changes that were to lead within a few years to the destruction of Freud's world of books. He had already suspected in 1932 that the rescue of the Verlag that year was merely postponing the inevitable. Shortly after despatching his call for help, he wrote to Ernest Jones on 26 April: "It is superfluous to say anything about the general situation of the world. Perhaps we are only repeating the ridiculous act of saving a birdcage while the whole house is burning."[59] In the spring of 1936, the Gestapo confiscated the stock of books of the Leipzig distribution firm of F. Volckmar, which included editions of Freud;[60] the Verlag thereby lost what had once been its most important customer base, the German book market, whose demand for psychoanalytic literature had admittedly fallen drastically since 1934.[61] The final enforced closure of the Vienna publishing house took place in 1938.[62] However, the legal process of liquidation was not completed until 1941.[63] Incidentally, the Vienna Psychoanalytic Society was closed down at the same time—an ironic confirmation of the close connection Freud had noted in his 1932 appeal between the fate of the Verlag and that of the psychoanalytic movement.

Looking back after his emigration, Freud wrote to the editor of *Time and Tide*: "After seventy-eight years, including more than half a century of strenuous work, I had to leave my home, saw the Scientific Society I had founded dissolved, our institutions destroyed, our Printing Press (Verlag) taken over by the invaders, the books I had published confiscated and reduced to pulp, my children expelled from their professions."[64] His enumeration of the misfortunes which had befallen him thus expressly included the destruction of the Verlag and the pulping of his books, and he placed these blows immediately alongside the persecution of his children.

[58]Cf. E. Freud, L. Freud, and Grubrich-Simitis, 1978, p. 282.

[59]Jones, 1957, p. 179.

[60]Hall (1988, p. 95ff.) has proved in detail that Martin Freud managed by tough negotiation to secure the return of the confiscated stocks of books a few months later and to convey them to Vienna. He evidently even obtained permission for part of the stock of Freud's works in print to remain with the distributor, in particular for possible sale abroad.

[61]Cf. Martin Freud's report on business trends in the *Internationale Zeitschrift für Psychoanalyse*, vol. 23 (1937), p. 189f., in which he also gives a detailed account of the circumstances of the confiscation and release of the books in the Leipzig warehouse.

[62]Concerning the contradictory information on the fate of the book stocks of the Internationaler Psychoanalytischer Verlag after its enforced closure—including in particular the stocks of Freud editions—cf. Hall, 1988, p. 99ff.; for further details and documents, see also Leupold-Löwenthal, 1988.

[63]Hall, 1988, p. 101f.

[64]1938c, p. 301.

2 London: From 1938 to 1960

Freud's youngest son, Ernst, had already emigrated to London with his family in 1933. After only a few years he was able to inform his father of the purchase of the summer residence called "Hidden House" in Suffolk, to replace the lost vacation home on the Baltic island of Hiddensee. Congratulating him, Freud wrote back on 17 January 1938: "It is typically Jewish not to renounce anything and to replace what has been lost. Moses, who in my opinion left a lasting imprint on the Jewish character, was the first to set an example."[1] When Freud himself went into exile a few months later, he in like manner immediately took steps to compensate himself for the loss of his world of books. In the first year of the war he had secured the services of the Amsterdam publishing house of Allert de Lange to bring out the original German edition of his work on Moses,[2] and that same year saw the foundation of the Imago Publishing Company in London, established in supreme defiance as the successor institution to the defunct Internationaler Psychoanalytischer Verlag.

The company was headed by the British publisher John Rodker. An intellectual like A. J. Storfer, Rodker had begun his career as a lyric poet, novelist, and translator of such authors as Lautréamont, Montherlant, Jules Romain, Henri Barbusse, and Magnus Hirschfeld. Sensing which trends of the modern movement were later to prove influential, he had also, in the course of his publishing activity, distinguished himself by his early advocacy of authors who were as yet substantially unknown, such as T. S. Eliot, James Joyce, Ezra Pound, Gertrude Stein, and Le Corbusier. He had been acquainted with psychoanalysis through Barbara Low since 1926 and met Freud after the latter's emigration to London. Considering that in the 1930s

[1]1960a, p. 436.

[2]The Dutch publishing house of Allert de Lange had founded this German-language publishing business under the same name in 1933 to cater to the publication needs of numerous emigrants. It was headed by Walter Landauer, who, together with Fritz Landshoff, had previously been coproprietor and codirector of the publishing firm of Kiepenheuer in Berlin. (Personal communication from Gottfried Bermann Fischer.) As stated earlier, Kiepenheuer had brought out an edition of the *Vorlesungen zur Einführung in die Psychoanalyse* [*Introductory Lectures on Psycho-Analysis*] under license as late as 1933, so that Freud was able to reestablish the link formed at that time. In 1939, Allert de Lange also published Marie Bonaparte's book *Topsy*, the translation of which Sigmund and Anna Freud had completed in that last fearful period in Vienna before the family received permission to leave the country.

psychoanalysis still belonged self-evidently in the cultural avant-garde, we should not be surprised by Rodker's decision to dedicate himself henceforth exclusively to the publication of the new German-language edition of Freud and other psychoanalytic texts through his newly established Imago Publishing Company, which operated for years as a one-man business. Like Anton von Freund in the days of the old Verlag, Marie Bonaparte, whom Rodker met at Freud's house,[3] made the work of the new publishing company possible by her financial support.

Once again, Freud's concern for the survival of the psychoanalytic journals seems to have been one of the principal driving forces behind the foundation of this publishing house. Under his editorship, the Imago Publishing Company started to bring out the journals' successor as early as 1939. As the terminally ill Freud said in his preliminary note: "The 1938 issue of the 'Internationale Zeitschrift für Psychoanalyse und Imago,' owing to political events in Austria, could not be published. After an interruption of more than one year, the two journals are now reappearing again, joined in one volume and with the combined title 'International Journal for Psycho-Analysis and Imago.' [. . .] The *one* journal will continue unchanged the traditions of both."[4]

Indeed, the *Zeitschrift* again came to be the medium for the first publication of new works by Freud. In the three years of its existence—it had to cease publication in 1941—it presented, among others, the following: in volume 24, "Der Fortschritt in der Geistigkeit" ["The Advance in Intellectuality"] from the third essay of the book on Moses; in volume 25, *Abriss der Psychoanalyse* [*An Outline of Psycho-Analysis*] and "Die Ichspaltung im Abwehrvorgang" ["Splitting of the Ego in the Process of Defense"]; and in volume 26 the letter to Freud's boyhood friend Emil Fluss. The last three contributions were published posthumously under the editorship of Anna Freud.

After Freud's death, Imago also brought out individual editions of some of his works in German;[5] they included *"Selbstdarstellung"* [*An*

---

[3]Cf. Bonaparte, 1956, p. 587.

[4]1939e. [*Translator's note*: English wording as given in Freud, E., L. Freud, and I. Grubrich-Simitis, eds., English version (1978), p. 319.]

[5]As though the intention were not only to rescue Freud's original texts but actually also to save German-language psychoanalytic literature as an entity from falling silent, the Imago Publishing Company in 1949 and 1950 published the German editions of the two contributions by Anna Freud and Dorothy Burlingham in which these authors elaborated the experience they had gained at Hampstead Nurseries during the Second World War: *Kriegskinder* [*Young Children in War-Time*] and *Anstaltskinder* [*Infants without Families*]. Anna Freud's classic *Das Ich und die Abwehrmechanismen* [*The Ego and the Mechanisms of Defense*] of 1936 and her *Einführung in die Technik der Kinderanalyse* [*The Psycho-Analytic Treatment of*

Autobiographical Study] in 1946, in a reprint of the edition published ten years earlier by the Internationaler Psychoanalytischer Verlag but with some changes in the illustrations; in 1947, *Zur Psychopathologie des All-tagslebens* [*The Psychopathology of Everyday Life*]; and, in 1950, the *Vor-lesungen zur Einführung in die Psychoanalyse* [*Introductory Lectures on Psycho-Analysis*]. The year 1950 also saw the publication of the first major body of correspondence, *Aus den Anfängen der Psychoanalyse; Briefe an Wilhelm Fliess; Abhandlungen und Notizen aus den Jahren 1887–1902* [*The Origins of Psycho-Analysis: Letters to Wilhelm Fliess, Drafts and Notes 1887–1902*], edited by Marie Bonaparte, Anna Freud, and Ernst Kris; this book gave a powerful boost to the process of biographical research on Freud and the historiography of psychoanalysis, in those days taking their first hesitant steps. Ernst Kris furnished substantial notes and an imaginative introduction; we are therefore indebted to him for the first critical edition of letters by Freud, which was in fact the first critical edition of any of Freud's texts.

However, there is no doubt that the Imago Publishing Company was established mainly for the purpose of rescuing Sigmund Freud's *Gesammelte Schriften* in the new guise of the *Gesammelte Werke*, later often called the Imago edition—that is, of seeing that his oeuvre was handed down in his "beloved mother-tongue."[6] How important this was to him can be inferred from a letter to Arnold Zweig dated 21 February 1936, in which he sought to help that writer, who had emigrated to Palestine, fallen into a crisis, and was considering moving to the United States: "In America too you would have to shed your own language, not an article of clothing but your own skin."[7] At any rate, the preamble of the contract concluded between Freud and the Imago Publishing Company on 16 May 1939 contains the following programmatic statement: "Whereas the Author's literary and scientific work consisting of 12 volumes entitled Gesammelte Schriften has been destroyed, the Publishers desire to republish it." We can see how literally this was originally meant from an early brochure in which the Imago Publishing Company announced and invited subscriptions for the project in the German language, with an English appendix, as a "new edition,"

Children] of 1927 were incorporated in the catalog of the Imago Publishing Company from the stocks of the defunct Internationaler Psychoanalytischer Verlag, as were the four volumes of the compilation of Sándor Ferenczi's works originally published in 1927 and 1938 as *Bausteine der Psychoanalyse*. [*Translator's note*: The contents of the volumes of the German and English editions of Ferenczi do not correspond.]

[6]1915*b*, p. 278.

[7]1968*a*, p. 122.

To the present-day reader, the most graphic testimony to Freud's unre-
lenting concern for the oeuvre is surely to be found in the letters he wrote to
his various correspondents. Those to Sándor Ferenczi, for example, include
hardly a single passage of any length without a reference to works in the
process of creation or to new editions and translations of works already
published. Much the same could be said of the terse, diarylike entries recorded by Freud for a few years of his life in the three volumes of *Prochaskas
Familien-Kalender*[22] that have come down to us, for the years 1916, 1917,
and 1918, and in the "Kürzeste Chronik,"[23] a kind of abbreviated diary
with very succinct entries, which he kept in the last decade of his life, from
1929 to 1939.

Prochaska's family calendars appeared at the time of the First World
War as annuals; they were a bizarre, illustrated amalgam of homespun
wisdom, edifying literature, and tales of hardship endured, accompanied by
some advertising. The volumes included a section of pages having a blank
line for every day of the year. Freud here recorded not only family matters
such as illnesses, birthdays, deaths, and visits, and the military distinctions
and captivity of his sons, who had been drafted into the army, but also the
political events then following each other in rapid succession, such as "Rev-
olution in Russia," "Beginning of the German offensive in the west," "Rev-
olution Vienna & Budapest," "Armistice with Italy—war over!", "Rev-
olution in Kiel," "Republic in Bavaria!!" "Republic in Berlin   Wilhelm
abdicated," "Ebert Chancellor for war   Armistice terms," "War ends—K.
Karl[24] abdicates," "Republic & union with Germany—endured panic." At
the same time, he staunchly continued to record the vicissitudes of his works
with meticulous accuracy and continuity: "Everyday Life 5th ed. finished,"
"Completed MS. of Lectures," "Vth edition of Int[erpretation] of Dr[eams]
announced," "Totem & Taboo Hungarian," "Karger[25] demands VIth ed.
Everyday Life," "Danish trans. of 5 Lectures[26] requested," "Lectures 2nd
ed. and Saṃlung IV."[27] The "Kürzeste Chronik" is made up of the same
mixture of personal and family events, political news, and the vicissitudes of
his works. In addition to such entries as "Pearls for Martha," "+ Mother

[22]Sigmund Freud Collection.

[23]Some pages from the "Kürzeste Chronik" have already been published in the volume
Sigmund Freud: His Life in Pictures and Words (E. Freud, L. Freud, and Grubrich-Simitis,
1978, pp. 270, 281, 288, and 335f.). The complete document, which comprises only twenty
pages in its entirety, appeared in 1992 (cf. Freud, 1976*m*).

[24]Emperor Karl I of Austria.

[25]The Karger Publishing Company in Berlin.

[26]"Five Lectures on Psycho-Analysis," 1910*a*.

[27]Volume IV of the *Sammlung kleiner Schriften zur Neurosenlehre* [Collection of Shorter
Writings on the Theory of the Neuroses].

died 8 a.m.," "Dozent position annulled—hormone injection," "Christmas in pain," "Anti-Semit. disturbances," "Republic in Spain," "Anschluss with Germany," "Hitler in Vienna," "Anna with Gestapo," "Acceptance by England assured," we see Freud again keeping a record of the growth and ever-increasing worldwide reputation of his oeuvre: "Norwegian Lectures," "Jokes in French," "Japan. translation 'Beyond Pleasure Principle,'" "Libidinal types begun," "Fem Sexuality finished," "French Illusion,"[28] "Chinese lectures," "XII volume Ges. Ausgabe [complete ed.]," "Postscript to Autobiographical Study," "Moses III begun again," and, finally, "Moses passed for press."[29]

Identifying with this dedication to the work, as here once again documented, the first successor generation of editors gave priority to the objective of ensuring that the writings of the founder of psychoanalysis remained available at all and were effectively preserved during the Second World War and the immediate postwar period. Editorial deficiencies and inconsistencies were accepted as inescapable realities in this situation—for instance, after Ernst Kris, a man thoroughly versed in the humanities, was compelled by wartime communication difficulties virtually to give up his collaboration on the edition following his emigration to the United States. In a letter dated 11 October 1969 to Alexander Mitscherlich, Anna Freud made the following candid admission about the *Gesammelte Werke*: "I know very well what the defects of the present German edition are; they can be excused only by the extraordinarily difficult conditions under which we produced it. Furthermore, we were at the time manifestly not very 'competent', nor did we have any competent assistants of any kind [. . .]."[30]

Anna Freud did not then mention that the editorial committee initially entrusted with the task, consisting as noted earlier of herself, Edward Bibring, and Ernst Kris, had in fact originally aspired to the production of a more ambitious edition. The Sigmund Freud Collection contains separate drafts by Edward Bibring and Ernst Kris of an appeal which, while undated, probably originates from 1939 or 1940. It shows that the intention at the time was to supplement "the new edition of the Gesammelte Schriften" with a "collection of Freud's letters and extracts from his letters, to comprise one or more volumes"; the relevant letters or passages were to be confined to those "in which matters of a scientific or related nature, in particular problems of psychoanalysis, are discussed." "We emphasize that personal communications are to be excluded from publication." The appeal—whether it

---

[28]*The Future of an Illusion* (1927c).

[29][*Translator's note*: Freud's word "imprimirt" is wrongly rendered in the published English translation as "printed" instead of "passed for press".]

[30]Alexander-Mitscherlich-Archiv, Stadt- und Universitätsbibliothek, Frankfurt am Main.

was ever sent out is unknown[31]—was manifestly directed to former Freud correspondents, who were asked to make available to the editors copies of the text of the letters in their possession. A possible use for the letters as sources in the editorial apparatus of the new Freud edition was indicated in passing: "(Suitable passages are also to be used as occasional notes in an apparatus of notes accompanying the works.)"[32]

[31]At any rate, an unpublished letter from Marie Bonaparte to Anna Freud dated 16 February 1940 (Sigmund Freud Collection) shows that the latter had asked her with which French colleagues Freud had regularly corresponded.

[32]The interest in Freud's letters which arose shortly after his death is also documented in the correspondence exchanged between Ludwig Binswanger and the Freud family in 1939 and 1940. In a letter dated 29 December 1939, Anna Freud informed Binswanger, who had previously suggested an eventual publication of Freud's letters, of her joint project with Bibring and Kris. Binswanger's response to her proposal that excessively personal matters could be omitted was that she should collect all kinds of letters and not just those with a scientific content (Freud, 1992a, pp. 250–52).

3 FRANKFURT: FROM 1960 TO THE PRESENT

Today, a half century after the end of the war, it is almost impossible to imagine the extent to which the Nazi regime succeeded in causing Freud's writings to disappear from the German book market and in banishing from the public consciousness the universe of thought he had brought into the world in his magnificent prose. Against this background, it seems an irony of history that his works were kept in a locked closet at the former Berlin Psychoanalytic Institute, which had been subjected to the repressive leveling process of *Gleichschaltung*, where they could be consulted by psychotherapy students if signed for, until the building burned down just before the end of the war.[1] It is a measure of the crippling aftereffects of the traumatic act of destruction directed against Freud's once so assiduous and successful publication policy that it took all of fifteen years before the initiative for producing editions of Freud's works in their original language moved from London back to the German-speaking world. Probably even more time would have elapsed had not the unexpected death of John Rodker compelled Freud's heirs, who themselves never returned from exile, to look for a new publisher and thereby to give up the relative independence in matters of publication by which Sigmund Freud had set so much store. At all events, anyone who wanted to read his writings in German after the war had to resort for many years to imports from the Imago Publishing Company.[2]

It was surely no coincidence that the first Freud paperback to be produced and marketed on a large scale in the Federal Republic of Germany, suddenly attracting the attention of young readers in particular to his thought—but not, incidentally, until 1953—was brought out by a returned émigré publisher, Gottfried Bermann Fischer, in the Fischer Bücherei, the regular-format paperback arm of the publishing house of S. Fischer, now

---

[1]Dräger 1971, p. 46.

[2]When the publishing house of Franz Deuticke brought out a new edition of the *Traumdeutung* [*The Interpretation of Dreams*] as its first postwar publication in 1945, drawing on the old rights in its possession, the fact went almost unnoticed, even though it was followed by a further edition in 1950. Deuticke published a new edition of the *Drei Abhandlungen zur Sexualtheorie* [*Three Essays on the Theory of Sexuality*] in 1947 and reprinted *Über Psychoanalyse* ["Five Lectures on Psycho-Analysis"] in the same year; these lectures were republished on the Deuticke list for the last time in 1951.

established in Frankfurt. The volume contained *An Outline of Psycho-Analysis* and *Civilization and its Discontents*, together with Thomas Mann's address in 1936 on the occasion of Freud's eightieth birthday. No other German publisher had until then approached Freud's heirs for a license.[3] The first edition of fifty thousand copies was sold out within a few months. A new edition followed the very next year, as did another Freud paperback, *The Psychopathology of Everyday Life*. For the latter, the publishers commissioned a foreword from Alexander Mitscherlich, the leading public protagonist of the difficult rebirth of psychoanalytic training and research in postwar Germany. Licensed paperback editions of *Totem and Taboo* and of *Jokes and their Relation to the Unconscious* followed in 1956 and 1958, respectively, again in the Fischer Bücherei.

In 1960, Gottfried Bermann Fischer followed up a tip from his attentive then-editor, Hans-Geert Falkenberg, who had heard of the intended sale of the Imago Publishing Company. Bermann Fischer immediately commenced negotiations with Marianne Rodker in London for the acquisition of world rights to Freud's works, excluding the English, Spanish, and Portuguese language areas. His resolve to assume henceforth the responsibility for publishing the German-language editions of Freud may well have originally been stimulated by some impressive meetings with the aged Sigmund Freud and ultimately by their common destiny as victims of persecution.

One of the conversations between the two men had taken place in Freud's apartment at Berggasse 19 during the publishing family's first years of exile, in Vienna from 1936 to 1938.[4] Even earlier, on 2 May 1935, Freud had told Arnold Zweig of a link with the publishing house: "At the instigation of the Fischer Verlag I have written a short address for Thomas Mann's sixtieth birthday[5] (6 June) [. . .]."[6] As Mann's publishers, Bermann Fischer and his wife had been present when Mann visited Freud at his summer residence in Grinzing on 14 June 1936 to give him a private reading of the commemorative address he had delivered at the Konzerthaus-Saal in Vienna on the occasion of Freud's eightieth birthday.[7] Finally, in the summer of 1938, Bermann Fischer approached Freud from Stockholm, the next stopping place of his publishing house in exile, with a view to securing the rights to Freud's book on Moses. When the author informed him that the rights had already been assigned, Bermann Fischer replied on 18 August: "I hope that another opportunity will one day arise for my publishing house to bring

---

[3]Personal communication from Bermann Fischer.
[4]Cf. Bermann Fischer, 1967, p. 124 and p. 376, as well as p. 130.
[5]1935c.
[6]1968a, p. 106.
[7]Mann, 1978, p. 316.

out one of your books. It would give me particular pleasure and satisfaction."[8]

This opportunity eventually came in 1960—not just for one book but for Freud's entire work. Looking back in his autobiography, the publisher confirmed that, having long deemed this oeuvre to be among the "fundamental creations of our century," he had seen the acquisition of the Freud rights as a "significant extension of the publishing house."[9] In the next few years he was also able to resume his connection with Ernst Freud, who was now responsible for the administration of the rights and remained so until his death in 1970. Bermann Fischer had known him since the 1920s, when, as a young architect, he had decorated and furnished the Berlin apartment in which the publisher lived with his family.

Not only the rights were transferred to S. Fischer when the contract was signed. The Imago Publishing Company's stock of Freud's books was also acquired and henceforth marketed from the Federal Republic. Before the contract was a year old, S. Fischer, in the first group of titles in its series of large-format paperbacks—a style new to the German-language book market—issued a Freud anthology, again selected by Alexander Mitscherlich, who also provided an afterword.[10] It was called *Das Unbewusste* [The Unconscious], with the subtitle *Schriften zur Psychoanalyse* [Papers on Psychoanalysis]. According to the laconic jacket text: "This volume is intended as an introduction to the many-faceted world of Freud's oeuvre, which is still virtually unknown in Germany twenty years after his death." This collection was followed a year later by another regular-format paperback: *Drei Abhandlungen zur Sexualtheorie, Und verwandte Schriften* [*Three Essays on the Theory of Sexuality, And Related Writings*], again selected and with an afterword by Mitscherlich. Freud's heirs had disapproved of the selection of texts in *Das Unbewusste*, so the contents of the paperback with the texts on the theory of sexuality were decided in consultation with Anna Freud.

In addition, under the simple title *Briefe 1873–1939* [*Letters of Sigmund Freud 1873–1939*], there appeared in 1960 the first major collection of personal correspondence spanning almost the whole of Freud's life; it was edited by Ernst Freud and his wife, Lucie, "in the hope that those who know Sigmund Freud only from his work shall receive here a portrait of the

[8]Both letters from Bermann Fischer are in the Sigmund Freud Collection.

[9]Bermann Fischer, 1967, p. 374.

[10]Attention is drawn to the coincidence that Alexander Mitscherlich, in collaboration with Fred Mielke, made the documents in the Nuremberg doctors' trial available to a wider readership for the first time in *The Death Doctors*, the original German edition of which, *Medizin ohne Menschlichkeit*, was published in the Fischer Bücherei in the same year.

man."[11] Ernst Freud had originally resolved to publish this selection of his father's *personal* letters as a "protest against Ernest Jones's biography" and "in fact against the will" of his brothers and sisters.[12] The book, a kind of autobiography in epistolary form, certainly exhibits editorial shortcomings of many kinds: for example, cuts were not identified clearly enough, let alone justified. Yet this anthology afforded the reader an early glimpse of the colossal massif of the letters that had issued from Freud's pen during his lifetime and aroused an almost hymnic echo from renowned critics in the feature supplements of the day, not least as a literary event. For instance: "We have reason to be thankful," wrote Walter Jens,[13] "our country has been made the richer by an important writer, now finally discovered; the German language has once again found its master. [. . .] Of its own accord, the life of a man who has changed our century perhaps more than any other unfolds in the [. . .] book." Or Friedrich Sieburg:[14] "We have been [. . .] enriched by a great life testimony. [. . .] These letters are magnificent and moving from the first day to the last. We read them with admiration, but also with shame at the fact that we were witnesses to a time which drove this great man into exile."

In 1962, S. Fischer also brought out an inexpensive edition of the Fliess documents, *Aus den Anfängen der Psychoanalyse* [*The Origins of Psycho-Analysis*], again in the new large-format paperback series.

Not long after I began work at S. Fischer,[15] I embarked in 1963/64 on a comparison of the *Gesammelte Werke* with the *Standard Edition of the Complete Psychological Works of Sigmund Freud*, issued under the general editorship of James Strachey in twenty-four volumes, which was then not yet complete; and I gave detailed reasons why the English edition was superior to the German. The *Standard Edition* had by then become known as the leading and indeed the only critical edition of the main part of the oeuvre. The comparison immediately led to the plan to make Freud's works available to the German-speaking reader in the future essentially in two versions: the specialist was to be provided with a new, lavishly presented *critical complete edition*, while the general reader—in particular, students

[11]1960*a*, p. x.

[12]Quoted from a letter to me dated 11 February 1968 on the occasion of the second, expanded edition of the volume.

[13]In *Die Zeit*, 17 February 1961.

[14]In the *Frankfurter Allgemeine Zeitung*, 12 November 1961.

[15]The following passages on the third phase of the editorial history inevitably have a more personal tinge because Freud editions have been one of my responsibilities as an editor at S. Fischer Verlag since 1963. Even after ceasing to be an employee of S. Fischer in the mid-1970s, I continued my editing of the work of Freud without interruption on a freelance basis, with the same responsibility as before.

in neighboring disciplines—would be offered an inexpensive *textbook edition* [*Studienausgabe*] in five or six volumes, with more systematically selected contents and a more extensive commentary than the individual regular-format and large-format Freud paperbacks hitherto published by Fischer Verlag.

The less ambitious second project, the *Studienausgabe*, reached the stage of implementation relatively quickly. Alexander Mitscherlich drew up an outline for the contents of the six volumes, based partly on the structure of the *Collected Papers*, the English-language Freud selection published in five volumes in 1924/25 and 1950. James Strachey was asked to consent to the reproduction in the *Studienausgabe* of extracts from the critical apparatus of his *Standard Edition*. He refused, justifying his decision in a letter to me dated 16 March 1964 with a radical critique of Mitscherlich's outline; it was in his view misguided to base our work on the questionable edition of the *Collected Papers*, which he deemed an "out-of-date relic which should be buried and forgotten as soon as possible." Strachey's letter was helpful because it made us fully aware that it would not be possible to reproduce overnight in Germany the Freud edition culture which had since evolved in England. At the invitation of Mitscherlich and of S. Fischer Verlag, James Strachey and his assistant Angela Richards declared themselves willing to coedit the *Studienausgabe*.

In 1966, Strachey and Richards put forward a plan for a completely different selection of works. Their aim was to allow the relatively uninformed reader to become thoroughly versed in all the main areas of the psychoanalytic oeuvre under the guidance of a considered *thematic* structure.[16] However, they were heedless of the fact that this would have resulted in a doubling of the number of volumes. The management of the publishing house objected. It was at the time impossible to foresee the enthusiastic reception that awaited Freud's work in postwar western Germany, and so there was considerable doubt as to the existence of a demand for such a comprehensive and hence relatively expensive selection of his writings. Almost inconceivably from today's standpoint, we did not at that time dare to use the title *Metapsychologische Schriften* [Metapsychological Papers] for volume 3 of the *Studienausgabe,* although it accorded with its contents, because we felt that the term "metapsychology" was completely unknown and would be more likely to meet with rejection than interest. Finally, it was feared that the *Studienausgabe* might ultimately compete with the projected

---

[16]Except where they present a single extensive work—e.g., volume 1 with the *Introductory Lectures* and the *New Introductory Lectures*, or volume 2, with *The Interpretation of Dreams—chronological* order is observed *within* individual volumes containing a number of different texts on a given theme.

critical complete edition. The editors therefore reduced the original twelve-volume structure to ten, albeit on condition that the publishing house undertake to bring out in its regular-format paperback series inexpensive ancillary editions of all the main works that had to be omitted "with extreme reluctance"[17]—in particular, the *Studies on Hysteria, The Psychopathology of Everyday Life, An Autobiographical Study,* and *An Outline of Psycho-Analysis.*[18]

Final corrections to the proposed selection were discussed, and the editorial principles to be followed[19] were settled. Under the title "Über mögliche Missverständnisse bei der Lektüre der Werke Sigmund Freuds" ["On Possible Misunderstandings in Reading the Works of Sigmund Freud"], Mitscherlich composed an introductory essay on the vicissitudes of psychoanalysis in Germany, accompanied by advice to the reader. Most of the detailed editorial work was performed over many years of intensive cooperation between Angela Richards (James Strachey having died in the spring of 1967) and ourselves at S. Fischer Verlag; the passages from the editorial apparatus of the *Standard Edition* were translated by Mitscherlich's assistant, Käte Hügel. The first two volumes of the *Studienausgabe,* numbers 8 and 10, appeared in 1969.[20] Throughout those years, all concerned were constantly aware of the paradox of our position, that the first comprehensive critical *German-language* edition of Freud was substantially based on the achievements of *English-speaking* editors. When we were deliberating on the order in which the editors' names should be printed, Strachey high-mindedly suggested that Alexander Mitscherlich should come first, arguing in a letter to me dated 25 January 1965: "My reason for wanting us to take back seats as editors of the paperback Ausgabe is merely that it will be absurd for a couple of unknown English people to set themselves up as editors of a German classic."

As for the much more comprehensive project for a new critical complete edition of Freud, it was clear from the beginning that this would be a long-term undertaking and that the first volumes were unlikely to be issued soon. It was therefore decided to complement the seventeen volumes of the *Gesammelte Werke* distributed and reprinted by S. Fischer Verlag with two

[17]Richards, 1969, p. 28.

[18]The *Abriss* [*Outline*] had been on the market since 1953 in that first Freud paperback, and *Zur Psychopathologie des Alltagslebens* [*The Psychopathology of Everyday Life*] since 1954.

[19]Angela Richards described them in the "Erläuterungen zur Edition" ["Explanatory Notes on the Edition"] (1969).

[20]As a part of the new series, edited by Thure von Uexküll and me, entitled *Conditio humana: Ergebnisse aus den Wissenschaften vom Menschen* [The Human Condition: Results from the Sciences of Man].

more volumes, volume 18, the *Gesamtregister* [general index], and an un-numbered *Nachtragsband* [supplementary volume].

The manuscript of the *Gesamtregister*, once in the possession of S. Fischer, proved not to be ready for typesetting. After a process of laborious correction coordinated by ourselves, volume 18 of the *Gesammelte Werke* appeared in 1968 as the first ever general index of Freud's works.

As to the *Nachtragsband*, we proposed to assemble in it all of Freud's psychological and psychoanalytic texts which for various reasons had not been included in the seventeen volumes of the *Gesammelte Werke*. In other words, pending the publication of the new critical complete edition, the *Gesammelte Werke* were to be brought into line with the *Standard Edition* at least as regards the actual text of the psychological and psychoanalytic part of Freud's oeuvre. This entailed the overcoming of certain difficulties. For a while, Anna and Ernst Freud opposed our intention to include in the supplementary volume Josef Breuer's contributions to the *Studies on Hysteria*—namely, the epoch-making case history of "Anna O." and the chapter entitled "Theoretical." They could indeed justifiably argue that Freud himself had wanted these passages to be excluded from the collected editions of his works published hitherto—no doubt partly because he did not wish to see his name associated with texts in whose composition he had not been involved even as coauthor. On the other hand, years before our discussions about the contents of the *Nachtragsband*, James and Alix Strachey, realizing that the reader would otherwise be presented with a mere torso of the revolutionary book, had integrated the Breuer pieces into their new translation of the *Studies* for the second volume of the *Standard Edition*. Anna and Ernst Freud eventually changed their minds and agreed to our intention. Angela Richards offered her services as editor of the *Nachtragsband*, so that the collaboration with the English editors became even closer.

However, let us return to what was at the time the more ambitious project, the critical complete edition of Freud. Being as yet relatively unfamiliar with editorial theory, we talked in those days simply of a "historical-critical" edition. It was, at any rate, to include the editorial achievements of James Strachey as embodied in his commentaries in the English edition; in other words, these were to be translated for the new edition and incorporated in its editorial apparatus. Second, it was intended, by means of additional notes on scientific and cultural history, over and above Strachey's contribution, to establish connections between Freud's concepts and methods and the European context of ideas. Third, the edition was to present not only all the texts from the psychoanalytic phase of Freud's creative life but also those from two major areas substantially unaccounted for by Strachey: the entire

substance introduced into the book since its first issue."[37] To give at least one more example, the same applies to the *Drei Abhandlungen zur Sexualtheorie* [*Three Essays on the Theory of Sexuality*], published in the fifth volume of the *Studienausgabe* in 1972, in which the reader is also enabled, by the identification and dating of the variants, to reconstruct the successive steps in Freud's revision of this work, which, together with *The Interpretation of Dreams*, is assuredly his most revolutionary; we can see how material was added in almost every new edition after the first in the light of the growth of his knowledge during the intervening period.

To facilitate their use for scientific purposes, the volumes were provided with particularly detailed indexes. An additional volume (*Ergänzungsband*) contains Freud's papers on technique and the theory of therapy. Ernst Freud had in 1968 already suggested the compilation of a bibliography of all of his father's publications—effectively, a continuation of the author's own early "Chronology," which was actually the first Freud bibliography. In 1974 Angela Richards presented such a bibliography in the last volume of the *Standard Edition*, which was edited by her and published after Strachey's death. She was able to base her work on Alan Tyson's and James Strachey's valuable earlier compilation dating from 1956, the "Chronological Hand-List of Freud's Works," to which, however, she added an alphabetical list of titles. Both lists were incorporated in the *Studienausgabe* in 1975, in a separate booklet in a German version adapted by Ingeborg Meyer-Palmedo; the volume was entitled *Sigmund Freud-Konkordanz und -Gesamtbibliographie* [Sigmund Freud Concordance and Complete Bibliography]. It also included detailed page number comparisons between the *Gesammelte Werke*, the *Studienausgabe*, and the *Standard Edition* to help the reader find corresponding passages in each of these three Freud editions. One point that emerges from the concordance is that more than two-thirds of the Freud texts contained in the *Standard Edition* are now also available, critically edited, in the *Studienausgabe*.[38]

As stated earlier, it had been intended since the fixing of the contents of the *Studienausgabe* to present in an ancillary list of the Fischer Taschenbuch Verlag [the regular-format paperback arm of S. Fischer] those of Freud's writings which had had to be omitted from the edition solely on grounds of length, notwithstanding their importance, during the years of publication of the *Studienausgabe* (1969 to 1975); the only exceptions were to be works

---

[37]Strachey, 1972, p. 15 [English: *S.E.* 4, p. xx].

[38]This reference work has appeared since 1989 in a revised and substantially expanded new edition under the title *Freud-Bibliographie mit Werkkonkordanz*. The revision of the bibliography incorporates the results of the searches of Gerhard Fichtner, now coeditor. The bibliography is continuously updated.

that had already been available for years as regular-format paperbacks. The *Studien über Hysterie* [*Studies on Hysteria*], including Breuer's contributions, appeared in 1970; and in 1971 I edited Freud's so-called autobiographical texts, accompanied by a critical apparatus, under the title *"Selbstdarstellung"; Schriften zur Geschichte der Psychoanalyse* [*An Autobiographical Study; Papers on the History of Psychoanalysis*]. The following paperbacks were also published in those years, albeit with the different, more formal intention of supplementing the *Studienausgabe*: in 1969, under the title *Darstellungen der Psychoanalyse* [Portrayals of Psychoanalysis], Freud's shorter summaries of his teachings, including "Five Lectures on Psycho-Analysis" (whereas the *Studienausgabe* contains all thirty-five *Introductory Lectures on Psycho-Analysis*, including the *New Introductory Lectures*); and in 1971, under the title *Über Träume und Traumdeutungen* [On Dreams and Dream Interpretations], another collection of shorter texts on the subject, together with *Über den Traum* [*On Dreams*] (whereas the *Studienausgabe* presents the full-length *Traumdeutung* [*The Interpretation of Dreams*]). In the years after the completion of the *Studienausgabe*, many more Freud titles were marketed as regular-format paperbacks.

On the occasion of the fiftieth anniversary of Sigmund Freud's death, at the end of the 1980s, the entire presentation of the oeuvre in regular-format paperbacks was revised. Some of the Freud anthologies published in the 1950s and early 1960s, whose contents appear to have been assembled somewhat arbitrarily, will not be reprinted in the future, the relevant titles being transferred to other compilations. More specific themes, such as clinical theory and therapeutic technique, are now reflected for the first time in individual paperback editions. In this new, systematic series *Sigmund Freud—Werke im Taschenbuch* [Sigmund Freud—Works in Paperback] (which comprises a total of twenty-eight volumes), almost all the psychoanalytic works and some of the preanalytic papers—namely, the monograph on aphasia and the cocaine studies—will be made available in inexpensive reading editions volume by volume over the next few years. All volumes are provided not only with bibliographic appendixes but also with new introductions and/or afterwords in which contemporary scholars—psychoanalysts, historians, sociologists, ethnologists, and philologists—connect Freud's works with more recent research, subtly reassess them, and describe their continued impact on a broad spectrum of modern intellectual life. Some volumes also contain additional building blocks for a future critical complete edition. For example, the volume including Freud's analysis of Wilhelm Jensen's short story *Gradiva* comprises Jensen's actual text, accompanied by the revealing marginal notes and underlinings made by

Freud on the pages of his copy as he read it; while the volume containing the work on Moses will for the first time offer a complete edition of the first version, the so-called historical novel.[39]

S. Fischer Verlag had received numerous requests from book clubs for a two-volume selection of Freud's works, with commentary, for the lay reader. When, at the end of 1974, I asked Anna Freud to make such a selection and supply the commentary, she agreed only on condition that she and I produce and issue the edition together. In the ensuing years, we discussed in detail the selection, the commentary, and the content of the editorial introductions and linking texts. Following an idea of Anna Freud, the first volume, *Elemente der Psychoanalyse* [Elements of Psychoanalysis], was structured around *The Question of Lay Analysis,* one of Freud's most lucid propaedeutic texts; we placed this essay at the beginning of the volume and presented the other Freud works in the same order as he himself there followed for his various themes in order gradually to introduce a person unversed in psychoanalysis to its fundamental principles. For the second volume, *Anwendungen der Psychoanalyse* [Applications of Psychoanalysis], which was intended to document "programmatically" the original scope of Freud's teachings beyond the confines of medicine, we based the order of the subject matter—from the study of literature, via the psychology of religion, to the theory of education—on passages from Freud's *An Autobiographical Study.* The *Werkausgabe in zwei Bänden* [Edition of the Works in Two Volumes] was published in 1978; it contains bibliographic and didactic notes, which also link the content with more recent psychoanalytic research.

To sum up, since the acquisition of the rights by S. Fischer Verlag, Freud's works have been published in the original language on three levels: first, in the form of hardcover books—as embodied both in the *Werkausgabe in zwei Bänden,* the only compact didactic introduction, and, in particular, in the *Gesammelte Werke,* as completed by the *Gesamtregister* [general index] and the *Nachtragsband* [supplementary volume], the only comprehensive edition of the psychological and psychoanalytic works, in volumes 1 to 17, which, as described, is a kind of publishing relic of the pioneering days in Vienna; second, in the form of large-format paperbacks—represented by the *Studienausgabe,* the only critical edition of a major part of the main oeuvre; and third, in the form of regular-format paperbacks—in a large number of individual volumes, comprising reading editions disseminated on a huge scale, which present almost the whole of the psychoanalytic oeuvre and some of the preanalytic works.

Numbers of copies printed and sold are, of course, an aspect of the

---

[39]See below, chapter 10, "First Versions."

destiny of books that is particularly relevant to the history of their impact, but it is one I cannot discuss in detail here. Ernest Jones's biography of Freud[40] contains many instructive indications of the number of copies of individual works sold during Freud's lifetime; we learn, for example, that the first edition of the *Traumdeutung* [*The Interpretation of Dreams*] comprised 600 copies, which sold very slowly over a period of eight years.[41] To give the reader at least some idea of the extent of the dissemination of Freud's works in paperback form in the German language, I may mention the total number of copies produced of three of these mass-market Freud paperbacks: by the end of 1991, forty-two printings, totaling 755,000 copies, had been made of the volume containing the *Abriss der Psychoanalyse* [*An Outline of Psycho-Analysis*] and *Das Unbehagen in der Kultur* [*Civilization and its Discontents*], published in 1953; the regular-format paperback edition of the *Traumdeutung* [*The Interpretation of Dreams*], first published in 1961, has run through twenty printings, with sales amounting to some 246,000 copies; and the *Vorlesungen zur Einführung in die Psychoanalyse* [*Introductory Lectures on Psycho-Analysis*], first published years later, in 1977, after the most tempestuous phase of Freud's reception in the German-speaking world and following the publication of the work in the first volume of the *Studienausgabe*, have so far had thirteen printings, amounting to a total of 88,000 copies.

Finally, it may be noted that several German-language editions of Freud were even published officially in the former German Democratic Republic, under license at the beginning of the 1980s; although in some cases accompanied by tendentious editorial commentaries, they nevertheless gave GDR readers direct access to some of the primary sources.[42]

The disclosure of Freud's letters, a process which had begun with the publication of the Fliess documents and the anthology *Briefe 1873–1939* [*Letters of Sigmund Freud 1873–1939*], continued alongside the presentation of the works proper. The correspondences with the following were published in succession: Oskar Pfister (1963), Karl Abraham (1965), Lou Andreas-Salomé (1966), and Arnold Zweig (1968); while the letters to Edoardo Weiss, first published in English in 1970, came out in German in

---

[40]Jones, 1953, 1955, and 1957.

[41]Jones, 1953, p. 395.

[42]For details, cf. Grubrich-Simitis, 1989, p. 906, note 115. When copyright protection for Freud's works expired in the GDR in 1989, the Leipzig publishing house of Johann Ambrosius Barth brought out, just before the unification of Germany, a collection of some of the shorter preanalytic writings under the title *Sigmund Freud (1856–1939) Hirnforscher · Neurologe · Psychotherapeut* [Sigmund Freud (1856–1939) Brain Researcher · Neurologist · Psychotherapist], edited by Ingrid Kästner and Christina Schröder.

resulting from laborious and sometimes painful struggles to achieve quality editions and to obtain the necessary personnel and funding; it was a matter of quiet persistence wresting what we could from awkward realities. However, we may legitimately assert that these polyphonic publications have contributed to the process of bringing Sigmund Freud's heritage to life in the German-speaking world today. There can admittedly be no certainty that this source of enlightenment has been reliably implanted in all its enduring vibrancy unless, in a new, fourth phase of the oeuvre's editorial history, we have a critical edition, commensurate with the author's status, of the works and of at least a selection of the letters, incorporating the building blocks assembled in the interim. After our exploration of the landscape of the manuscripts, I shall sketch out the contours of such an edition in part III of this book.

PART TWO

Landscape of the Manuscripts

I was miserable the whole time

and deadened the pain

by writing—writing—writing.

—Freud to Sándor Ferenczi,
2 January 1912

4 WRITING — WRITING — WRITING

The letters to Wilhelm Fliess not only are the log of the genesis of psychoanalysis but also contain Freud's most compact description of his own creative process. "I have never been able to guide my intellectual work," he wrote.[1] But he had plainly learned at an early stage to entrust himself more or less passively to the obscure rhythm that governs the preconscious and unconscious workings of the mind—to wait again and again, often for a long time, until he was seized by a kind of inner urgency, a mood in which isolated ideas and inklings no longer withdrew below the threshold of consciousness but came together in rapid bursts and ultimately crystallized into pregnant configurations. These are described by Freud almost as if they were living things imbued with a dynamic of their own controlling their growth and movement, as if he were merely placing himself at their disposal as a container. He himself used the metaphor of birth to characterize the terminal phase of the creative process, which he portrayed as involving "frightful labor pains."[2] However, the preparatory phases were not marked by a constant state of well-being either. In order to feel them getting under way in the first place, he needed the stress of a moderate level of mental and/or physical pain, the tension of that "modicum of misery"[3] that was "the optimal condition for my mental activities."[4] This was required not only for the exercise of his cogitative faculty but also for the composition of felicitous prose. For instance, he writes to Fliess on 6 September 1899 from Berchtesgaden, where he was spending the summer, during the period when he was working on *The Interpretation of Dreams*: "My style has unfortunately been bad because I feel too well physically; I have to feel somewhat miserable to write well."[5]

Traces of these fundamental prerequisites for the initiation and successful continuance of the creative process are also to be found in the more intimate of Freud's subsequent correspondences, especially in that with Sándor Ferenczi. Here too, many passages testify to his willingness to wait patiently, as if scenting the air, in a kind of intermediate state between passivity and activity. The structure of the German language may well have

[1]1985c, p. 313.
[2]Ibid., p. 278.
[3]Ibid., p. 181.
[4]Ibid., p. 146.
[5]Ibid., p. 370.

been conducive to this attitude, thanks to its wealth of verb forms expressing the passive direction of behavior, but also because it allows active clauses to be instantly transformed into passive ones and vice versa, not to mention the specific passive forms that make possible a blurring of the passive and active voices.[6] Because he was aware of the fertility of this humble attitude of not forcing things along, Freud distrusted any work he wrote to order. For example, he makes the following disparaging remark about the short study entitled "The Psycho-Analytic View of Psychogenic Disturbance of Vision," written in 1910 as a contribution to a Festschrift in honor of the sixtieth birthday of his friend the ophthalmologist Leopold Königstein: "It doesn't amount to much, like everything done on request."[7] He preferred to surrender to his very own internal rhythms until the "good fortune" of an idea or the outline of a theory came to him. "The question of taboo ambivalence," he reported during his work on *Totem and Taboo*, "suddenly came together a few days ago, almost snapped in with an audible 'click,' and since then I am practically giddy. My interest has been extinguished for the moment, and I have to wait until it gathers itself together again." Or, during the gestation of *Inhibitions, Symptoms and Anxiety*: "Genesis: like a novel serialized in a newspaper, the author allowing himself to be surprised by each installment. [. . .] The stuff is so badly written that it must probably be rewritten; for a long time the question was whether it should remain unwritten. But fate has dictated otherwise."

The only thing he would force himself to do was to make time for reflection and writing. He called both activities "work", whereas almost everything else was dubbed a "nuisance"—giving lectures, writing letters, chairing meetings, reading books, attending congresses, and even treating patients. "Unfortunately, I get to work so little that I have to force myself again and again to get into the proper mood. That harms my style as much as do my many hours of association with people who speak German badly." Freud therefore strove actively and consciously again and again to find his way back from the nuisances to the work. Yet nuisance and work were not serious antitheses. After all, he gleaned the material for his writing mainly from the therapeutic dialogues with his analysands. And when he succeeded in balancing nuisance against work, a precarious internal equilibrium seemed at the same time to be assured. At any rate, one way or another, he was intensely busy; as he himself put it, it was good for him "not to have a

---

[6]Cf. Grubrich-Simitis, 1986*a*, p. 289.

[7]This quotation and the many formulations from the correspondence with Ferenczi in this and the next two paragraphs are taken from Freud's letters of 12 April 1910 (1992*g*, p. 265), 1 February 1912 (ibid., p. 340f.), 14 August 1925, 4 May 1913 (ibid., p. 482), 13 February 1919, and 2 April 1911 (ibid., p. 265), respectively.

single hour of the day for self-contemplation." When unoccupied, he tended to feel dull and empty.

The other prerequisite for his creativity, that "modicum of misery," is also alluded to many times in the correspondence with Ferenczi. Freud repeatedly stresses that in order to produce anything he needs "a bit of discomfort from which I have to extract myself." In this way, over and over, there manifestly arose something like a charge of yearning, a utopian impulsion, directed toward an ideal of perfection in regard to beauty of language and clarity of thought.[8] Freud had come to a good accommodation with this silent, background unhappiness as the spur to his creativity. There is perhaps an element of wise acceptance of his own mental wounds in his injunction to Ferenczi, who was always so anxious to be cured, with its allusion to C. G. Jung's "complex mythology": "Man should not want to eradicate his complexes but rather live in harmony with them; they are the legitimate directors of his behavior in the world."[9] A few weeks after this letter, written on 17 November 1911, he notes on the second day of the following year, as if for the sake of illustration: "I was miserable the whole time and deadened the pain by writing—writing—writing."[10]

It is perhaps tempting to reflect on the sources of that modicum of misery. The reader's attention should not be focused on the well-known *external* factors, such as the poverty of his origins, anti-Semitic discrimination, outsider status due to violation of taboos and critique of institutions, political persecution, and attacks on his lifework. Neither, however, do I claim to offer a conclusive hypothesis about the unconscious dynamics of Freud's creativity. Remaining as it were on the surface, I shall describe only some of the more conspicuous phenomena which, according to the evidence of the documents, fairly consistently accompanied the bringing forth of the oeuvre. Just occasionally, where there seems to be positively no alternative, the odd conjecture about underlying *internal* conflicts will be woven into the narrative.

A combination of three factors appears to be essential to the development of creativity at the highest level, and all three of them surely came together in Freud. The first is supreme intrinsic talent, the principal elements of which are the potential to make complex, novel combinations of signs and a finely tuned sense of rhythm, form, and material. The second require-

---

[8]Freud's sense of beauty had developed early and was not confined to his style. For example, when he was just twenty-three years old, describing the nerve specimens resulting from his modified isolation technique, he explicitly and with palpable delight refers to their "beauty" (in "Notiz über eine Methode zur anatomischen Präparation des Nervensystems" ["A Note on a Method of Anatomical Dissection of the Nervous System"] [1879a]).

[9]1992g, p. 314.

[10]Ibid., p. 325 [published translation modified].

ment is that a degree of successful mothering shall have been received at the beginning of life, promoting the development of the basic ego structures as a precondition for symbolization, sublimation, and the tolerance of frustration. Third, there must have been traumatic experiences of loss and discontinuity in the relationship with the initially reliable primary object, and these must have occurred before the completion of the process of self-object differentiation; in other words, early mental wounds must have been inflicted, leaving scars and resulting in a permanent relative permeability of the ego boundaries. If the boundaries of the ego remain permeable in this way, perceptual latitude is effectively increased in relation both to the unconscious and to external reality, albeit at the cost of lifelong psychic fragility.

These highly simplified formulations, in which the emphasis is placed on the traumatic element, are here framed largely in terms of Margaret S. Mahler's theory of development, but a Kleinian approach could also be adumbrated. In this case, the modicum of misery would relate to the experience, in a kind of mourning, of depression not defended against, something that is conditional upon an adequately developed tolerance of depressive fantasies and anxieties and on trust in the subject's own reparative capabilities—in other words, the "depressive position" must, so to speak, be within reach, and it has to be possible to work through it again and again in the creative process. It must be conceded, however, that psychoanalysis, of whatever school, has difficulty in accounting for the *formal* constitutive aspects of both artistic and scientific creativity—which are combined in Freud's work. The charges once brought by Flaubert against Sainte-Beuve and Taine as critics can equally well be leveled at not a few psychoanalytic studies of art: "that they don't take sufficient account of *Art*, of the work itself, of its construction, of its style, in short of everything that constitutes beauty."[11]

As for the third determinant of creative achievement, early traumatization constantly impelling toward self-stabilization, this may in Freud's case have consisted in a sudden inner turning away of his mother from her firstborn in the second year of his life. It was at this time that Freud's younger brother, Julius, died in infancy, and his mother, then pregnant with her third child, had to cope not only with the death of her second child but also with the loss of one of her brothers, who had died almost simultaneously. The mourning work associated with this twofold bereavement must have resulted, at least temporarily, in a quite abrupt diminution of the young mother's capacity for empathy, thereby unleashing in the infant storms of affect which placed an excessive burden on his budding ego. While

[11]Flaubert and Turgenev, 1985, p. 46.

it is beyond the scope of this book to go into the details of Freud's early biography and its repercussions in his texts,[12] it is perhaps worth pointing to the possible connection between his productive unhappiness and that no doubt traumatic irruption into the development of his ego before the process of separation was complete. Such a link can, of course, not be proved. Again, it is well to bear in mind an objection raised by Freud in a letter of 16 September 1930 to Ferenczi in relation to the studies of trauma on which Ferenczi was then engaged: "The new views on the traumatic fragmentation of mental life to which you allude seem to me to be most ingenious [. . .]. My only reservation is that, given the extraordinary synthetic activity of the ego, it will be virtually impossible to speak of trauma without at the same time dealing with the reactive cicatrization. The latter, after all, also gives rise to what we see, whereas the traumas themselves must be inferred." At any rate, Freud's texts may be said to be partly the result of repeated successful attempts to come to terms with an inner state of distress, with mostly unconscious anxieties, never to be entirely allayed, about getting lost, about starving, and about death.

What, in this context, was the function of writing—in the concrete sense of motor activity? Already in the Fliess period, Freud had distinguished between *two* intellectual states: one in which he did nothing but listen very closely to his patients—that is to say, in which he empathized, perceived, and registered—and a second, in which he drew conclusions and made notes.[13] We can discern here a precursor of the distinction which he later[14] recommended that the analyst make between two attitudes: on the one hand, analysis on the basis of evenly suspended attention, without taking notes, and on the other, the work of synthetic cogitation, which remains dependent on a written record. The act of writing was manifestly a concomitant of the creative process in Freud from quite an early stage.

While preparing the facsimile edition of Freud's essay "The Theme of the Three Caskets" in the mid-1970s, I asked Anna Freud about her father's

---

[12]Cf. Grubrich-Simitis, 1991, p. 35ff., for some further details.

[13]This practice of writing down seems to have begun even earlier where his self-analysis is concerned. As a result, Freud was clearly able not only to simulate or provide a substitute for something of the objectivizing and onward-driving power of the dialogue between analyst and analysand, but also to moderate the inhibiting criticism that usually comes into play very rapidly in self-observation. He had already reported in *The Interpretation of Dreams*: "[. . .] I myself can do so very completely, by the help of writing down my ideas as they occur to me" (1900a, p. 103). He later also commended this technique to his daughter, as we can see from a letter from Anna Freud to her father dated 7 August 1921: "Now at last I also believe you when you say that dream analyses, if made by oneself, can only be done in writing." (The correspondence between Sigmund and Anna Freud has not yet been published; this translation is based on Ingeborg Meyer-Palmedo's transcription.)

[14]1912e, p. 114.

writing habits. As far as she could then recall, he had always begun to set down a work only at a relatively late stage—that is to say, after it had matured within him in every respect, down to the finest details of its definitive linguistic form, so that, effectively, all he needed to do was copy it from a textual image stored within him. This picture has since proved to be incorrect. It may have been the result of a retroactive idealizing tendency—for when Anna Freud was a member of the editorial committee for the *Gesammelte Werke*, she had stated in 1940 in the foreword to the seventeenth volume that it had been Freud's custom to make notes and jot down ideas as a "starting point for subsequent works."[15] As we shall see, the documents prove that the works were hardly ever produced according to the model of divine inspiration; as a rule, there were a number of different stages, each recorded in writing, in a process of consuming hard labor, which often progressed in fits and starts. "[. . .] for me it has almost always been an agonizing struggle. Why should it be any better for you?" Freud confirms in a letter dated 6 December 1915 to Ferenczi, who had complained to him of the difficulty of definitive formulation. Although Freud never made any secret of his writing habits—after all, he describes them repeatedly in his letters—his students clearly tended, even during his lifetime, to idealize the alleged facility of his production. In an interview given decades later, for example, Sándor Radó was still referring to the virtual absence of corrections in the manuscripts: it had been breathtaking to see how Freud had simply dashed them off without first making a draft.[16]

As with any writer, writing carried a powerful cathexis for Freud. It was also highly susceptible to disturbance. He sometimes suffered from writer's cramp, in which he recognized a phenomenon of resistance. Even minor changes in his handwriting were a source of intense concern for him, as if they were harbingers of the loss of "all ability to work and to struggle"[17] which he feared throughout his life. For example, toward the end of the First World War, on 17 February 1918, he noted in a letter, again to Ferenczi: "The fact that my handwriting is now rapidly deteriorating (perhaps the cold has something to do with it?) will not have escaped you." A few weeks later, he was able to inform his friend with a sense of relief that the "spoiling" was now attributable mainly to the arthritis of advancing years. Under

[15]P. viii.

[16]Radó was talking about fair copies of successive new works as they came into being, which Freud occasionally sent to Ferenczi for criticism and which Ferenczi used to read and discuss with Radó. The interview was conducted in the 1960s by Bluma Swerdloff as part of the Columbia Oral History Project. This material has recently been published by Paul Roazen and Bluma Swerdloff under the title *Heresy: Sandor Rado and the Psychoanalytic Movement.* Cf. p. 44f.

[17]1966a, p. 51.

even more extreme external stress, in 1938, shortly after his arrival in exile, he again blamed an impairment of his handwriting on an organic cause: this time disturbances of the urinary function.[18]

Yet even when Freud was sure of his handwriting, he was sometimes plagued by a *"horror calami."*[19] Certain external conditions—protective circumstances in time and space—were necessary to overcome this dread, this fear of the pen. They included the following: the expectation of a period without disturbance—that is, days without patients and, on weekdays, predominantly evenings and nights; a tranquil sanctum of his own, well shielded from the living area of his apartment and the family routine—that is, the study that adjoined his consulting room; a chair specially made to support his body in certain postures while he sat at his desk; a fog of cigar smoke around him; the silent presence of objects which condense the past and bring it to life in the here and now—that is, the books and antiques, in particular the Egyptian, Etruscan, Roman, and Chinese bronze statuettes and terracotta figures ranged two-deep on his desk, which he literally faced eye to eye as he worked, and whose ceremonial solemnity must have both challenged and mirrored him; and finally, specific writing implements—heavy fountain pens and colored wax crayons—and his unusually large sheets of paper.

However, such protective circumstances in time and space were afforded not only by Freud's main residence in the Berggasse. He could also find them in those segments of his vacations when he was not traveling but staying at a single summer residence with his family—for instance, in Berchtesgaden, Aussee, Karlsbad, Klobenstein, Badgastein, and later Semmering. According to the evidence of the letters, a considerable proportion of the oeuvre actually came into being during these "nuisance"-free phases—at least in broad outline; on his return, Freud would make bibliographic additions, insert the text of quotations, and perform checks and corrections of all kinds. But it was while on holiday, as he once wrote to Ferenczi, that he would finally react "to the billions of impressions which I had to absorb from ten people for nine hours a day for nine months, but admittedly not in due proportion, otherwise I would surely be able to produce volumes."[20] Immediately upon arrival at his holiday destination, Freud would normally rest for a while. Then he would devote himself to the reading matter he had brought with him and begin to get himself in the mood for creative work. Once again, particular surroundings were necessary: "a nice little place in the woods close by where one can read and take

[18]See the beginning of chapter 6.
[19]1985c, p. 127.
[20]Letter of 21 July 1922.

Freud's writing desk at Berggasse 19.   [Fig. 4.1]

notes"[21] and, for the work of writing proper, a comfortable room to himself in the boardinghouse or hotel, where he could set up a "writing corner." The familiar writing implements, on which Freud felt dependent, were taken along. In a letter to his daughter Anna from the Hungarian resort of Lomnic on 19 September 1918, he says: "If you see Sachs, remind him to bring me the fountain pen. My good one is broken, and I can hardly write."

In D. W. Winnicott's terms, these specific arrangements could be called the "facilitating environment" of Sigmund Freud as a writer; they could also be seen as his "location of cultural experience,"[22] of creative intercourse with cultural objects, distinguished by Winnicott as a third realm, additional to that of external reality, on the one hand, and instinct-driven internal reality, on the other. Winnicott placed this realm in the "potential space" which, at the beginning of life, at one and the same time links and separates the baby and the mother, the self in the process of constitution and the object that provides support—literally an intermediate space which, where it opens up, is an essential prerequisite for any play and creative work, the

[21]1992g, p. 300.
[22]Winnicott, 1967.

variable handling of symbols. Winnicott, as we know, also assigned the use of transitional objects to this space. Perhaps the particular writing implements and especially the large sheets of paper really did perform a similar function to that of transitional objects in the creative process. When asked why he had opted for such a striking, grand paper size, Freud is said to have replied that, if he had to resign himself to so many restrictions in life, he wanted at least to have space and freedom while writing.[23] The reference to restrictions may conceivably, among other things, have been an allusion to his agoraphobic traits, which Reik has portrayed empathically for us in another book.[24]

At any rate, these special surroundings and specific implements manifestly gave Freud the courage to repeat, in the commencement of each work, something whose outcome was never certain: to surrender, in that state of tension in which ideas are as yet inchoate, mere inklings, and not ripe for formulation, at first to the threatening experience of dependence, non-differentiation, and chaos; but then, reactivating traces of his own very early object experiences, *both* traumatic *and* successful, to detach himself from this condition in a kind of "struggle for liberation"[25] through language in statements of ever-increasing lucidity—for naming is always a form of separation too—and finally to attain intellectual autonomy. Once this process of differentiation was under way, he seems to have been attended by the pleasure of control, joyful relaxation, and a delightful feeling of being entertained—that is, all the affective qualities of creative play. In these buoyant phases, Freud was also plainly able to write very quickly.[26] The fact that such self-configuration took place *autonomously*, yielding, where successful, something completely new which perhaps could not be lost, filled him, at least temporarily, with satisfaction and confidence.[27]

[23]Reik, 1956, p. 22. All the full-page facsimiles reproduced in this book are thus appreciably reduced in scale. The same applies to the extracts comprising only a few lines. For a faithful reproduction of the size of the paper and of Freud's handwriting, color, typography, etc., the reader is referred to the facsimile edition of the essay "The Theme of the Three Caskets" (1913*f*).

[24]Reik, 1949, p. 16.

[25]1992*g*, p. 240.

[26]Jones, 1957, p. 138.

[27]Even if Freud's creative process is described here predominantly in terms of the handling of separation conflicts, this does not, of course, rule out the genital, generative aspects that can probably be discovered at the root of any creative activity; the reader will recall the birth metaphor mentioned at the beginning of this chapter. The relevant capacity is, moreover, bisexual. "I am beginning to write something out of boredom," he says in a letter to Anna Freud dated 20 April 1927, "but I do not yet know whether it will be viable." Here Freud is in effect identifying equally with a father who can initiate life and with a mother who is prepared to carry the child to full term but is not yet certain whether growth will proceed.

One of the theaters of this struggle for liberation—in almost physical terms—was Freud's relationship to his newly emerging work. As a rule, except in the case of contributions written to order, he would work with fervent exclusiveness and unparalleled intensity on *a single* book, *a single* essay. A particular formulation in which this state of fusion is expressed appears again and again in the letters. "Nothing but the dream," he wrote to Fliess[28] from Berchtesgaden during the composition of *The Interpretation of Dreams*. While immersed in the "Psycho-Analytic Notes on an Auto-biographical Account of a Case of Paranoia," he informed Ferenczi: "I am Schreber, nothing but Schreber."[29] Again, while setting down *Totem and Taboo*, he asserted on several occasions: "I am totally totem and taboo" and "I have just been totally omnipotence, totally a savage. That's the way one must keep it if one wants to get done with something." It is as if he were saying that only by such an intimate symbiosis with a text of this kind, only by truly sinking his teeth into it, would he ultimately be able to detach himself from it.

In Freud's case, this not only libidinal but also aggressive cathexis of a new work waxed and waned in a number of stages. In the process, writing as a motor activity seems to have performed an indispensable function, at first increasing and then diminishing its intensity. As stated, writing was one of the mainstays of his creative process, helping to inspire it from quite an early stage. When he was able actually to see his thoughts in written form, as it were to confront them face-to-face, then he finally had a concrete target for his self-criticism; he was, as he once confessed to Ferenczi,[30] proud of this capacity, which he regarded as, next to his courage, the best thing in him, causing him to be extremely selective in publishing his works; without it he could easily have published three times as much. But it was in this way that the oeuvre ultimately came into being: it was precisely by writing—making *notes* and sketching out *drafts*—that he would feel his way toward new works, which he would nurture for a while like pieces of himself, after which he would elaborate them into *fair copies* and gradually send them out into the world. As we shall see, although some notes and drafts have come down to us, the fair copies make up the bulk of the documents preserved from the genesis of the works. These fair copies also represent the stage of transition to the public text of the printed version.

Some surviving galleys show that Freud as a rule made final corrections

[29]Letter of 3 December 1910 (1992g, p. 239); the next two quotations are taken from letters to the same addressee dated 11 August 1911 (ibid., p. 300) and 30 December 1912 (ibid., p. 457), respectively.
[30]In the letter of 17 October 1910 (ibid., p. 227).

and additions of both content and style when proofreading.[31] At this stage, he liked to use his colleagues as a kind of intimate public: he would circulate galley proofs—whereas he would entrust his manuscripts only to his very closest associates—and request criticism. However, it was only when a work went to press and was published that he felt he had really separated from it. There are indications in his letters that he tended to react with fatigue and depressive withdrawal when he had finished correcting the galleys. For example, at the end of the discussion with Ferenczi about the galley proofs of *Totem and Taboo*, he writes: "My thoughts are now fleeing from it." And when *The Ego and the Id* was being printed: "Now I am in the familiar depression after all the proofreading."[32]

[31]This is true in particular of the galleys of the *"Selbstdarstellung"* [*An Autobiographical Study*], which actually do include some significant amendments to the text. However, relatively minor corrections, in some cases in a different hand, are also to be found in the galleys of "Der Humor" ["Humor"], "Fetischismus" ["Fetishism"], "Die Feinheit einer Fehlhandlung" ["The Subtleties of a Faulty Action"], "Die endliche und die unendliche Analyse" ["Analysis Terminable and Interminable"], "Moses, ein Ägypter" ["Moses an Egyptian"], "Wenn Moses ein Ägypter war . . . " ["If Moses was an Egyptian . . . "], and the obituary for Lou Andreas-Salomé. The galleys of *Die Zukunft einer Illusion* [*The Future of an Illusion*], on the other hand, are uncorrected. Some chapters or parts of chapters of the fourth volume of the *Sammlung kleiner Schriften zur Neurosenlehre* (namely, chapter 26 and parts of chapters 25 and 27) are preserved in the form of corrected page proofs.

[32]These two statements are contained in letters dated 26 June 1913 (1992g, p. 496) and 17 April 1923, respectively.

5 VICISSITUDES OF THE MANUSCRIPTS

Having finished correcting his proofs, Freud seems to have abruptly lost interest in his manuscripts, which he no doubt felt belonged to the private sphere of his life. From then on, as described in part I of this book, his undivided attention was devoted to the published work and its future. No sooner did he have the printed version in his hands than he discarded the handwritten originals once they had served their purpose. The resulting losses included the manuscript of the book of the century, the *Traumdeutung* [*The Interpretation of Dreams*],[1] as Freud explicitly confirmed in a late letter to Abraham Schwadron dated 12 July 1936: he had "handed [it] into the wastebasket."[2] Earlier still, on 8 July 1929, he had stressed in a card to Israel Spanier Wechsler,[3] a New York neurologist, that the manuscript of the *Drei Abhandlungen zur Sexualtheorie* [*Three Essays on the Theory of Sexuality*][4] also no longer existed.

The practice of destroying his manuscripts[5] does not seem to have really come to an end until 1913/14, although Freud gives the date as 1905 in his letter to Schwadron. However, the manuscripts of a number of important works from earlier decades have also survived, although no doubt more by chance than otherwise. These include the sheets on which he wrote down the studies "Charakter und Analerotik" ["Character and Anal Erotism"], "Über infantile Sexualtheorien" ["On the Sexual Theories of Children"], "Die 'kulturelle' Sexualmoral und die moderne Nervosität" [" 'Civilized' Sexual Morality and Modern Nervous Illness"], "Allgemeines über den hysterischen Anfall" ["Some General Remarks on Hysterical Attacks"], and "Formulierungen über die zwei Prinzipien des psychischen Gesche-

---

[1] All that survives, as will be seen from the chapter on the notes, are manuscripts of a number of additions to later editions of the work.

[2] Cf. Gay, 1988, p. 612.

[3] Sigmund Freud Collection.

[4] Once again, only copies of the manuscripts of some notes to later editions of the book have survived: for example, of part of the 1920 note on the question of inversion (1905*d*, p. 146), or of the famous footnote from the same year on the Oedipus complex as the nuclear complex of the neuroses (ibid., p. 226, note 2).

[5] This refers to his routine treatment of the actual handwritten sheets on which he recorded his works. Apart from this, Freud is known to have gone through all his papers systematically at various stages of his life and to have destroyed large parts of them on each occasion; he did this for the first time in 1885 and for the last time in 1938, before his emigration.

hens" ["Formulations on the Two Principles of Mental Functioning"] as well as the manuscripts of the "Rat Man" and Schreber case histories, the study of Leonardo, and the third and fourth essays of *Totem und Tabu* [*Totem and Taboo*].[6] The papers and notes once enclosed with the letters to Wilhelm Fliess—texts not intended by the author for publication and made public only after his death—also survive in manuscript form.[7] Conversely, other documents of central importance from the early decades of Freud's creative life, over and above the manuscripts of *The Interpretation of Dreams* and of the *Three Essays*, have been lost; these include the fair copies of the case history of "Little Hans," the *Gradiva* study, the technical papers "Zur Dynamik der Übertragung" ["The Dynamics of Transference"] and "Ratschläge für den Arzt bei der psychoanalytischen Behandlung" ["Recommendations to Physicians Practicing Psycho-Analysis"] as well as the metapsychological paper "Einige Bemerkungen über den Begriff des Unbewussten in der Psychoanalyse" ["A Note on the Unconscious in Psycho-Analysis"].

The sequence of surviving material becomes almost complete only from 1913/14. There are just a few obvious gaps. For example, the original pages of the following are missing: *Massenpsychologie und Ich-Analyse* [*Group Psychology and the Analysis of the Ego*],[8] "Der Realitätsverlust bei Neurose und Psychose" ["The Loss of Reality in Neurosis and Psychosis"], "Die Feinheit einer Fehlhandlung" ["The Subtleties of a Faulty Action"], and the first of the three essays on Moses, "Moses, ein Ägypter" ["Moses an Egyptian."]. One will also search in vain for the fair copies of "Zur Psychologie des Gymnasiasten" ["Some Reflections on Schoolboy Psychology"], "Vergänglichkeit" ["On Transience"], "Dostojewski und die Vatertötung" ["Dostoevsky and Parricide"], and "Warum Krieg?" ["Why War?"]. These last four titles were contributions written by Freud to order, brought out together with texts by other authors, and not sold as specialized psycho-

[6]The Sigmund Freud Collection does, however, contain a photocopy of the fair copy of parts of the second essay (sections 3 and 4, although the beginning of section 4 is located somewhat earlier in the manuscript than in the printed version). The collection also includes parts of the fair copy of chapters 3 and 4 of *Zur Psychopathologie des Alltagslebens* [*The Psychopathology of Everyday Life*] in photocopy form.

[7]The undated manuscript "Kritische Einleitung in die Nervenpathologie" ["Critical Introduction to Neuropathology"] should also be mentioned in this connection; it was presumably written in the second half of the 1880s, and only extracts from it have been published so far (1983g). It was discovered in the estate of Wilhelm Fliess's son. Only a photocopy of the original exists in the Sigmund Freud Collection.

[8]The Sigmund Freud Collection contains only photocopies of a fragment of the manuscript of this work: the top halves of the torn-through manuscript pages 72 to 76 from the fair copy of the tenth chapter, "Die Masse und die Urhorde" ["The Group and the Primal Horde]."

analytic publications. He may have neglected to ask for his manuscripts back after they had been set in type,[9] as he otherwise seems to have done from 1913/14.

The reason for the change in Freud's treatment of his manuscripts during that period was evidently a dawning awareness of their autograph value. Just before the First World War, he had learned from Paul Federn that the Morgan Library in New York was interested in acquiring his manuscripts to add to the collection established by the American banker John Pierpont Morgan. Although this project came to nothing, manifestly because of the war,[10] Freud henceforth kept his manuscripts. Not long after his first operation for cancer, his nephew Edward L. Bernays wrote him from the United States that he had been approached by the Morgan's librarian. Freud replied on 27 November 1924: "I would not object at all. I cannot imagine what the value of such manuscripts might be. For me, at all events, they are worth nothing and I am quite ready to turn them into tangible assets, should a connoisseur turn up. But of course, it would have to be worthwhile, if only for the sake of prestige."[11]

Although nothing came of the plan even after this second attempt, further inquiries of this kind continued to reach Freud in the ensuing years. At the end of the 1920s, for example, Israel Spanier Wechsler suggested that he might bequeath his manuscripts to Jerusalem University. Freud, recalling the former occasion, adopted a temporizing attitude, not without self-irony, in his reply of 8 May 1929: "Your assumption that this university is dear and important to me is correct, but it may be that we do not agree about the assessment of such manuscripts. To me they do not mean anything; it actually would never have occurred to me to offer them to the University as a gift. I used to cast them into the wastepaper basket after they had been printed until one day someone suggested that they could be put to another use. This man told me that among the rich there are fools who, in the event of my becoming famous, would be willing to pay cash for such pages covered by my hand. Since then I have been preserving them and am awaiting

[9]This is certainly true of the epistolary dialogue with Albert Einstein published under the title "Warum Krieg?" ["Why War?"] in 1933. The manuscript of this work came under the hammer at Sotheby's in New York at the end of 1990; according to the catalog, it was "Sold by Authority of the Trustees of an Educational Institution." The secretary of the International Institute of Intellectual Cooperation of the League of Nations, Leon Steinig, who had initiated this correspondence, seems to have previously sold the pages preserved in his possession to the educational institution. The document has now been acquired by a private American collector for $165,000; this has unfortunately precluded its addition to the body of manuscripts in the Library of Congress.

[10]Cf. a letter from Freud to Paul Federn dated 24 January 1915 (photocopy in the Sigmund Freud Collection).

[11]1965b, p. 272.

such pleasant consequences of my fame, bearing in mind that there is no other way of my leaving or presenting anything to our own institutions such as the *Verlag*, the Viennese Institute, or the Berlin Sanatorium; indeed, such a legacy might be quite welcome to my seven grandchildren. Before the war I was told that a well-known collector of waste paper was actually considering the acquisition of my rubbish."[12] When the Jewish National and University Library approached Freud directly from Jerusalem with the same request in 1936, he suggested that the library contact his daughter Anna after his death, as she would inherit his books and papers.

Freud on this occasion again confirmed his "antipathy to personal relics, autographs, collections of handwriting specimens, and everything that springs from these"; although he had been persuaded to keep his manuscripts, he did not like to occupy himself with them.[13] These were not just empty words. Freud's behavior toward his colleagues, for example, indicates that he really did not share the general esteem for manuscripts and that, to the end, he did not treat them with any particular reverence. Here are two examples. When he sent Sándor Ferenczi the draft manuscript of his twelfth metapsychological paper in 1915, he left it to him whether to discard or to retain it. And the unpublished correspondence with Max Eitingon shows that, over the years, Freud had—presumably at Eitingon's request—given him three manuscripts: no less than those of *Jenseits des Lustprinzips* [*Beyond the Pleasure Principle*], the *"Selbstdarstellung"* [*An Autobiographical Study*], and *Das Unbehagen in der Kultur* [*Civilization and its Discontents*].[14] Later, he plainly forgot which manuscripts he had given away. When in 1934, to his irritation, a purveyor of pictures and autographs offered for sale the manuscript of the short paper "Ein religiöses Erlebnis" ["A Religious Experience"], he on 27 November not only informed Eitingon that the Internationaler Psychoanalytischer Verlag had since acquired the pages for the sum of one hundred schillings[15] but also inquired: "I am now pursued by the probably insignificant idea that I might once have given these sheets to you at your request. How then might they have gone astray? But I did give you a manuscript once. Now which one was it?"[16] In his reply, Eitingon reminded Freud of those much more important gifts, and

---

[12]1960a, p. 387.

[13]Gay, 1988, p. 612.

[14]The gift of the latter manuscript seems even to have been noted in the "Kürzeste Chronik," which contains the following entry for 24 December 1929: "Christmas—Eitingon 'Discontents.'" All three manuscripts are now in the Sigmund Freud Collection; unlike the others, they are bound. Eitingon thus not only had them bound but evidently also saw to it that they were ultimately returned.

[15]However, this manuscript is not in the Sigmund Freud Collection today.

[16]Translated from a transcription made available by Sigmund Freud Copyrights.

shortly afterward Freud was able to report the outcome of his successful investigations: the former director of the Verlag, A. J. Storfer, had put the manuscripts—in fact several of them—on the market. So Freud had also failed to notice that he had not had several of his manuscripts back from his own publishing company on completion of the production process.

It therefore comes almost as a surprise that, at least since 1913/14, most of the manuscripts have remained together and have been preserved. According to information supplied by his daughter Anna,[17] Freud ultimately bequeathed the now precious papers to his children; the place of his daughter Sophie, who died young, was taken by her son Ernst. Except for those belonging to Anna Freud, the manuscripts were acquired many years ago by the American Psychoanalytic Association and, to protect them once and for all from sale and dispersal, assigned to the Sigmund Freud Collection—that is, to the Library of Congress. Anna Freud completed the collection when she donated her one-sixth portion to the Library of Congress in the mid-1970s. However, it had been agreed that all manuscripts would remain in Hampstead as long as Anna Freud lived. When I first perused the papers in 1975/76, they were still kept in Freud's study, preserved in big leather boxes. After Anna Freud's death in 1982, they were temporarily accommodated at a London bank before being handed over to the Manuscript Division of the Library of Congress in 1986. The Library of Congress is now their permanent home.

The large collection "Writings, 1877–1985 and undated"[18] contained

[17]She gave me this information in connection with the preparations for the facsimile edition of "Das Motiv der Kästchenwahl" ["The Theme of the Three Caskets"].

[18]Three bundles of manuscripts of Freud's translations are, incidentally, also cataloged under this heading. The first, dating from the earliest stages of his scientific career, comprises passages from Jean-Martin Charcot's *Leçons sur les maladies du système nerveux* [German title: *Neue Vorlesungen über die Krankheiten des Nervensystems, insbesondere über Hysterie* (New Lectures on Diseases of the Nervous System, with Particular Reference to Hysteria)] (1886*f*). The second contains part of the translation of Israel Levine's book *The Unconscious*, published in London in 1923. Freud had a high opinion of this work and may have inspired its translation by his daughter Anna, which was published by the Internationaler Psychoanalytischer Verlag in 1926. In the first part of his book, Levine introduces authors who had concerned themselves with the unconscious *before* Freud; they included the English writer Samuel Butler with his theory of an "unconscious memory." Jones (1957, p. 239) and Strachey (1957, p. 205) have already pointed out that Freud had not wanted to let anyone but himself translate precisely this passage. This was not out of any particular esteem for Butler but merely because Butler, with his reference to the physiologist Ewald Hering, gave Freud an opportunity to pay a debt of gratitude to a genuine precursor: in a translator's note of his own and through the addition of a quotation from Hering, Freud expresses his view that Hering was indeed one of the thinkers who, before Freud himself, had understood something of the unconscious activity of the mind (cf. *S.E.* 14, p. 205). The manuscript also proves that Freud himself translated not only the Butler passage but also the following section, "General Conclusions," probably with a certain pride because Levine comments in it that the conceptions of the

in Series B is accessible. It will only later be possible to determine whether the series of the Sigmund Freud Collection currently[19] identified by the initials A, E, F, Z, ZR, and Zpat include further manuscripts of direct relevance to the genesis of the oeuvre, as access to these parts of the collection is still substantially closed. However, the *systematic* exploration of the bulk of the manuscripts from Series B that are now no longer restricted surely itself remains a task for the future.

The details discussed in the following chapters of part II are extracts, examples from the results of my studies, selected and arranged with a view to providing the reader with a coherent and as far as possible entertaining account. As for the variants, I came across them as a rule during the course of more or less random, isolated comparisons between manuscripts and printed versions—that is, comparisons involving relatively short passages. However, some of my investigations were inevitably based on topics associated with my earlier research on Freud, such as drive/trauma, fantasy/memory, and archaic heritage/phylogenetic construction; a person who has been engaged with Freud's texts for any length of time will never lose his bearings when exploring these autographs. In the case of a number of writings, especially late works, I have compared manuscript and published version not only in passages chosen more or less at random but in their entirety and word for word. What seemed to me to be unpublished I attempted to decipher. Even so, what follows is hardly more than a preliminary survey of the landscape of Freud's manuscripts. In it, I take no account of such documents as handwritten notes on patients from the time of his medical training, lecture registration sheets, and the like, or of the vast body of letters, although this material is indirectly relevant to the context of the oeuvre. The following chapters are presented in chronological order of the three typical stages of the dynamic characterizing the genesis of Freud's texts: notes, drafts, and fair copies.

---

unconscious of all these forerunners, from Leibniz via Schopenhauer to Hartmann and Nietzsche as well as Butler himself, bear "the marks of vagueness and speculative thought" (p. 42). The third bundle comprises the manuscript of a major part of the translation of Marie Bonaparte's book *Topsy, Chow-Chow au Poil d'Or* [in German: *Topsy; Der goldhaarige Chow* (Topsy, the Golden-Haired Chow)], the result of another collaboration with his daughter Anna, which was brought out in 1939 by Allert de Lange, the Dutch publishing house which served the needs of exiled German-language writers, as stated in part I of this book.

[19]That is, at the time of my last visit to the Library of Congress in February 1992.

6 Notes

When the editors of the *Gesammelte Werke* brought out a volume of Freud's posthumous writings in 1941, they also presented a short collection of his notes.[1] The two-page manuscript of these notes, preserved in the Sigmund Freud Collection, bears the title "Ergebnisse, Ideen, Probleme. London Juni" ["Findings, Ideas, Problems. London June"]. The entries, dated with the month and day of the month only, were manifestly set down in 1938, the year Freud went into exile. Comparison of the manuscript with the published text reveals a number of editorial interventions, made without comment. The modernization of spelling and punctuation and the expansion of abbreviations may be deemed an obvious course, and one misreading that distorts the sense was surely unintentional.[2] However, proper names are also disguised, and one entry has plainly been shortened.[3]

The editors claim to have reproduced only a selection from that set of notes. A parallel reading of the manuscript and the printed version shows that only two notations were omitted. The first, recorded on 24 June, is autobiographical and deals with the relationship mentioned earlier, that between writer's cramp and symptoms of the urinary system:[4] "24/6 The only borrowing from graphology, in 1909, 53 y old in New York I had a

---

[1] 1941*f*.

[2] In the entry for 20 July, "Erspuren" (Freud's usual abbreviation for "Erinnerungsspuren" ["memory traces"]) has been misread as "Erbspuren" and consequently mistranslated as "inherited vestiges" (ibid., p. 299).

[3] The note of 16 June (p. 299) ends in the manuscript with the words: "Example: Dorothy in the first flush of love for James the gardener."

[4] [*Translator's note*: The author explains in the German edition of this book that in the following all quotations that are to the best of her knowledge hitherto unpublished have been transcribed letter by letter. Working from these transcriptions, I have done my best to reproduce the fragmentary, unpolished nature of the notes as realistically as possible. Where a word is truncated (e.g., "hy") and the author has completed it (e.g., as "hy[sterisch]"), I have reproduced this exactly (e.g., as "hy[sterical]"). However, because an English-speaking person would be unlikely to omit letters in the middle of a word (e.g., "Bearbeit[un]g"), I have always rendered such instances by a complete English word. I have tried to abbreviate and condense in the way a native English speaker would have done. In most cases I have not reproduced headings and titles in the original German; the use of an English heading or title does not imply that the original was not German.] Line breaks in the original are not as a rule followed. All additions by the present author appear in square brackets; however, editorial comment is confined to a minimum. Question marks in square brackets indicate uncertain readings. Some of Freud's occasionally idiosyncratic spellings and other writing habits [in the original German] are explained in more detail in chapter 8.

sudden prostate swelling with nonpulsating urge to urinate; at the same time, something quite new for me, a writer's cramp, which disappeared after some weeks (or months?). Now, again and more intensely afflicted with the same disorder, I notice the conspicuous deterioration and impediment of my handwriting. The old urinary symbolism of writing persists." The other omitted note is dated 22 September and reads as follows: "22/9 For origin of Eros—possibility that when life arose there was at same time a disintegration into m & f[5] substance, which as Plato surmises[6] have since wanted to unite. Though not everything fits in with this. Origin of Eros & death would thus be the same. But whence the simultaneity of the two events?"

In their foreword to the seventeenth volume of the *Gesammelte Werke*, the editors state that "Ergebnisse, Ideen, Probleme" ["Findings, Ideas, Problems"] constitutes "the only sheet" from Freud's "diary-like" notes to have survived: "All similar notes from previous years were destroyed by Freud himself before his departure from Vienna."[7] This wartime account dating from 1940 was no doubt consistent with the editors' impression of Freud's literary remains at the time. In my studies in the Sigmund Freud Collection I discovered that an abundance of other notations have also been preserved, partly as original manuscripts and partly as photocopies, and indeed that there exists a *body of notes* by Freud that have not yet been brought to light. Up to now we knew only that Marie Bonaparte, who was staying in Vienna in 1938, had acted to mitigate the effects of Freud's preemigration destruction of his papers: she had asked the family's house-keeper, Paula Fichtl, to recover discarded manuscripts from the wastebasket and give them to her. It may one day be possible to reconstruct from the correspondence between Anna Freud and Marie Bonaparte whether the princess returned the notes to the heirs after the war and what part of the material to be described in the following pages owes its survival to this rescue operation. Certainly not all of it, for there are indications that Freud himself kept some such papers and took them with him into exile.

Many of the notes preserved are dated by month and day of the month, and in some cases also by year. This, together with variations in the handwriting, shows that they stem from different phases of Freud's creative life. Some of them go back to preanalytic times, to his work on hysteria in the early 1890s. The writing materials used also vary, and some examples are already quite fragile. Freud set down quite a few of his notes on slips or relatively small, thin pieces of paper, while others were made on his usual large, strong

[5] Abbreviation: masculine and feminine.
[6] Reading uncertain; possibly "surmised."
[7] 1941*f*, p. viii [in *G. W.*, vol. 17].

sheets; they are almost always written in ink. Still others survive in the form of fragments torn on more than one side and sometimes reassembled with tape; their preservation may be due to Marie Bonaparte's rescue operation. However, there are also bundles of sheets on which Freud either wrote down his ideas direct or pasted strips of paper containing notes he had manifestly cut out before from other, no doubt earlier, collections of notations. The notes are as diverse in length as in their other formal aspects: they range from single words to quite extensive textual entities which almost constitute drafts, including in between the form of the—as it were—scientific aphorism, as already embodied in the "Findings, Ideas, Problems" included in the volume of posthumously published works.

To give the reader as vivid an impression as possible of the intensity of semantic condensation of such medium-length notations, a similar, earlier collection, again comprising two pages,[8] is reproduced below as facsimile 6.1 and translated; the individual texts were set down between December 1911 and January 1914:

Ideas & Discoveries

[1911]	5 Dec.	Primitives show mental impulses in their orig. completeness & ambivalence
	6 Dec.	Determinatives in the dream which are not translated
	10 Dec.	Series formation in neuroses is analogous to kinship among savages.
	10 Dec.	Anxietey arises when libido is withdrawn from a f[antasy]. Is that correct? How can it be proved? Perhaps only from an ucs [fantasy]?
	17 Dec. (4th[9] in addition)	There are 3 types of onset of neurosis, a)through frustration, b) through demands of reality, c) through inhibition in development. Combination of these.
	19 Dec.	Phobias (hy[sterical] and ob[sessional]) ჟistinguished by projection of internal complexes onto outside world.
	19 Dec	Disbelief in ob[sessional neurosis] replaces amnesia in hy[steria].
	31 Dec.	All internal restraints were once external resistances—Phylogenetic explan[ation] of repression.

---

[8]The Sigmund Freud Collection contains only a photocopy of the original manuscript.
[9]Add: type of onset.

First page of 'Ideen u[nd] Entdeckungen' ['Ideas & Discoveries'].   [6.1]

	31 Dec.	Genesis of sense of guilt perfectly analogous to that of anxiety, organic.
	31 Dec.	Fragmentary dreams consist of the associated symbols.
1912	15 Jan	Provenance of frequency of father accusation.
	19 Jan	Taboo comes from ambivalence.
	1 March	Sense of guilt from ~~soc~~erotic factor of social feelings. (important!).
	1 March	Simile of telephone for treatment.
	5 March.	Conscience arises from excess of ambiv. impulses, phylogenetically fixed?
	16 March	Secondary elaboration the root & paradigm of delusion formation.
	31 May	Role of fantasy comes from [before?] development of ego.
	6 June	Bisexual solution of infantile phobias.
	11 June	Theme of 3 sisters choice.
	12 June	Cordelia is death.
	19 June	Confirmation of connection bt. symbol & devel. of language (change of meaning).

[Second page:]

	Oct 1913.	The self-observing agency & Silberer's works—Delusion of being watched. The pregenital organization
	28 Oct.	Masochism of castration threat, sadism of eavesdropping on coitus.
	Jan 14.	Connection between masoch[ism] and castration Impotence, anal erotism

It would take us too far from our subject to attempt to retrace step by step the relevant processes of transformation; however, anyone familiar with Freud's oeuvre will, on reflecting about these ideas and discoveries, recognize that, like the genes of a germ cell, these concise sentences or parts of sentences contain in concentrated form the information that was to control the growth of the works that came into being during the same period: for example, of *Totem and Taboo* as well as "Types of Onset of Neurosis," "Observations and Examples from Analytic Practice," "Recommendations to Physicians Practicing Psycho-Analysis," "The Theme of the Three Caskets," and "On Narcissism: An Introduction."

Apart from the fact that it will not be possible to assign many undated notations to their correct place until further research has been conducted on this segment of the manuscripts, even an attempt to give an outline description of the various bundles of notes in chronological order would be beyond the scope of this chapter. Let us instead highlight some selected thematic areas, so as to illustrate the characteristic features and rich variety of this body of notes. The briefest selection of the headings with which Freud himself preceded many of his notes will suffice to show that they reflect the entire breadth of his thought:

Fear of being alone
The Sphynx
Speleologists
A true children's story
Children overlook the "how"
Word bridges
Hysterical stammering
Obsessional thought & compulsive action
Double meaning of symptoms
Moaning
Transference & impediment
New formula for the task of the treatment
Occurrence & absence of fantasies
Fantasies as the antithesis of memories
Organization of the Ucs.
The metapsychology of the beyond
Lost tendencies in art
A source of anti-Semitism.
How the difficult problem of dreaming of the mother's
    death is solved

The six thematic regions illuminated below in brief or at greater length—notes from his clinical work, notes on linguistic phenomena, on dreams, and on civilization, key words for particular works, and quasi-autobiographical reflections—occupied Freud throughout his life; such notations have therefore survived from various phases of his creativity. Roaming at will back and forth through the decades, I should therefore like, first, to offer a close-up picture of the pointillistic fine structure of the body of notes, taking a number of individual elements as examples, and, second, to draw attention to some higher-order configurations, which can be discerned only from a somewhat greater distance.

A considerable proportion of the double and single sheets and of the two sides of cut-out pieces of paper are filled with notes on occurrences from treatment sessions—that is, with the untold riches of the material thrown up daily by the therapeutic interaction between Freud and his patients.[10] "As regards instances, I write them down from memory in the evening after work is over."[11] And indeed, these notes do not comprise comprehensive and continuous accounts of sessions. In this respect they differ from the well-known, compact Original Record of the case of the "Rat Man" dating from 1907/08.[12] Freud seems to have used notations of this kind in the form of vignettes, sometimes of the utmost brevity, to gather material for theoretical considerations in the process of emerging or, by means of this assiduous compilation of details, to put himself on the track of higher-level conclusions.

The patients are often identified only by their first names but occasionally also by surname or, alternatively, by first name and the initial of the surname; and it is not unusual to feel that one recognizes figures familiar from the published work. Many a statement by an analysand is recorded verbatim. For example: "The attack is an extract from the history, says patient." In a ten-point enumeration of theoretical results of research on hysteria also preserved among the notes, we find an echo of this female patient's words: "The hysterical attack corresponds to a memory from the patient's life; it consists of the return of the scene experienced and the like, and the associated expression of the emotion." From this, as from the other nine points, those acquainted with Breuer and Freud's published contributions on hysteria can trace links with the five-point list "On the Theory of Hysterical Attacks"[13] dating from 1892, with the Lecture and Preliminary Communication "On the Psychical Mechanism of Hysterical Phenomena,"[14] and ultimately with the *Studies on Hysteria*.[15] One of the resulting

---

[10]However, a number of notes show that from the beginning his interest was not confined to the *reconstructed* child, which, in work with adult patients, gradually assumes concrete form during the course of an analysis; many actually contain fresh, direct observations of children and vividly illustrate how Freud's perceptual genius also extended to the *direct* reality of the infantile in the here and now. It may be recalled in this connection that Freud had developed at an early stage into an experienced observer of children during his many years of work at Kassowitz's pediatric institution, as is documented in his writings on child neurology.

[11]1912*e*, p. 113.

[12]Cf. the new transcription by Ingeborg Meyer-Palmedo in G. W., Nachtragsband, pp. 509–69, and the description of this manuscript in that volume's editorial introduction.

[13]1940*d*.

[14]1893*h* and 1893*a*.

[15]1895*d*.

gains will be an impression of the energy of Freud's theorizing in this famous collaboration which initiated the genesis of psychoanalysis.

However, testimony to the quotidian toil of Freud's clinical work is also borne by his strenuous reflection on all the forms of manifestation of obsessional neurosis, on obsessional thought and compulsive action, and on the underlying logical processes. The same applies to the notes on "an entire class of symptoms which have not yet been described, which lie between unsuccessful repression & sublimation, those of successful repression with cicatrization." Among these Freud counted, for example, not only tricks of the memory and prejudices, but also hobbies and monomanias.

Again and again his empirical prudence, his disciplined caution in the process of hypothesizing is documented—for instance, how he watched for "clues" in the clinical material that would make it easier for him, in his exploration of the etiology of the neuroses, to assess the importance of real traumatic experiences, on the one hand, and of pathogenic fantasies, on the other. This key question, which as it were triggered the genesis of psychoanalysis in the 1890s, occupied Freud throughout his life. Contrary to the notorious simplifications and falsifications of today's anti-Freud polemicists,[16] which have had such an enduring media impact, he never disputed the possibly pathogenic effect of real traumatic events and experiences and of the associated memories and their further elaborations.[17] The notes that have come down to us include, for example, the following passage under the heading "Occurrence & absence of fantasies": "I have a case in which I should like to take almost everything as actual memory, i.e., one which thereby differs from all others in their wealth of fantasies. That cannot be due to the cessation of masturb., which is best documented precisely in this case. But perhaps it is because a continuous series of facts to be repressed extends here to the age of 12–14 y., [whereas] in the others the real experiences break off very soon[,] still within the prehistoric period. The patient concerned shows herself during the treatment to be protected against any therapeutic effect of the work by considering the memories found to be untrue, rejecting any connection between them and her conscious memory, & not thinking any more of the treatment. She did not feel there was anything odd about the father's behavior or give any particular thought to it. How did she manage that?" Again and again, here as in countless other notes, Freud emphasizes ignorance: "(not comprehensible)" or "Still very obscure—Non liquet," the legal expression that Freud also used repeatedly in his published work when something was unclear.

Early notes, jotted down almost a century ago, directly convey to the

[16]Cf., for example, Masson, 1984.
[17]For further details, see my study "Trauma or Drive—Drive and Trauma" (1988).

present-day reader, for whom all this is now taken for granted as part and parcel of the very foundations of psychology and who is no longer able to conceive of thinking without such fundamental knowledge, the full weight of the revolutionary discovery of the ubiquity and depth of transference processes and of the development of the basic elements of psychoanalytic technique. The notes show Freud calling himself to order: "I still too readily forget that everything unclear is transference." Under the heading "Transference & impediment," the first entry contains another exhortation to self-discipline and precision: "That must be taken more sharply." He continues: "1). First, the t[ransference] should not be attacked as long as it does not present an impediment. 2). It becomes an impediment earlier than in spontaneous cases owing to the focusing of attention, 3). owing to the tendency to form resistances that results from the work, & owing to its outstanding fitness for this[,] 4). owing to its intensity or as soon as it attains too great an intensity[,] 5). owing to its negative sides[,] which are developed to a greater or lesser extent. I used to be inclined to ascribe the impeding nature of the transference entirely to the last factor, but this [is] not tenable, much more complicated. After all ΨA [psychoanalysis] is at a disadvantage compared with suggestive treatment, because it makes the tr[ansference] negative early on [and] provokes conflicts, but through the overcoming of these it has a curative effect."

The early search for a completely new kind of approach to his patients and their communications had dominated Freud's thought, not only in the consulting room but elsewhere, and even permeated his private reading. The extent of this preoccupation is documented by an undated entry headed "Citate u Analogien" ["Quotations & analogies"]: "For the proper attitude to the work of interpretation: Burckhardt. Hist. Greek Civilization p 5, intense effort is actually least likely to secure the desired result here; quietly attentive listening with steady diligence takes one further."

[6.2]

This is not only reminiscent of certain characteristics of the process of writing in Freud, but also contains the germ of the later technical concept of "evenly suspended attention"[18]—that is, a first delineation of the typical attitude toward the patient's communications that is enjoined upon the

[18]Cf. in particular 1912*e*.

analyst. As it happens, Freud mentioned the same inspiring reading matter in a letter to Fliess dated 30 January 1899: "For relaxation I am reading Burckhardt's *History of Greek Civilization*, which is providing me with unexpected parallels."[19]

Another undated note from the same period is headed "Double meaning of symptoms": "If we assume that symptoms can come into being only in the case of conflict, the condition can be stipulated that the symptom arising must correspond at the same time to both of the currents present in the conflict by a kind of double meaning. This condition combines with another, which states that the symptom must correspond at least to a sexual wishful situation, [and] may also express all other memories and motives. Example: Y's vomiting. It probably represents pregnancy, and in addition, as a sex. situation & through the comparison of head with rump, the ejaculation of the lovers she lacks. The latter meaning serves the lustful current which was for so long the dominant one in her, but by vomiting she is deprived of food, wastes away, gets ugly, so that she cannot attract any lover, as a punishment. The punishment is inflicted on her just as artfully as she tormented her lovers, in that her sexuality shows itself, but she must not enjoy anything of it.—When Helene A. runs away from concert & theater, this also seems to have a double meaning. She is fleeing from temptation, but is also obeying an old idea that the lovers meet at the lavatory for their tryst, & by (going out) beforehand[,] she summons the other to come after her, as she probably heard in the childhood scene."

Extracts from this record, here set down in abbreviated form for private use and therefore not understandable in every detail to the present-day reader, did eventually find their way into the published text. The vomiting example had already been mentioned by Freud in a letter to Fliess of 19 February 1899—this in turn enables us to date the notation—on the brand-new discovery of the multiple meaning of the symptoms: "A symptom arises where the repressed and the repressing thought can come together in the fulfillment of a wish." He continues enthusiastically: "This key opens many doors. Do you know, for instance, why X.Y. suffers from hysterical vomiting? Because in fantasy she is pregnant, because she is so insatiable that she cannot bear being deprived of having a baby by her last fantasy lover as well. But she also allows herself to vomit, because then she will be starved and emaciated, will lose her beauty and no longer be attractive to anyone. Thus the meaning of the symptom is a contradictory pair of wish fulfillments."[20]

[19] 1985c, p. 342. Cf. below, p. 266f. The note can be fairly precisely dated from the date of the letter and from the year of publication of Burckhardt's work (1898).
[20] 1985c, p. 345.

It is well known that the Fliess letters were published posthumously against the wishes of their author. However, Freud himself made the ideas outlined in the notation and in the letter accessible to the public before the turn of the century in the seventh chapter of *The Interpretation of Dreams*[21]—carefully closing some of the yawning gaps in understanding that remain in the note and additionally dramatizing the dialectic of wish fulfillment and incapacity for enjoyment by a classical comparison from his reading of Plutarch: "I can therefore make the quite general assertion that *a hysterical symptom develops only where the fulfillments of two opposing wishes, arising each from a different psychical system, are able to converge in a single expression.* [. . .] Examples would serve very little purpose here, since nothing but an exhaustive elucidation of the complications involved could carry conviction. I will therefore leave my assertion to stand for itself and only quote an example in order to make the point clear, and not to carry conviction. In one of my women patients, then, hysterical vomiting turned out to be on the one hand the fulfillment of an unconscious fantasy dating from her puberty—of a wish, that is, that she might be continuously pregnant and have innumerable children, with a further wish, added later, that she might have them by as many men as possible. A powerful defensive impulse had sprung up against this unbridled wish. And, since the patient might lose her figure and her good looks as a result of her vomiting, and so might cease to be attractive to anyone, the symptom was acceptable to the punitive train of thought as well; and since it was permitted by both sides it could become a reality. This was the same method of treating a wish-fulfillment as was adopted by the Parthian queen towards the Roman triumvir Crassus. Believing that he had embarked on his expedition out of love of gold, she ordered molten gold to be poured down his throat when he was dead: 'Now,' she said, 'you have what you wanted.' "[22]

The second example in the note on the double meaning of symptoms, the one concerning the phobia of Helene A., might be an idea that occurred to Freud later or rather a record of a *new* understanding, in terms of the double meaning of symptoms, of the troubles of a patient he had treated some years earlier. Helene A. may conceivably be identical with a woman patient already described by Freud in his 1894 paper "The Neuro-Psychoses of Defense," albeit there in the context of a theoretical argument about the dislodging and transposition of affects.[23]

Many notes document Freud's fascination with language and his linguistic genius in a way that is even more directly word-related than the one

[21]James Strachey has already drawn attention to this (1966b).
[22]1900a, p. 569f.
[23]Cf. 1894a, p. 54.

on the double meaning of symptoms. They appear as vestiges of an ongoing, multidimensional process of translation—from the symptom to the unconscious conflict, from the manifest to the latent dream content, from the transference constellation to the childhood scene, from the primal fantasy to real phylogenetic events. Under the heading "How hy[steria] approaches the roots of language" he writes: "Actually psychoneurosis. One of my pat[ients], who had fallen ill after a quarrel with his brother Richard, from then on showed a pathological aversion to everything that reminded him of this brother[.] He did not even want to think of getting rich, because the brother's name was Richard. He himself thought this compulsion a ridiculous detail due to the similarity in sound of the word & of the initial letter. But now L. Geiger (Origin of Language) shows that 'rich' comes from the same root as the similar syllables in the names Heinrich, Friedrich, Richard, and the Latin Rex."

We unexpectedly come across the first record of linguistic equations with which we are familiar from the published works—for example, madeira—materia—mater, that is, how wood (madeira in Portuguese) "came to represent what is maternal and female."[24] Or puns from dreams, like the following under the heading "Old dr[eam] of Irma.": "The mother says to her & her friends: Well, now each of you will make a dessert remark (bonbon—bon mot)." These are examples of that "syllabic chemistry," which was the expression once used by Freud to denote this kind of releasing and recombining of verbal elements.[25]

[6.3]

Many of the notes testify to the importance of the semantic and syntactic aspects of language in the functioning of unconscious psychic processes. On both sides of one sheet Freud noted down "Different styles of indirect representation," including verbal representation, representation of meaning, representation of relations between concepts or events, direct symbolization, and representation by vignettes. Each of these categories is then characterized concisely, even telegraphically. On verbal representation, for example, he writes: "a) Verbal representation, usually where a thought preserved in words is to be represented. 1). Disguising of each word (concept) in a sentence, of a memory, or in series of sentences which has this

241916–17a, p. 159; cf. also 1900a, p. 355, and 1913d, p. 282, note 2.
251900a, p. 297, note 1.

word in common. In the latter case the word is usually used with do[26] multiple meanings, so as not to betray oneself too quickly. The subsequent sentences betray the word more and more, gradual approach to the wording." The comment on direct symbolization is laconic: "A dirty path which many take[.] Abstract through sexual[?] concretum."

However, because dreams so often resort to direct symbolization as their means of representation, this phenomenon continued to command Freud's attention long after the first publication of *The Interpretation of Dreams*. By far the largest number of additions he made to subsequent editions of the great book are indeed devoted to the subject of symbolism in dreams. At the beginning of Section E in the sixth chapter, fully written out only for the fourth edition, of 1914, Freud explicitly stresses that, while he had recognized the presence of symbolism in dreams from the very beginning, it was only by degrees and as his experience had increased that he arrived at a full appreciation of its extent and significance, under the influence of the contributions of Wilhelm Stekel.[27] Many traces of this learning process can be found in the notes. The "3 Sammelbögen" ["3 sheets of collected ideas"] dating from 1909 contain the following terse sentence on symbolism in dreams: "It goes much further than I thought." And the first entry in a fairly long list in which symbols are presented in parallel with what they symbolize reads: "Staircase is a coitus hewn in stone."

[6.4]

This is followed in this document and other notes by numerous examples of further symbols—smooth walls, tooth, necktie, hat, bridge, and so forth—often embedded in the texts of the actual dreams or actual analyses

[26]Freud was presumably at first going to write "doppeldeutig" [having a double meaning].
[27]1900a, p. 350.

from which Freud gleaned them. The beginning of a typical two-page note of this kind takes the following form:

[6.5]

The full text reads as follows:

Dream symbols: building, staircase, shaft.

He goes for a walk with his father in a place which must certainly be the Prater, as the Rotunda can be seen, with a small annex in front of it, to which a captive balloon is attached, though it looks rather limp. His father asks him what all this is for; he is surprised about this but explains it to him. Then they come into a courtyard which has a large sheet of tin laid out in it. His father wants to pull off a piece of it, but first looks round to see if anyone might notice. He tells him he need only tell the foreman and he can then take some without any bother. A staircase leads down from this yard into a shaft, whose walls are cushioned in soft material, rather like a leather armchair. At the end of this shaft is a longish platform & then another shaft begins. . . . . . .

Analysis. Rotunda etc., he immediately says, is his genitals, the captive balloon is the penis, whose limpness he has reason to complain of. [So rotunda = bottom, annex = scrotum].[28] Situation in this part of the dr.[eam] must be reversed. He questions the father about the function of the genitals. Since this never actually happened, the dr[eam] thoughts must be taken as a conditional: "If I had asked my father for sexual enlightenment" . . . (Probable continuation: he would not have told me the truth anyway.) The second scene centers on pulling off, which in turn, as is clear from the context, means masturbation. The masturbation is displaced onto the father, and for this purpose reproaches [are] used, which he is accustomed to make to his father concerning dubious business practices. The "tin" is an allusion to the merchandise in his father's business. The secret of masturbation is expressed very boldly by the opposite. (It can be done openly). The father's dishonesty as a businessman can surely also be used for the interpretation: he would have deceived me just as he deceives his customers. He

[28]Freud's square brackets.

immediately interprets the shaft as a vagina. He practiced intercourse for a while, but then gave it up and now hopes to resume it with the aid of the treatment. This according to his own idea is the meaning of the platform between the two shafts.

It is noteworthy that climbing down here becomes a symbol of coitus, as is otherwise that of climbing up a staircase.

The dream corresponds to a frequent type in which the dreamer surveys his sexual life, the biographical dream.

17. 4. 10.   Freud

Readers wishing to trace the repercussions of this note in the published work will find it, almost verbatim but with some additions to complete the account and to facilitate understanding, in the "Additions to the Interpretation of Dreams"[29] published the following year, 1911, in the newly established *Zentralblatt für Psychoanalyse* as well as in *The Interpretation of Dreams*, as supplementary material for the third edition,[30] and in the *Introductory Lectures on Psycho-Analysis*.[31]

As has already been indicated, in the chapter on the vicissitudes of the manuscripts, Freud threw away the manuscript of *The Interpretation of Dreams*, so that it is lost to research. However, on the basis of the many notes on the subject of dreams that have escaped destruction, it will be possible in the future not only to adduce evidence of certain elements from the genesis of the book of the century—for example, Freud's notes on his reading—but also to reconstruct more precisely than would be possible by a mere comparison of editions the stages of the process of revision to which the author subjected his magnum opus over a period of some three decades.[32] A few more examples will now be given to demonstrate this to the reader.

The first decade of the century—that is, the time between the first publication of *The Interpretation of Dreams* and the appearance of the revised second and third editions—was plainly a fertile period for the glean-

---

[29]1911*a*, pp. 608–10 [in *S. E.* in 1900*a* only; see next note] (*Zbl. Psychoanal.*, vol. 1, p. 190f.).

[30]1900*a*, pp. 364–66.

[31]1916–17*a*, p. 194f.

[32]As it happens, even the manuscripts of a number of later additions appearing in revised editions of *The Interpretation of Dreams* are preserved in the Sigmund Freud Collection. These include the 1911 addition to Section (G) "Absurd Dreams—Intellectual Activity in Dreams" in the sixth chapter (1900*a*, p. 430f.), from "There is another kind of absurdity, which occurs in dreams of dead relatives, [. . .]" to "[. . .] precisely what necessitated the dream's absurdity." The Sigmund Freud Collection also contains, on two double sheets, the manuscript of "Additional Examples of Dream-Interpretation," part of which was subsequently integrated into the book.

ing of material. Again and again, Freud during this time seems to have sought a dialogue with his newly acquired colleagues and students and to have involved them in a collective working process. Indications to that effect are to be found in the *Minutes of the Vienna Psychoanalytic Society*. For instance, the following is recorded in the minutes for 3 March 1909: "PROF. FREUD would like to call attention to a certain kind of dream, and to ask everyone whether this dream is known to him and what is his interpretation of it. Usually, these dreams deal, in numerous variations, with *climbing down a smooth wall or the outside of a house*. The dream usually ends in a feeling of anxiety when the ground is about to be reached."[33] Even if Freud had by this time probably already forwarded the amendments for the second edition of *The Interpretation of Dreams* to his publisher, he was clearly still engaged in making additions to the section entitled "Typical Dreams" in the fifth chapter. These typical dreams are closely connected with the theme of symbolism in dreams discussed above, in that Freud took it that their stereotyped scenarios had the same meaning in every dreamer, so that they could be interpreted in broad outline without the specific associations of the dreamer. He also hoped that this uniformity would provide clues to the understanding of the supraindividual, perhaps phylogenetic, sources of the language of dreams.

It is to this context and period of research that an undated two-page note preserved in the Sigmund Freud Collection as a photocopy seems to belong.[34] Its form suggests that Freud had searched his memory for typical dreams of his own—a discipline to which he perhaps thought colleagues should subject themselves with the object of fixing the results in writing and appending their signature to them.

My individual characterization of dreams.

(Typical dreams).

Freud

I should like to distinguish between dreams with sensations & others. The first group include: flying, falling, swimming, paralysis, the second is well known. Death of relatives, examination, nakedness, Oedipus dream, perhaps also money dream, travel dream, going through a flight of rooms.

My stock of dreams with sensations is poor. I cannot remember flying, or swimming[,] as particularly frequent. I often have[35] the falling

---

[33]Nunberg and Federn, 1967, p. 170.

[34]The original manuscript was recently auctioned by Christie's; part of it is reproduced in the catalog (1989*f*).

[35]Corrected from "hatte" [had].

dream, in crude form in the past, but now with the refinement that I have to climb out of the window down the façade of the house using the projections of sills etc to the street, during which a painful sensation of falling comes over me.—Dreams of paralysis have become very rare indeed in the last few years, having been common but not very clear-cut in earlier years.

I have never had the Oedipus dream undisguised, but reported a disguised anxiety dream with this meaning in the Interpretation of Dreams. I can remember only a single example of the ~~dream~~ ^{death} of living relatives. Shortly after the birth of my youngest girl, I dreamt, without an affect of anxiety, that her little predecessor was dead but lying rosy-cheeked in the cradle. I remembered in the analysis that, as an 8 y[ear-old][?] boy I had crept along after the birth of the last sister (who corresponds in the sequence to my youngest daughter) to the cradle of her predecessor, ~~and~~ who was then 1 y old and sleeping rosy-cheeked[,] & thought as I did so: now you are no longer the youngest.

The dream of nakedness was very common in my case & occurred in many kinds of interesting forms, even in military garb. It too has disappeared in the last few years. I still had the exhibitionistic inclination corresponding to it in the years of my puberty. I see as its derivatives the difficulties which I encounter at times when I have something to publish, but also the compulsion to publish intimate things which ultimately forces itself through.

The most familiar kind of typical dream for me is the examination dream, which has made the usual progress from the Matura [school-leaving examination qualifying for university] to the Rigorosum [oral examination for doctorate]. During the last few years, in which I have had to struggle so much for recognition & probably been deeply wounded by criticism, this dream has positively proliferated & given me an opportunity to attempt to interpret it. I still hold that it appears before anticipated & feared humiliations, but, by the use of an idea found I know not where, have now succeeded in understanding it better and take it as a consolation in relation to anticipatory anxiety.

For I read somewhere that examination dreams feature only examinations which one ^{has} passed and never ones ~~which~~ in which one has failed. This is true in my case. I failed in the third Rigorosum in forensic medicine, but have never dreamt of this subject. The Rigorosum dream is usually about the preliminary exams, botany &—a particular torment—zoology. In botany I was in danger with Wiesner because I could not recognize a single plant; my good theoretical knowledge then saved me. I wanted (for reasons of justified anxiety) to run away from zoology; but Claus, whom I met in the corridor, took me by the arm, urged me to stay, and gave me the questions which were bound to lead to a distinction. A similar part was played in the Matura dream by the history examination; I dodged the danger by a bold maneuver & passed the exam with flying colors. So the dream seems to console by relating the present anxiety to occasions when the anxiety proved to be un-justified. The text of this consolation: What are you afraid of then? You were afraid then too & are now a doctor or professor anyway! is misunderstood by the Cs, wh. takes it as a protest against the nonsensi-cal aspect of the dream[.]

I do not know the dream of finding money. In earlier decades I often had travel dreams in which one most wonderful landscape followed another; since I began to travel (1895), they have become rare. I did not often see well-known landscapes or cities in dreams—on one occasion Rome before I became acquainted with it, from an engraving, and another time Florence, exactly as I had already seen it.

Moving through a flight of rooms is one I have if anything had frequently, but it has not so far proved amenable to interpretation.

Readers themselves may trace some of the derivatives of this "characteriza-tion of dreams" by Freud in the metamorphoses of *The Interpretation of Dreams*; however, it also contains autobiographical and dream material that does not recur in any of the published versions. The fact that only extracts from the plethora of empirical material accruing from the treat-ment of patients, self-analysis, observation of children, and cooperation with colleagues actually found their way into Freud's public texts is con-firmed by many notes. Here is another example.

On 13 January 1908 Freud had recorded on a sheet of paper—pre-served only as a fragment—a dream accompanied by reflections on its transference meaning, evidently stemming from the treatment of the "Rat Man." The posthumously published "Original Record" of this analysis includes only entries dated 7 and 20 January 1908.[36] If we consult the manuscript of that "Original Record," it becomes clear beyond doubt that the note of 13 January was not, say, detached from it subsequently; instead, Freud kept it separate from the beginning, presumably because he found this dream significant from an aspect independent of the case history. Indeed, the sheet carries a heading of its own: "How people dr[eam] of a dead person[,] absurd." Shortly afterward, Freud added a passage[37] to the second and third editions of his dream book, published in 1909 and 1911, respectively,

[36]1955a, pp. 316–18.
[37]1900a, p. 430f.

in the section headed "Absurd Dreams" in the sixth chapter, in which he deals with the representation of dead persons in dreams and in particular with the feature, which also characterizes the dream of the Rat Man's, that the dreamer can immediately bring back to life a person initially represented as dead. However, Freud does not mention the Rat Man dream at this point but quotes other examples, some of which have themselves already been recorded in the notes. So the note on the dream of 13 January 1908 probably belonged to a more comprehensive collection of evidence which Freud used to support his hypotheses on this subject and from which he drew only to a limited extent for his published work.

Again, the very title of a two-page note dated 12 December 1911 immediately gives an impression of this assiduous collating activity: "Sammlung zum Traum" ["Collection on dreams"]. Under concise headings such as "Dream within a dream," "Occurrence of symptoms in the dr[eam]," "Preferred dream situation," Freud recorded dreams of his own and of analysands. Quite a few of these notations, elaborated to a greater or lesser extent, were in turn integrated into later editions of *The Interpretation of Dreams* and/or published in the series "Observations and Examples from Analytic Practice." The precursors of many an element in this collection[38] can be readily identified in these notes. For instance, the first of the published examples, "Dream with an Unrecognized Precipitating Cause," corresponds in the relevant manuscript to the note "Dr[eam] without visible cause." The printed version of 1913 reads: "A good sleeper awoke one morning at a summer resort in the Tyrol, knowing that he had had a dream that the Pope was dead. He could think of no explanation of it. During the morning of the same day his wife said to him: 'Did you hear the dreadful noise the bells made early this morning?' He had not heard it but had evidently dreamt about it. The interpretation which his dream gave of the bells was his revenge on the pious Tyrolese. According to the newspapers the Pope was slightly indisposed at that time."[39] We learn from the telegraphic version in the notes that this was a dream of Freud's own—still more evidence of the extent to which his own person always remained involved in the process of observation. The note is worded as follows: "I dr[eamt] in Klobenstein: The Pope has died. No explanation. That morning Martha asked: Did you hear the dreadful noise of the bells early today? I didn't. Pope was ill at time. Revenge on Tyrolese."[40]

[38]For instance, entries 2 and 19 to 22 (1913*h*, p. 194 and p. 197f.).

[39]Ibid., p. 194.

[40]However, when in 1914 Freud also added this example to the fourth edition of *The Interpretation of Dreams* (1900*a*, p. 232), he no longer disguised the fact that it was a dream of his own; nor did he do so in the *Introductory Lectures* (1916–17*a*, p. 94).

[6.6]

Many more pages could be filled with examples from the abundance of such records of dreams and dream interpretations. They constitute yet more evidence of how Freud throughout his life expected new insights to accrue from dream material. It was something he literally hoarded. And these private, hitherto silent documents make it clear that, having once found his *via regia* to knowledge of the unconscious, he was indeed not to deviate from it to the end of his days. He never lost the conviction, formed early in his career, that on this royal road he had been granted an "understanding of that most marvelous and most mysterious of all instruments,"[41] our mental life.[42]

Yet the entire cosmos of Freud's thought, not only his research on dreams, is represented in the notes. Here and there, albeit mainly as an isolated instance, the scintilla of an idea for the works on the theory of civilization flares up momentarily. Once again, here are some examples: "Men cannot tolerate being bereft of parents[,] & so they create a new parental couple from God and nature: foundation, ultimate foundation of religion [is] man's infantile helplessness." And—already in 1905: "Religion as obs[essional] neurosis—private religion—." Or: "If something for which a people reproaches itself from its past later recurs ucs., then [it is] as a reproach to another [people]. [. . .] Exact analogy with the situation in individual psychology, paranoia, which is in a similar position with just such reproaches[.] Persecution mania. Self-reproaches projected onto others." And, as if to illustrate such projective processes in society, although included in another bundle of notes entitled "From older notes from 1897 on," we find the following under the heading "A source of anti-Semitism": "The fact that anti-S[emitism] is generated in the nursery is clear. Irma has a physical horror of any Jew. When she was a child they said (in Ofen[43])[,] if there was

[41]1900*a*, p. 608.
[42]It should also be mentioned that the other normal phenomenon used by Freud to study the action of unconscious forces, that of parapraxes, is another recurring theme in the notes.
[43][The German name for Buda, the western part of Budapest.]

any trace of incontinentia alvi on a child's vest: the Jew has wiped his mouth on it again."

[6.7]

Or consider another note analyzing aspects of civilization: "Uneducated people & savages overestimate ψ [psychic] achievements, which are not very familiar to them: symbolization, verbalization, fantasying[,] as the common people here do the printed word[,] and ascribe magic powers to all these effects. Minimum real significance coincides with maximum esteem."

Finally, here is a note on the theory of art: "The primary aspect of the drive for art is no doubt artistic aptitude, the capacity for transformation & expression, which must be physiologically determined. But in ψ [psychic] terms the motive for exploiting this capacity originally belongs to the drive for mastery, in that the image produced is deemed in every respect to be a substitute for the orig[inal], and was prob[ably] also originally intended to give the creator power over it, so that here a lost tendency of art might be sought. The same of course [applies] in the case of a loved object; here too creation is in the service of the component of mastery. A priori [there are] two kinds of art, [one which] creates a likeness & [one which] is intended to express feelings. The first [is] more primordial & easier to understand; the second no doubt [has its] origin in the wooing of love, but hardly the only one[?], also in the expression of social feelings: ceremonial, dance, the stage, music. Abundant of course in the service of the function of love." At this point in the same bundle, there follows a slip of paper that Freud had evidently cut out from other, probably earlier, notes and on which he had written the line "Taken from 4 notebooks from 1901.[44] on." This cut-out slip begins with the following entry: "1.—Idea that art was originally always tendentious & that these tendencies have been lost (religion, defense."[45]

---

[44]The period after the year is actually present in the manuscript. Freud clearly added the final word, "on" ["an" in German], when he realized that he wanted to make extracts from notes written after 1901 too.

[45]The enumeration ends with the parenthesis left open.

As if in direct line of descent from the above, the Sigmund Freud Collection elsewhere contains a photocopy of a note with the explicit title "Lost tendencies in art," comprising a whole page of detailed collected thoughts on such tendencies—that is, on the religious, political, and social functions that art was required to perform in earlier times: as pictorial magic, votive offering, cult object, song of praise, sign of property, tribal mark of distinction, and so on. However, Freud does not seem to have followed up these ideas in his published work; there is merely a brief general reference in *Totem and Taboo*.[46] An intention recorded in a note on 15 May 1904, to write something about the "sexual character of classical architecture," was also not translated into reality; indeed, he had at the time already added the realistic proviso "although when & how is not clear to me."

The notes by which Freud wrote his way toward the many works that did come to fruition record a number of stages in the process of genesis of each. Seed from which his book *Jokes and their Relation to the Unconscious* sprang can be found on the back of one of those pieces of paper that Freud cut out of earlier notes and pasted onto a new sheet. He was concerned only with the front, which contains a fresh vignette from a session with a woman suffering from obsessional symptoms. For this reason, the text on the reverse, which did not seem to him to be worth preserving and to whose line sequence he paid no heed when he cut it out, survives solely as a fragment. Truncated lines indicate that Freud, perhaps inspired by his research on dreams, was engaged in reflections on the techniques of the riddle, taking as his example the daldal riddles[47] thought up by his former philosophy teacher Franz Brentano, and that it was only from this base that he began to contemplate a contrasting comparison with the techniques of the joke. The situation is thus the exact opposite from that in the eventual book on jokes itself, in which this comparison is relegated virtually to the status of a footnote, very much to the detriment of the riddle.[48] Still concerned with riddles, Freud continues in the note: "Pleasure gain connected with the work of solving. Originally nontendentious nature of riddle.—Conditions of convertibility[.] But ideas won't go any further today. It is an uninspired day." Could it be that what follows on this sheet was written down the next day? For it already contains, in a veritable explosion of ideas, the fundamentals of the structure and main theses of the book on jokes:

[46]1912–13a, p. 90.
[47]Cf. 1905c, note 6 on p. 31f.
[48]Cf. 1905c, p. 31f., note 1, and p. 67, note 1.

a). Technique of joke.

b). Psychogenesis of joke

c). Tendency of joke.

d). Joke & comic, humor

e). Joke & riddle.

f). Theory of pleasure in joke.

Joke —— comic — riddle ⎞

ucs.   pcs — cs.   ⎠ perhaps

also irony

satire

etc.

Important aspect of characterization of diff. kinds of
pleasure gain through psychic localization.

Book of riddles by Mises, Polle.—Aspects:

Joke lies in technique—de-joking [the joke]

Psych. localization.

Economy theory

Laughing with oversaturation

Preliminary stage of jesting.

a) Lifting of inhibitions.

b). Orig[inal] sources of pleasure.

[6.8]

Two more of those pasted slips merit our interest in connection with the
book on jokes. One of them is headed "A true children's story," and reads:
"Three children, an older girl, two small boys (age to be inserted later)[.]
The older boy warns the younger of an inadvertency of dress. If you do not

behave, you will get ill and have to take Bubizin. Bubizin is not a new alkaloid, but came about as follows. When his sister was ill, the boy heard that she had to take Medizin (Mädizin) [that is, for a Mädi—little girl]; he therefore assumed, since the difference between the sexes already pervades this world for him, that a little boy [Bube] would by analogy have to take Bubizin.—The events in this story happened a few weeks ago at Strakowitz in Bohemia." The other slip of paper, on which Freud later added the child's age, probably after inquiring about it, reads: "The hero of Bubizin is 2½ y. old." He probably remembered this old true story when he came to write the seventh chapter of the book on jokes, on the species of the comic, while seeking an example of the irresistible effect of the naïve, especially in children's comments. He may have written the episode down in the form in which it was impressed on his memory without even consulting the text of the earlier note, as the published version shows some characteristic discrepancies,[49] even if the verbal joke "Mädizin/Bubizin," which arose from the child's honest attempt to draw a serious conclusion, has been preserved.[50]

Only the earliest beginnings of the genesis of the "Contributions to the Psychology of Love" can be reconstructed from notes, which, as it were, bear witness to the moment when Freud put to himself a "new central problem: psychology of human love" and immediately began to record "some material," including a "First collection on love life." Examples of its concise entries are: "Riddle of love is [the] awakening of the infantile"; "The enigmatic [object] sought in first love [is] like a blood relationship, specifically like [that] between mother & child"; "Being in love is the normal psychosis—"; "Transition from delusion of grandeur to sexual overestimation in men. This lacking in women"; "Genital vanity analogous to penis narcissism"; "Estimations of the sexes for each other at diff. ages"; "Coquetry as staying at [the stage of] forepleasure." These are followed by a reminder to himself to take care in his observations—no doubt also a warning against overhasty theorization: "Most is still lacking, but it cannot be done systematically; it must be tracked down as and when opportunity allows."

When Freud was in Karlsbad for the cure in the summer of 1914, he wrote to Ferenczi on 17 July, just a few days before the outbreak of the First World War: "So here we are again at the warm springs, enjoying the heat and rain as they come [. . .]. I [. . .] have begun to study Macbeth; he has been tormenting me for a long time and I have not so far found the solution. It is strange; I surrendered Macbeth to Jones years ago, and am now as it

[49] Ibid., p. 183.

[50] The fact that Freud continued to be interested in the phenomenon of jokes after the publication of his book is illustrated by two sheets bearing the title "War jokes," an anthology compiled during the First World War, now also in the Sigmund Freud Collection.

were taking him back. Obscure forces are at work here." Freud's notes do indeed include two pages[51] begun on the previous day, the first lines of which read as follows:

[6.9]

Macbeth.   Karlsbad.
——————   16.7.14.

Present day for royal dramas, it is the time
of the wars with Spain.

This bundle also includes some further photocopied documents, namely, a sheet written ten days later, on "26/7," again headed "Macbeth," and another sheet, the original of which is torn, written on both sides and entitled "The prototype of Lady Macbeth," dated "30/9 14." The notes testify to Freud's careful rereading of the play, his comparing it with other Shakespeare dramas, and his study of historical sources and secondary literature. In the record of his own initial thoughts and questions, it is easy to identify precursory formulations for the second section of the paper "Some Character-Types Met with in Psycho-Analytic Work," published two years later. As we know, Freud tried to illustrate the type of person who is wrecked by success by the character and fate of Lady Macbeth.[52] All the basic notions for understanding—or, as the case may be, for the inability to understand—the change in the nature of Lady Macbeth, which, to judge from the course of the drama, takes place within a period of a few days, are adumbrated: childlessness; division of the features of a single personality between two roles, so that Macbeth and Lady Macbeth actually embody a *single* figure; and the drawing of a parallel between Lady Macbeth and Elizabeth I. "Elizabeth, murderess of Mary Stuart, also a guest, died childless, had to make son[53] [her] heir. Elizabeth is Lady Macbeth[.] Her last hours[.]"

---

[51]Preserved in the Sigmund Freud Collection as photocopies but presumably originally written on both sides of a single sheet.

[52]1916d, pp. 309–33.

[53]James I, son of the executed Mary Stuart.

As emphasized in the letter to Ferenczi quoted above, the drama of *Macbeth* had already occupied Freud much earlier; and he did not cease to wrestle with the secrets of that great play once the paper on character types had been published. This is documented by one of those cut-out slips of notes pasted individually onto a larger sheet, which contains the following conjecture, formulated in jocular terms: "If Jul. Caesar, Hamlet & Macbeth so permit, I should like to believe that Shakespeare was himself suffering from hallucinat[ions] around this time & was haunted by the ghost of his father. The father exerted an overwhelming influence on him; his rehabilitation was the practical goal of his life. Macbeth would then come down to himself, as the Lady does to Elizabeth." These lines may well originate from the context of the essay "The 'Uncanny,' " which appeared in 1919—that is, after the end of the war.[54]

Initial preparatory notes for the study "A Seventeenth-Century Demonological Neurosis," published in 1923, have also been preserved. This, as will be shown, is a work from which documents of all three phases of the typical genetic dynamic of Freud's texts have been preserved: two sheets of notes, large parts of the draft, and, finally, the fair copy. The notes, which survive in a photocopy, consist of key words, probably set down by Freud during his reading of the copy made available to him of the *Trophaeum Mariano-Cellense*, the manuscript from which he drew the material for his interpretation of the demonological neurosis of the painter Christoph Haitzmann. As with clinical notes which constituted the basis of subsequently published case histories, Freud did not elaborate everything contained in the notes on the demonological neurosis in the draft or fair copy. The first of the two sheets of notes is dated "5 Nov 22." and bears the title "Bond with the Devil." Freud begins with an exhortation to himself: "Look at figures & describe them." This is a reference to the eight pictures by the painter contained in the manuscript, of the various appearances of the Devil together with their captions. Freud excerpts and points up these captions.[55] Based on an appraisal and evaluation of the different sources, there then follow further detailed notations on the bonds with the Devil and their wording as well as on details of the painter's life and of his case history. These notes thus constitute a compact inventory of the basic material that Freud was to develop and interpret in the draft and the fair copy.

The bundle of notes on *Totem and Taboo* is unusually voluminous. It is therefore discussed here, at the end of our description of the notes associated with the origins of specific individual works. This bundle contains countless

[54]Cf. 1919*h*, p. 250.

[55]He also wrote brief characterizations of the paintings on a separate sheet.

astonishing snapshots documenting Freud's tentative reflections as he prepared his first great book on the theory of civilization, and in particular the famous fourth essay, "The Return of Totemism in Childhood." This final essay constitutes the climax of the work, containing as it does the hypothesis about the murder of the primal father in the prehistoric family and the genesis of the sense of guilt and of cultural institutions. Again, as already indicated, it remained one of Freud's favorites among his own writings throughout his life. A note dated "30/3 13" records the beginning of the essay in telegraphic form:

[6.10]

Totemism

Prelim. ΨA, wh. discovered overdeterm., needs
no warning against tracing origin to single
source. Here origin of religion—synthesis
can show relative importance [of] factor discussed here[.]
Totem in Essay I. Main laws repeated. two
Basis [of] organization, place of a religion.
—Suspicion that tot[emism] goes far, was perhaps general
(quote lit. Reinach). Two points need
explanation 1). Animal [plays] this part 2) Exogamy
—Many theories[,] now read Wundt, then other
reading matter mentioned there—Non liquet.

The reader will easily be able to expand the note—translated above without emendation—if he reads it in conjunction with the first three paragraphs of the printed version of the fourth essay:

There are no grounds for fearing that psychoanalysis, which first discovered that psychical acts and structures are invariably overdetermined, will be tempted to trace the origin of anything so complicated as religion to a single source. If psychoanalysis is compelled—and is, indeed, in duty bound—to lay all the emphasis upon one particular source, that does not mean it is claiming either that that source is the only one or that it occupies first place among the numerous contributory factors. Only when we can synthesize the findings in the different fields of research will it become possible to arrive at the relative importance of the part played in the genesis of religion by the mechanism discussed in these pages. Such a task lies beyond the means as well as beyond the purposes of a psychoanalyst.[. . .]

In the first of this series of essays we became acquainted with the concept of totemism. We heard that totemism is a system which takes the place of a religion among certain primitive peoples of Australia, America and Africa, and provides the basis of their social organization. As we have heard, it was a Scotsman, McLennan, who in 1869 first drew general attention to the phenomena of totemism (which had hitherto been regarded as mere curiosities) by giving voice to a suspicion that a large number of customs and usages current in various societies ancient and modern were to be explained as remnants of a totemic age. Since that date science has fully accepted his estimate of totemism. Let me quote, as one of the most recent statements on the subject, a passage from Wundt's *Elemente der Völkerpsychologie* [. . .]: "In the light of all these facts, the conclusion appears highly probable that at some time totemic culture everywhere paved the way for a more advanced civilization, and, thus, that it represents a transitional stage between the age of primitive men and the era of heroes and gods."

The purpose of the present essays obliges us to enter more deeply into the nature of totemism. For reasons which will presently become clear I will begin with an account given by Reinach, who, in 1900, sketched out a *"Code du totémisme"* in twelve Articles—a catechism, as it were, of the totemic religion [. . .].[56]

[56]1912–13*a*, p. 100f.

This is followed by detailed statements on the part played by animals and finally, a few pages later, by some comments on exogamy.

Comparison of the text of the notation with that of the printed version again demonstrates the technique of extreme contraction with which Freud was accustomed to set down his initial ideas. Other surviving notes inform us that between the sketching of the first outline and the subsequent elaboration of the opening passage of the fourth essay there really did lie that intensive and extensive learning process that Freud enjoined upon himself at the end of the note: "now read Wundt, then other reading matter mentioned there." Once again, he had added "non liquet." Certain suspicions, gradually crystallizing hypotheses, were no doubt already stirring within him, but it was necessary first to inform himself comprehensively about the status of the contemporary debate in the fields of ethnology and sociology on the topics of interest to him: totemism, exogamy, the horror of incest, the prehistoric family, and so on. On some of these sheets of notes Freud thus seems, under the headings of such major topics as "Incest" or "Derivation of exogamy," to have assembled the views of different scholars together with promising bibliographic references.

However, a high proportion of the material contained in the bundle consists of notes on his reading of *individual* sources. On these pages, Freud wrote down the name of the author and the title of the book he was studying at any given time. On the left he jotted down the numbers of the pages on which he had come across something that appeared to him significant; he characterized the arguments concerned in a few key words, underlined phrases here and there or excerpted quotations, which would occasionally be in English or French; and he noted down bibliographic references, sometimes highlighting them by the use of Greek letters. He would embark on a passionate expedition of reading, probably lasting no longer than a few weeks or at most some months, to follow up such bibliographic references, as is documented by still other study notes, for example, on works and theses of J. J. Atkinson, Charles Darwin, E. Durkheim, J. G. Frazer, or A. Lang—so to speak reading his way on from author to author, from book to book.

To illustrate the structure of these reading notations, here are, first of all, two extracts from notes that Freud set down during his study of "Wundt. Elemente d.Völkerpsych[ologie] II Chap[ter] p 116"; the reader will immediately recognize elements of the passage quoted above:

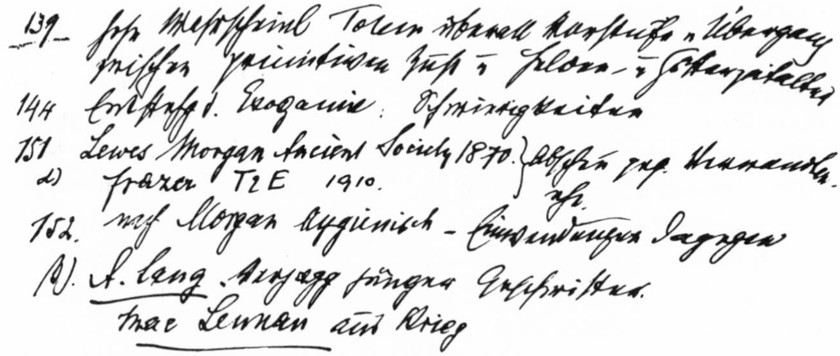

[handwritten facsimile]

[6.11]

139: high prob[ability] totem[ism] everywhere paved way for & [represented] transitional stage between primitive states & era of heroes & gods

144 Genesis of exogamy: difficulties

151 Lewes Morgan Ancient Society 1870.
  α) Frazer T[otemism] & E[xogamy] 1910. } Horror of inmarriage.

152 according to Morgan [this is] hygienic—objections to this
  β) A. Lang. Expulsion of younger siblings.
     Mac Lennan from war.

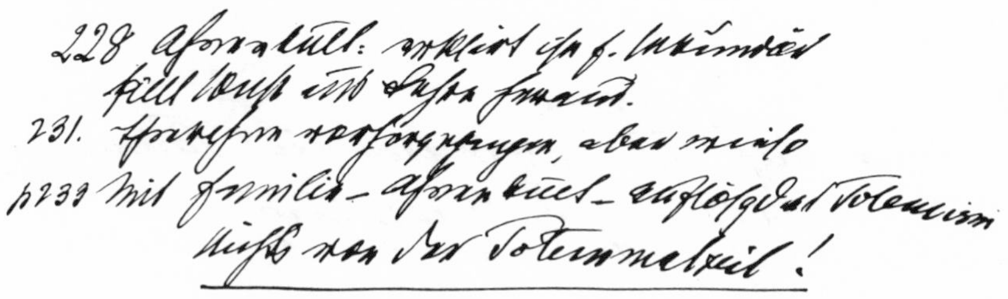

[handwritten facsimile]

[6.12]

228 Ancestor cult: declares it secondary
     otherwise does not fit theory.

231. Animal ancestor preceding, but how

p 233 With family—ancestor cult—dissol. of totemism
     Nothing about the totem meal!

The exclamation "Nothing about the totem meal!" no doubt betrays Freud's disappointment with his reading, which is understandable considering that one of his main aims in the fourth essay of *Totem and Taboo* was to track down the phylogenetic roots of the unconscious primal fantasies of castration, parricide, and incest with the mother or, put differently, concrete dramatic and traumatic events in the prehistoric family that might by Lamarckian evolutionary mechanisms have left their precipitate in the primal fantasies and still be present in the mental life of present-day man in the form of an archaic heritage, causing turmoil within. It is fundamentally a matter of Freud's attempt to link the models of trauma and drive in his reflections on the etiology of the neuroses.[57] There are two reasons the totem meal may have interested him so much. First, it implies an actual sacrificial killing which the perpetrators experience ambivalently, on the one hand celebrating it triumphantly, but on the other bemoaning it with a sense of guilt and mourning; and, second, the communal devouring of the victim represents a physical form of internalization, concretistically paving the way for identification with the lost one.

A sheet dated "1/4 13" containing notes that Freud clearly made while reading the article on the totem or on totemism in the *Encyclopaedia Britannica,* an authority he held in high esteem, ends in like manner with the impatient question, emphasized by underlining: "Where totem meal?" It therefore comes as no surprise that in his notes he recorded with particular care the small number of sources in which the totem meal was in fact mentioned. The sheet on the first and second volumes of Salomon Reinach's *Cultes, mythes et religions* even has the rubric:

[6.13]

Reinach
essential for references to totem meal
& rejection of descent

Here are just a few of these entries:

"13. Totem marque distinctive caractère sacré reside
non dans l'individu mais dans l'espèce
just as in animal phobias.[58]

[57]Cf. Grubrich-Simitis, 1988.

[58]It will be recalled that it was children's animal phobias, as a displacement of fear of the father, that put Freud on the track of *Totem and Taboo.*

14. Sacrifice from totem meal. Then sacrifice to God
     Human sacrifice.
16. Passages on this. Pausanias
[. . .]
59 Robertson Smith's proof that sacrifice
    is the totem animal.
T[ome] II. Mort d'orphée
    Rob. Smith Sarrasin's totem meal"

Freud must have felt a lifelong debt of gratitude to this W. Robertson Smith. When Ernst Simmel, who had emigrated to Los Angeles, composed six introductory lectures on psychoanalysis for the university public in that city and sent the manuscript to Freud for his opinion in 1938, the latter urged him, a quarter century after the publication of *Totem and Taboo*: "Don't forget Robertson Smith[,] whose discovery I merely took up."[59] And in the printed text of the fourth essay, he had paid veritable homage to this man who, in his *Lectures on the Religion of the Semites,* had in effect served him up the totem meal he had been seeking: "William Robertson Smith, who died in 1894—physicist, philologist, Bible critic and archaeologist—was a man of many-sided interests, clear-sighted and liberal-minded. In his book on the *Religion of the Semites* (first published in 1889) he put forward the hypothesis that a peculiar ceremony known as the 'totem meal' had from the very first formed an integral part of the totemic system. At that time he had only a single piece of evidence in support of his theory: an account of a procedure of the kind dating from the fifth century A.D. But by an analysis of the nature of sacrifice among the ancient Semites he was able to lend his hypothesis a high degree of probability. [. . .] I will now attempt to extract from Robertson Smith's admirable work those of his statements on the origin and meaning of the ritual of sacrifice which are of decisive interest for us. In so doing I must omit all the details, often so fascinating, and neglect all the later developments. It is quite impossible for an abstract such as this to give my readers any notion of the lucidity and convincing force of the original."[60]

What enthralled Freud about Robertson Smith's remarks, a few trains of thought from which he reviews in the published text of the fourth essay, was already recorded in telegraphic form in the copious private notes he made on his reading. In both notes and essay, he also allowed the scholars who had refused to attribute such importance to the concept of the totem

[59]These handwritten corrections are in the Sigmund Freud Collection. They will be published shortly in German in the context of the correspondence between Sigmund Freud, Anna Freud, and Ernst Simmel, edited by Ludger M. Hermanns and Ulrich Schultz-Venrath.
[60]1912–13*a*, p. 132.

meal to have their say. But Freud remained undaunted and proceeded in the ensuing fifth section of the essay—adducing supporting hypotheses from Atkinson and Darwin on the primal condition of human society—to his great phylogenetic construction, giving free and undisguised rein to his imagination: "Let us call up the spectacle of a totem meal of the kind we have been discussing, amplified by a few probable features [. . .]."[61] Once again he describes the ceremonial slaughter of the totem animal by the clansmen and the highly charged ambivalence that pervades the communal totem meal, which ushers in the identification with the killed animal. Only now, however, does he link this depiction with the psychoanalytic conclusion that the totem animal is a substitute for the father, thereby establishing "an unsuspected correlation between groups of phenomena that have hitherto been disconnected":[62] in the prehistoric family, a violent primal father who wanted to keep all the females for himself castrated or drove away his sons as they grew up. "One day the brothers who had been driven out came together, killed and devoured their father and so made an end of the patriarchal horde. United, they had the courage to do and succeeded in doing what would have been impossible for them individually. (Some cultural advance, perhaps, command over some new weapon, had given them a sense of superior strength.) Cannibal savages as they were, it goes without saying that they devoured their victim as well as killing him. The violent primal father had doubtless been the feared and envied model of each one of the company of brothers: and in the act of devouring him they accomplished their identification with him, and each one of them acquired a portion of his strength. The totem meal, which is perhaps mankind's earliest festival, would thus be a repetition and a commemoration of this memorable and criminal deed, which was the beginning of so many things—of social organization, of moral restrictions and of religion."[63]

Of course, while this scenario is initially sketched out here in broad outline like a woodcut, Freud was to develop and refine it further in the subsequent passages of the essay. Yet this barely mitigates the exceedingly speculative, quasi-mythological character of the construction.[64] The extreme contradictions of Freud's emotional relationship with his work are

---

[61]Ibid., p. 140.

[62]Ibid., p. 141.

[63]Ibid., p. 141f.

[64]It is worth noting here that this scenario, like the whole of Freud's neo-Lamarckism, is by no means a frivolous fancy on his part. It is to a certain extent a construction born of embarrassment or despair. Freud could not but imagine the timeless power of the unconscious as anchored in hereditary dispositions, in the soma. What is still for the time being completely beyond the scope of the concepts of the natural and social sciences, he attempted to grasp at least in mythological notions (cf. Grubrich-Simitis, 1987, 1988, and Lorenzer, 1986).

documented in particular by the letters he wrote to Sándor Ferenczi in the early summer of 1913. On 4 May he says: "I am now writing about the totem with the feeling that it is my greatest, best, and perhaps my last good thing. Inner certainties tell me that I am right."[65] And four days later: "I haven't written anything with so much conviction since the Interpretation of Dreams."[66] But a more sober mood soon prevailed. "I have retreated far from my initial high opinion of the work," he told Ferenczi on 12 June, "and am, on the whole, dubious about it."[67] A fortnight later, on 26 June: "I consider the matter on the one hand too beautiful, but on the other hand, times and things are too obscure and to a certain extent beyond the pale of sure assessment."[68]

The manifest text of the fourth essay has since been shown by modern ethnology to be absurd. This was demonstrated in detail not long ago by Mario Erdheim,[69] who at the same time emphasized that *Totem and Taboo* was one of those books that had to grow old in order for their radicalism to be recognized. In his view, the work's radicalism lies not only in the fact that Freud was for the first time systematically seeking traces of his discovery, the unconscious, in the structures of society and civilization, but also, and in particular, in its potential for casting a bright light on problems of our own present-day society; Erdheim therefore recommends that the book be read in completely new ways. For our purposes, however, it is important mainly because—as will be shown elsewhere—the phylogenetic construction does indeed act like an intellectual magnetic field which was to exert its force again and again in the later writings. If only for this reason, the bundle of notes that, in addition, contains compact sketches of parts of the third and fifth sections as well as of the sixth and seventh sections of the fourth essay merits detailed discussion in this chapter. It has occasionally been conjectured that *Totem and Taboo* should be seen partly as Freud's reaction to the secessions of his pupils, and in particular to the conflict with the "parricidal" son C. G. Jung, which was then approaching its climax. But the notes that have come down to us do not seem to contain any evidence for such an autobiographical connotation.[70]

The notes in the Sigmund Freud Collection so far accessible for study do not explicitly deal with the external[71] and internal events of Freud's life at all.

[65]1992g, p. 482.
[66]Ibid., p. 483.
[67]Ibid., p. 491.
[68]Ibid., p. 496.
[69]Erdheim, 1991; cf. also Wallace, 1983.
[70]However, see below, p. 210 and p. 214.
[71]In contrast to, for example, the so-called "Kürzeste Chronik."

All the same, we do come across occasional hints of biography, autobiography, or self-reflection in these working papers. For example, Freud jotted down a few lines on the "paranoia" of his former friend Fliess and noted the following about Jean-François Champollion, the decipherer of hieroglyphics and founder of Egyptology: "Champollion very interesting. A real genius[,] not just through the favor of his disciples, as I am now becoming for a while. Confirms my idea that only the idée fixe makes a discoverer of one. 'Everywhere I see myself in Egypt.' Holding fast to the wishes of one's youth is the only way to lend strength to intention, i.e., as with Schliemann. One could initiate a collection: the importance of infantile wishes."

When we examine the backs of the slips of paper that Freud occasionally cut out of notes made in other contexts and pasted onto new sheets, manifestly because he wanted to pursue further the thoughts recorded on the front, we find that certain of the fragments of text concerned have the character almost of a diary.[72] For instance, a Saturday entry for 25 December—the year is 1909—records that he felt within himself "some strength for impudence"; he had also been impudent "in the polemical parts of the lectures at Worcester."[73] His verdict on psychoanalysis, as presented in these five lectures, is: "It is after all a truly colossal building & actually altogether mine. The Japanese dwarf fir in the middle of the room also puts me in a cheerful humor. Unfortunately, I shall not be able to keep it. By spending so much money at Christmas, I am really putting myself in the mood for work." In the next paragraph, we read: "I am quite unused to having an hour at my disposal for free work. Shall I get on with my dear Leonardo?[74] America[75] is already in its envelope, the sexual theory finished and put aside,[76] both of them polished off in great haste. I am fed up with the eternal repetitions."

A similarly candid note by Freud on his likely reaction to a threatened polemic against him and psychoanalysis in the periodical *Die Fackel* stems from about the same period: "Strange, the attitude of my ambition to it now. I am very clearly looking forward to it & shall be very sensitive to the expected criticism. Behind it [lies] annoyance at such popularity & [my] own stupidity." This last point is no doubt a reference to the Vienna Psychoanalytic Society's discussion on 12 January 1910 of Fritz Wittels's lecture "The 'Fackel' Neurosis," a pathography, not to say a "vivisection," of the

---

[72]The fragments of these slips of paper are currently not in the correct order in the Sigmund Freud Collection; however, they belong together, as quoted in the following.

[73]"Five Lectures on Psycho-Analysis," 1910a.

[74]1910c.

[75]This is a reference to the American version of the "Five Lectures on Psycho-Analysis."

[76]The additional passages for the second, expanded edition of the *Three Essays on the Theory of Sexuality*, 1905d, which appeared in 1910.

writer Karl Kraus, which had provoked this polemic. Another, still more intimate note, again about Fliess, which has, however, been cut and is therefore not completely legible, reads: "Inserted because occurred to me in the interim. I now know the reason for the uplifting effect of the trip to Sicily,[77] [. . .] complete liberation from Fliess [. . .]."

Much of this actually sounds like an ongoing quiet soliloquy designed for his own encouragement. For instance, a cut fragment of a sentence reads: "The Ucs[78] perhaps for the holidays & then all right to coin technical terms. More boldness all round." Another: "Draw out the entire infantile history by the infantile mem[ories] like a net by the cork floats." Perhaps the aphorism "Great deeds are the preserve of those who can do no other" also belongs to this more autobiographical context. Elsewhere, at the end of some fairly long clinical notes, we find proud exclamations: "Such insights do indeed have something satisfying about them" and "Deep insights."

[6.14]

To conclude this chapter, which conveys something of the range and diversity of the notes, here are a few words by way of summary. Freud's habit of making notes is mentioned again and again in his letters. As early as 9 November 1899, he informed Fliess that he was "making notes on the results of my four analyses every evening,"[79] commenting shortly afterward that he was keeping "a kind of diary"[80] on a specific treatment. These were actually finger exercises for a completely new kind of description of the internal world. One of the aims of this approach was, as he put it in a letter to C. G. Jung on 6 June 1907,[81] to lay bare "the architectonics of the cases"—even if his judgment of his success was on the whole skeptical: "To be sure of making everything absolutely clear, I tried to show all the complications and consequently got stuck every time."[82] Only later did he come to regard these shortcomings as inherent in the material and in the difficulties of its verbal communication. Even in his old age, when he wrote *An Outline*

---

[77]Freud means the journey with Ferenczi in September 1910.
[78]Presumably the metapsychological paper "The Unconscious."
[79]1985c, p. 385.
[80]Ibid., p. 388.
[81]1974a, p. 59.
[82]Ibid.

of Psycho-Analysis, he began the chapter entitled "The Internal World" programmatically as follows: "We have no way of conveying knowledge of a complicated set of simultaneous events except by describing them successively; and thus it happens that all our accounts are at fault to begin with owing to one-sided simplification and must wait till they can be supplemented, built on to, and so set right."[83]

However, the primary function of making notes was for Freud no doubt to record impressions and gather material. On the one hand, this abundance of details was intended to restrain his tendency toward premature systematization, toward the overhasty marshaling of facts into "series" and "formulae," and toward imaginative speculation. Shortly after sending the draft of the highly speculative, later rejected twelfth metapsychological paper to Ferenczi for criticism, Freud in effect called himself to order in this respect in a letter to him dated 31 July 1915: "It is my contention that one should not make theories—they should descend upon one as unbidden guests while one is engaged on detailed investigations [. . .]." And, indeed, the notes did, so to speak, constantly remind him of the need to pursue such detailed investigations. But, on the other hand, they served him directly for the storage of this material, so that hypotheses and theories could subsequently crystallize out of it, by a kind of additive effect, along the lines of the description he had once given in the study "The Disposition to Obsessional Neurosis": "This is the starting-point of the small new fragment of theory which I have formulated. It is of course only in appearance that it is based on this one observation; actually it brings together a large number of earlier impressions, though an understanding of them was only made possible by this last experience."[84] In other words, the notes helped Freud gradually attain "that simplification, without either ignoring or doing violence to the facts, for which we strive in scientific work."[85]

Again and again as we read the notes, we come across evidence of the working of Freud's scientific vigilance, of how it in effect adopted a *multiple focus* depending on the particular theoretical problems with which he was grappling at any given time. He himself explicitly pointed out that there were "dates, the text of dreams, or particular noteworthy events which can easily be detached from their context and are suitable for independent use as instances."[86] The use of these instances in a given text, quite often after they had been stored away for years or even decades, ultimately gave rise, in the

[83] 1940*a* [1938], p. 205.
[84] 1913*i*, p. 320.
[85] 1930*a*, p. 119.
[86] 1912*e*, p. 113.

published text, to a kind of hidden multidimensional architecture of material spanning the oeuvre as a whole, a structure that will probably not be revealed in its entirety until the private notes have been fully disclosed.

Last, the making of notes was sometimes motivated by the sheer joy of recognition, the delight of the collector, by the hope that in this way, through his exchanges with his colleagues, an unending supply of new, more and more graphic, and increasingly conclusive evidential material could be teased out. With this in mind, Freud wrote to Ferenczi on 6 January 1913: "Under the title 'Collection,' I will now send you more frequently such experiences from my practice, which are suitable for being singled out and which I myself ask to be put in order, i.e., occasionally matched up with similar things. You do the same, and if others follow our lead, then with time we will put together a nice ψα [psychoanalytic] picture book."[87] Just three months later, on 10 April 1913, he writes: "I have [. . .] put together from your and my little notes a first series 'Observations and Examples,' with which you can also begin, whatever you want."[88] The collection mentioned, of twenty-two notations, twelve of them from Freud's pen, did indeed appear in the same year in the *Internationale Zeitschrift für ärztliche Psychoanalyse* under the title "Erfahrungen und Beispiele aus der analytischen Praxis" ["Observations and Examples from Analytic Practice"].[89] All the same, what he published here, "without waiting to be worked over from a more generalized point of view,"[90] was not a verbatim extract from his handwritten notes. In the case of some of the examples, it is possible, as stated, to identify the pithier, even more succinct preliminary formulations in the "Sammlung zum Traum" ["Collection on dreams"] of 12 December 1911.

In other words, the notes were and remained strictly private documents. Leafing through them today, one has the impression that Freud was accustomed, from the beginning of his working life, to retain this preliminary stage of his published oeuvre, unlike the drafts and fair copies. From time to time—and presumably not only in 1938 while preparing to emigrate—he seems to have sifted through them and discarded some. Anything he had not yet turned to account in his published writings but still intended to pursue, or considered worth keeping for other reasons, he would cut out or excerpt; he occasionally numbered such extracts or cutouts and/or structured them by means of marginal remarks. He presumably threw the rest away.

The compilations surviving under the headings "From older notes from

[87]1992g, p. 460.
[88]Ibid., p. 477.
[89]1913h.
[90]Ibid., p. 194.

1897 on" or "Taken from 4 notebooks from 1901. on." argue in favor of his use of this technique. The last of the numbered entries in the latter collection reads: "7. Act of birth ̶c̶a̶u̶s̶e̶ ̶o̶f̶ source of anxiety. Macduff." Under this comes the line: "This from 1901." The notation once again confirms Freud's early concern with the drama *Macbeth* or, more precisely, with the traumatic birth of the avenger Macduff; but, furthermore, the fact of his extracting this early note and explicitly dating it with a year could also be interpreted as a reaction to Otto Rank's theory of the etiological significance of the trauma of birth, the subject of violent controversy when it was made public in 1923/1924, and could therefore be used as a clue to the date when Freud in this case looked through and culled his notebooks. This perusal and culling would then sometimes have had the character of an inventorization, a personal historiography of his ideas. Of course, these are mere conjectures.

There can be no doubt, at any rate, that the notes, as an initial informal fixing of his observations, impressions from his reading, ideas, and thoughts, performed an indispensable function for Freud over many decades. They were the dependable companions not only of his research but also of his work as a writer. From this point of view, there is every reason to believe that at least a part of the body of notes, here described for the first time, was taken into exile by Freud himself.

7 DRAFTS

Drafts embody the second stage of the dynamic that characterizes the genesis of Freud's texts. They are the detailed preparatory manuscripts from which the fair copies of the works he published directly issued. Freud himself used the word "Entwurf" [draft] to designate this type of text.[1] In line with this definition of the "draft" category, the manuscripts discovered in the context of the letters to Wilhelm Fliess and published only after Freud's death will not be considered here.[2] Neither shall we be concerned with the numerous sketches and tentative formulations that he tried out in his various correspondences before, during, and after setting down a new work, when attempting to describe the project currently in hand to the addressee.

Manuscripts that Freud so to speak used as models from which to prepare his fair copies are easily recognizable. They are sheets on which the text—usually written in ink and recorded telegraphically or at least in a manner characterized by numerous abbreviations—has been crossed out diagonally in blocks.[3] The author, in composing the fair copy, may well have had the appropriate draft beside him on his desk, marking it paragraph by paragraph with those diagonal lines to indicate the extent of his progress in transposing the matter recorded in the draft into the definitive form of the fair copy.[4]

As already indicated, only a small number of drafts and passages from drafts prove to have survived. There are in all five relatively extensive documents, here enumerated in chronological order of their genesis. First, among the manuscripts in the Sigmund Freud Collection, I happened upon the draft of the lecture "Wir und der Tod" ["Death and Ourselves"], which Freud delivered to the "Wien" Lodge of the Jewish B'nai B'rith on 16 February 1915.[5] Second, in 1983, I found among some papers of Sándor Ferenczi the

[1]Cf., for example, 1985a, p. xvi.

[2]1950a/1950c and 1985c; the "Kritische Einleitung in die Nervenpathologie" ["Critical Introduction to Neural Pathology"] (1983g), which dates from the Fliess period and was not intended by Freud for publication, will also not be considered, although it shows many of the characteristic features of a draft, such as abbreviations.

[3]As an example, cf. the facsimile of the draft of the Übersicht der Übertragungsneurosen [Overview of the Transference Neuroses] (1985a, p. 24ff.), and facsimiles 7.1 and 7.2.

[4]The form of certain of the fair copies—for example, that of the study of Leonardo— suggests that Freud occasionally cut out pieces from the draft or also from the notes and pasted them into the fair copy; the relevant passages are quotations that he had already reproduced in full in the preliminary versions, which this expedient saved him from having to copy again.

[5]This may conceivably be the text that Schur (1972, p. 292, note 9) mentioned as "a

draft of the twelfth metapsychological paper of 1915, "Übersicht der Übertragungsneurosen" ["Overview of the Transference Neuroses"], the fair copy of which, although written down, remained unpublished by the author and is now considered to be lost. Third, as already stated in the chapter on the notes, the Sigmund Freud Collection includes the draft, composed in 1922, of "Eine Teufelsneurose im siebzehnten Jahrhundert" ["A Seventeenth-Century Demonological Neurosis"]. Fourth, in that collection I was also able to identify the draft of *Das Ich und das Es* [*The Ego and the Id*]. Fifth and last, among the Moses manuscripts in the Library of Congress is the draft of some passages of the third essay of *Der Mann Moses und die monotheistische Religion* [*Moses and Monotheism*]—namely, the three sections in which Freud draws an analogy between, on the one hand, his construction of the genesis and effects of monotheism in terms of the psychology and history of religion and, on the other, the etiology of the neuroses.[6]

I have already edited[7] or described in detail[8] elsewhere the second and fifth of these drafts, so that a fuller discussion is not necessary here. I shall have relatively little to say below about the draft of the lecture but should like to draw the reader's attention mainly to the drafts of the "Demonological Neurosis" and of *The Ego and the Id* and to compare the two.

The first sheet of the twelve-page draft of "Wir und der Tod" ["Death and Ourselves"] bears the date "7/2 15."[9] The document is of interest because it shows that Freud first sketched out his lectures too in draft form and because it so to speak documents an early phase in the genesis of the second part of "Thoughts for the Times on War and Death." As we know, "Wir und der Tod" and "Our Attitude towards Death"[10] are almost identical in the substance of their ideas;[11] they differ primarily in their rhetorical structure,

---

nearly complete version of this lecture"; he claims to have come across it in Freud's library. However, Schur seems not to have carried out his intention to publish it.

[6]There are indications that the manuscript of the late work *An Outline of Psycho-Analysis*, which dates from 1938, should also be counted among the preserved drafts. However, because this work in other respects belongs to the context of the posthumous publications, I shall leave the discussion of this assumption for chapter 11.

[7]1985*a*.

[8]Grubrich-Simitis, 1991, p. 14ff. and p. 99ff. (revised 1994 edition, p. 20ff. and p. 100ff.).

[9]It is preserved in the Sigmund Freud Collection only in the form of a photocopy, in which the characteristic diagonal lines are, however, clearly visible.

[10]In 1915*b*, pp. 289–300.

[11]An even earlier sketch for some of the theses in "Wir und der Tod" ["Death and Ourselves"] and "Our Attitude towards Death" can be found in Freud's letter to the Dutch psychopathologist and essayist Frederik van Eeden dated 28 December 1914, written, that is to say, a few months after the outbreak of war (1915*g*). For more details of the circumstances of the lecture, the printed text of which the author has again made accessible, cf. Nitzschke, 1991.

and in particular in the way Freud addresses his specific audiences. However, some of the material in the lecture—for instance, the drawing of a parallel between the bloodlust of primitive man and our own archaic aggression—is formulated more robustly and more uncompromisingly, albeit with greater irony and wit, than in the essay. In a letter dated 8 April 1915, Freud in fact informed Sándor Ferenczi that he would shortly be forwarding the manuscript of "Wir und der Tod": "I wish to send you a bold lecture, inspired by gallows humor, which I have delivered here at the Jewish club (in the press). But please return it to me immediately, because, being a very popular piece, it is in great demand and available only in the singular." Freud is here manifestly referring to the fair copy of the lecture,[12] which he had prepared from the draft and which he now already had back from the typesetter. The draft in fact records his train of thought in appreciably abbreviated form. Comparison with the version of the lecture printed in the *Zweimonatsbericht für die Mitglieder der österreichisch israelitischen Humanitätsvereine B'nai B'rith* [Bimonthly Newsletter for the Members of the Austrian Jewish Lodges of the B'nai B'rith] shows that it bears roughly the same relation to it as the draft of the "Demonological Neurosis" does to the relevant fair copy, as will be described in detail below. However, a sarcastic concluding remark to be found in the draft of the lecture evidently did not find its way into the fair copy of "Wir und der Tod." It reads: "That brings me to the end & I can return from the subject of death to the more immediate details of our lives. I know what awaits me first. At the forthcoming fraternal dinner, one of you will be called upon to thank me for this lecture. May I express my brotherly sympathy to the poor fellow, as I have not made it easy for him. He will have to be profuse in the social conventions of praise &, in so doing, will be entitled to say to himself, in the deeper layers of his mental life: the devil take him, he has thoroughly spoilt my appetite."

Freud here intended to make a pun on an earlier passage in the draft of the lecture, on death wishes: "By the day and by the hour, we eliminate in our thoughts all those who stand in our way, who have impeded us or offended us. The remark 'the devil take him,' which so often forces itself past our bloodless pallid[13] lips as a shadowy interjection, is meant in deadly earnest by the deep layers of our mental life.[14] For every offense committed against us, the Ucs, like the Dracon[ian] law, has only the death penalty. Our Ucs murders for a trifle. Fortunately all these wishes have no power, other-

---

[12]It has not survived, whereas the fair copy of "Thoughts for the Times on War and Death" is in the Sigmund Freud Collection.

[13]This word ["abgeblasste(n)" in German] is written underneath "bloodless" ["blutleere(n)"] and was presumably inserted later.

[14]The next two sentences are noted in the margin.

wise mankind would have died out long ago, & not [even] the best, the wisest, the most beautiful & the fairest would still be alive." The relationship between the draft and the eventual text of the lecture as printed in the *Zweimonatsbericht* will now be illustrated for the reader as an example by the relevant passage from the printed version: "In the silence of our thoughts, we eliminate by the day and by the hour all who stand in our way, who have offended or harmed us. The words 'the devil take him,' which so often pass our lips as a feeble interjection, and which really mean 'death take him,' are meant in deadly earnest by our unconscious. Indeed, our unconscious murders for a mere trifle; like the old Athenian legal code of D r a c o, it knows no penalty for transgressions but death, and there is a certain consistency here, for every injury to our omnipotent and overweening ego is, after all, at root a crime of lèse-majesté. It is indeed fortunate that all these wicked thoughts possess no power. Mankind would otherwise have died out long ago, and not even the best and wisest among men, or the most beautiful and fairest of women, would remain in existence."[15]

Let us now describe and compare the other two, more important, drafts. Like the draft of the twelfth metapsychological paper, that of "A Seventeenth-Century Demonological Neurosis" seems to owe its preservation to chance. The manuscript originally consisted of twenty-two numbered pages; pages 5 to 8 are now missing.[16] At one point on page 9 of the manuscript of the draft, in the midst of the text, Freud has indicated by an "etc." and a long horizontal line that he has skipped a passage here.[17] All the existing pages exhibit the characteristic feature of the drafts: they are each crossed out from top to bottom with a number of oblique lines traced in red pencil. Except for the first four pages of one double sheet, they were all torn and reassembled later with adhesive tape; this tape has, however, now dried up and become detached, so that the draft consists of a large number of fragments. It is not clear who in the past tried to stick the torn

---

[15]1915*i*, p. 48.

[16]Reconstruction from the fair copy and the printed version shows that the pages concerned are those on which Freud describes in detail, on the basis of the sources, the circumstances under which the painter Christoph Haitzmann, who fell into a depression after his father's death, sells his soul to the Devil (1923*d*, p. 80ff.). The Sigmund Freud Collection includes not only the original manuscripts of the "Demonological Neurosis"—i.e., draft and fair copy—and the photocopy of the notes, but also copies of a total of four torn-off bottom halves of sheets which evidently belong to the context of the draft. Two of these fragments come precisely from that part of the draft manuscript that is missing today.

[17]The passages concerned are those dealing with ambivalence toward the father and the reflection of this emotional split in the antithesis of God and Devil as well as in Haitzmann's symptoms (in the printed version, 1923*d*, pp. 85–88). The two other half-sheets mentioned in the previous note concern this part of the draft manuscript that was skipped and presumably elaborated later.

manuscript together again. However, it may be assumed that it was Freud himself who tore the sheets and discarded them—perhaps during that process of culling his papers before his departure into exile.

The title of the draft manuscript, "Eine Teufelsverschreib[un]g im 17 Jahrhundert" ["A Bond with the Devil in the 17[th] Century"],[18] differs slightly from that of the published text; it was therefore only in the fair copy that Freud disclosed his approach—namely, to look at "this bond with the Devil as if it were the case history of a neurotic"[19]—by using from the outset the title "Eine Teufelsneurose im 17ten Jahrhundert" ["A 17th-Century Demonological Neurosis"].[20] Comparison of the fair copy with the draft shows that the latter is in fact a sketch in which even the finest details of Freud's ideas are elaborated. He had written to Sándor Ferenczi in 1915, concerning his "Overview of the Transference Neuroses," that the fair copy followed the draft sentence by sentence and deviated from it only slightly[21]—and the same applies to the "Demonological Neurosis." To illustrate that the draft is in the nature of a sketch and to exemplify the relation it bears to the fair copy, both versions of the first paragraph are shown below.

It reads as follows in the draft: "Expectation [of] seeing through many things easily has been afforded us valuably by child neuroses. Similar [to] neuroses from earlier times. Prepared not to find them under same names as nowadays, not surprised to find them in demonolog[ical] trappings, as in unpsychological modern days in hypochondriacal [trappings], disguised as illness. As we know, Charcot identified the manifestations of hy[steria] in portrayals of possession preserved [in] art, but not in the histories, [would have] not been difficult to find subject-matter of neurosis in them if more attention paid them at time. (Was done in individual cases, St. Theresa etc.)."

The corresponding passage in the fair copy reads:[22] "The neuroses of childhood have taught us that a number of things can easily be seen in them with the naked eye which at a later age are only to be discovered after a thorough investigation. We may expect that the same will turn out to be true of neurotic illnesses in earlier centuries, provided that we are prepared to recognize them under names other than those of our present-day neuroses. We need not be surprised to find that, whereas the neuroses of our un-

[18]Cf. facsimile 7.1 of the first page of the draft.

[19]1923d, p. 79.

[20]The reader is reminded that the notes for this work also bear the title "Teufelsverschreibung" ["Bond with the Devil"].

[21]1985a, p. xvi.

[22]The printed version in this case is identical with that of the fair copy, except for minimal differences of spelling and punctuation.

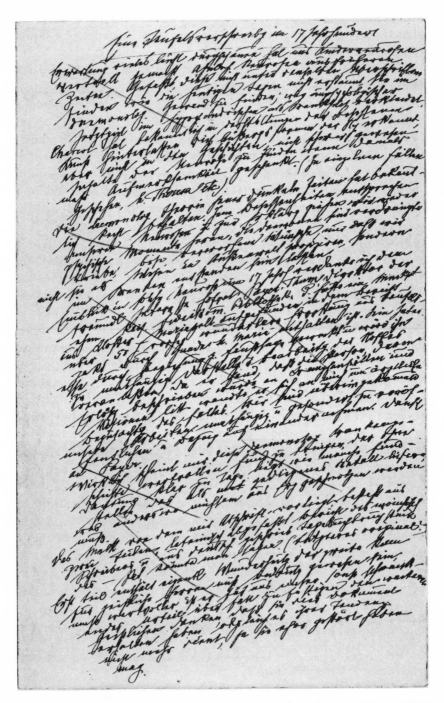

First page of the draft of the "Teufelsneurose" ["Demonological Neurosis"].　　[7.1]

psychological modern days take on a hypochondriacal aspect and appear disguised as organic illnesses, the neuroses of those early times emerge in demonological trappings. Several authors, foremost among them Charcot, have, as we know, identified the manifestations of hysteria in the portrayals of possession and ecstasy that have been preserved for us in the productions of art. If more attention had been paid to the histories of such cases at the time, it would not have been difficult to retrace in them the subject-matter of neurosis."

So if the fair copy is superimposed on the draft, the latter emerges like a skeletal silhouette, as in an X-ray image, revealing the ideas presented in the paper. Except for the parenthesis about Saint Theresa, the final text features all the elements of the bony structure of the draft, but fleshed out by soft tissues into a complete and natural linguistic body. On the whole, it is indeed the language and style of the text that are reduced in the draft to a mere sketch. Articles, pronouns, conjunctions, adverbial modifiers, auxiliary verbs, punctuation marks, and so on are often omitted, infinitives are rendered in abbreviated form, and word repetitions are not avoided. Conversely, all essential ideas are already recorded faithfully in the draft.

The work to be accomplished in the transition from draft to fair copy was therefore predominantly literary, that of a writer. It concerned not only fleshing out the linguistic bones to form a complete body or dropping certain ideas subsequently found to be distracting, but also structuring of text in such a way as to increase tension and impart rhythm. For instance, additional paragraphs, sections, and subtitles have been inserted. Certain material that in the draft still featured in the main text has been transferred in the fair copy to footnotes, thus slimming down and bringing into sharper focus the principal lines of thought, now unburdened by details such as references. Freud's meticulous honing of his style has a similar effect: word repetitions are almost always avoided in the fair copy; the rhetorical dialogue structure, which involves the reader and enhances the plausibility and coherence of the text, is intensified; and his use of metaphor is polished.

Examination of the draft of *Das Ich und das Es* [*The Ego and the Id*] reveals a different situation. The divergences from the draft of the "Demonological Neurosis" begin with the history of its preservation. As with the draft passages for the third Moses essay, Freud himself plainly wished to keep these sheets, as they are included unmutilated among the fair copies. The manuscript, in all thirty-two pages long, is written on both sides of double-size sheets of paper. Twenty-nine of these pages and the first section of page 30 again show the characteristic feature of Freud's drafts: they are crossed out in blocks with diagonal lines,[23] usually in blue pencil, but occasionally in red. Then follow about two pages of short notations under the subtitle "Ancillary questions, themes, formulae, analyses." On the left-hand side of the first page of the manuscript, next to the title, Freud has recorded the date when he began to write the draft: "23 July 22." At the bottom of page 31 is the time marker "9 Aug 22.", with the terse comment, "Thus far complete.—"[24] Only a few days earlier, Freud had noted in a letter to Otto Rank dated 4 August, again as it were in a state of wide-awake passivity, that the new work "has progressed fairly far in draft, otherwise waits for moods and ideas without which it cannot be completed."[25] On "13/8" and "30/8," he jotted down a few afterthoughts on the last page of the manuscript. At any rate, the actual text of the draft was set down in little more than a fortnight. Furthermore, the author must have begun work on the fair copy immediately afterward because according to the date on its last page he finished it by "2. Sept. 22."

The Ego and the Id is, as we know, the last of Freud's major theoretical works. The model of the psyche, of its structure and functioning, that it introduces is so innovative and formative in its intrinsic potency that the year of publication of the brief text, 1923, literally marks a watershed in the psychoanalytic literature. Shortly before his cancer was diagnosed, Freud had embarked upon his groundbreaking metapsychological labor, which was forced on him by the insight, based on years of clinical experience, that the ego and the unconscious are not antagonistic spheres, but that the ego too contains functional regions that must be characterized as uncon-scious—for example, defense or resistance. In this work of theoretical re-stratification, the first topographic model of the mental apparatus (distin-guishing among unconscious, preconscious, and conscious) was superseded by the second (with the id, the ego, and the superego as its agencies); how-ever, Freud at the same time reflected the impact of his new conceptualiza-tions on the theory of instinctual drives, made the phenomenology of the unconscious sense of guilt more specific, and deepened his comprehension of the mechanisms of identification and sublimation; and he introduced the term "superego," which, although since varied and extended many times over, remains a cornerstone of psychoanalytic thought to this day.

To what extent are the drafts of the "Demonological Neurosis" and *The Ego and the Id* comparable? Both stem from the same period of Freud's creativity and even from the same year, 1922. A connection may have existed on the level of the author's energy budget in that, after the intellec-

---

[23]Cf. facsimile 7.2 of the first page.
[24]Cf. facsimile 7.3 of page 31.
[25]As quoted in Gay, 1988, p. 407.

First page of the draft of *Das Ich und das Es* [*The Ego and the Id*]. [7.2] tual strain of composing the major work of metapsychology, he was perhaps seeking some relief in the detective game of testing the categories of neurotic etiology on an enthralling piece of history, which had at this time been called to his attention by a chief librarian in Vienna. "'Ego and Id' is currently maturing," Freud noted in a letter to Sándor Ferenczi written on 25 January 1923, while he was working on the "Demonological Neurosis," as he also informed his friend. However, the two works differ not only in their status in the canon of the Freudian oeuvre. The relation the drafts bear to the relevant fair copies is also not the same. In the case of *The Ego and the Id,* there is a much wider gulf between the texts of the draft and of the fair copy.

This discrepancy is most obvious in the concluding passage. Whereas the last paragraph of the draft of the "Demonological Neurosis" differs from the definitive version only in a few minimal linguistic details, passages corresponding to the final pages of the draft of *The Ego and the Id* will be sought in vain in the fair copy. Rather, it seems that in case of the latter Freud gave up the coherent sketching that constitutes the work of drafting proper and returned to an earlier stage in the genesis of the work: the jotting down of isolated ideas and aphoristic germinal formulations. For instance, while page 28 of the manuscript already contains the subtitle "Addenda & Additions," the line "Ancillary questions, themes, formulae, analyses" on page 30 is a clear indication that what follows is in the nature of notations.

The author indeed asks questions—for example: "How far it is legitimate to postulate separation of ego & id and superego in animals" and "whether sublimation is really conditional on identific[ation] or whether this process is only [an] isolated case." He notes such themes as: "Emphasize relation bt. phylogenesis & superego more strongly"; "idea of vertical breakdown of ego." He formulates central statements—for example, "Only what was already cs, i.e., stems from p[erception], can become cs. Making a thought cs = dressing it up as if it were being heard"; "All knowledge originates from surface, from the ego; i.e. from p[erception]"; "Ego is essentially bodily. Id becomes ego is perhaps formula of hypoch[ondria]." And he attempts the briefest of summaries of the contents of *The Ego and the Id*: "The work combines 1) Groddeck's ideas of the It with 2). the assumption from Beyond [the Pleasure Principle] of the two classes of instinctual drives & 3) the fact of the ucs sense of guilt, [and] adds new assumption on 4) mechanism of desexualization (sublimation), on 5). presence of a defusion and rests on a new insight 6) of the replacement of object cathexis by identification."

Yet many an element in this collection of notes does recur, transformed to a greater or lesser extent, in the fair copy. As an unmistakable derivative of the penultimate entry in the draft, dated "13/8,"—"Ego sycophantic,

Page 31 of the draft of *Das Ich und das Es* [*The Ego and the Id*]. [7.3]

opportunistic—Lloyd George"—the following sentence appears on page 34 of the fair copy: "In its position midway between the id and reality, it [the ego] only too often yields to the temptation to be sycophantic, opportunistic and lying, like a politician who sees the truth[?] but wants to keep his favorable place in public opinion." Other building blocks were clearly incorporated only in later works. It is probable even that Freud kept the draft of *The Ego and the Id* mainly because of this appendix of notes, perhaps imagining that he might wish to return later to one or another of its ideas; for this reason, exceptionally, he treated this draft in the same way as he otherwise did his notes.[26]

In fact, in other passages too the distance between draft and fair copy is appreciably greater than in the case of the "Demonological Neurosis," the two versions of whose text differ mainly in language and style. Although a degree of parallelism is also discernible at the beginning between the draft and the fair copy of *The Ego and the Id,* they begin to drift apart toward the end of the second and in the third chapter.[27] By the fourth chapter and, in particular, the fifth, there are no more than occasional points of contact between them. In this case, then, the draft does not have the character of an X-ray image. It is more like a quarry, whose crude, disparate blocks were not sorted, hewn, and assembled by Freud into novel, higher-order structures until the stage of production of the final text. Even in the fair copy, almost every line betrays the drudgery of the innovative process of thinking and formulating. This manuscript does indeed make a more restless impression than most of the other fair copies. It preserves the traces of corrections of all kinds—deletions, rearrangements, textual additions on separate sheets or strips of paper, and so on. One indication of the extent to which the author was moving over unfamiliar ground is the fact that lengthy passages, even of the draft text, are written out relatively fully. In other words, the draft does not exhibit the otherwise typical omissions and abbreviations, discussed in detail in relation to the draft of the "Demonological Neurosis," which, after all, signal how sure of himself the author felt regarding the subsequent expansion of even the briefest jottings. Some of the formulations in the draft of *The Ego and the Id* that are still rough-hewn, apodictic, and unhedged with reservation appear in the fair copy in milder form, more carefully supported by evidence, and phrased with greater caution. It is as if Freud, in order to be understood, had moved some way backward in the direction of conventionality, not out of opportunism but in order to diminish the risk,

[26]This argument no doubt applies equally to the draft, mentioned earlier, of certain passages of the third Moses essay because this too ends with a similar appendix of notes (cf. Grubrich-Simitis, 1991, p. 15ff. and p. 99ff.; revised 1994 edition p. 21ff. and p. 100ff.).

[27]The headings of the third, fourth, and fifth chapters also differ in the two versions.

associated with innovations of this magnitude, of putting himself beyond the pale of comprehension in the scientific community.

Once the draft and the fair copy have been critically edited—to the best of my knowledge, this is the only case in which two of the principal stages in the genetic dynamics of a constitutive text of psychoanalytic theory are documented in full—the reader will see from detailed comparison with the printed version that Freud's efforts to achieve maximum precision had by no means abated when he finished the fair copy. They even extended to the process of correcting the galley proofs. The fair copy and the printed text of *The Ego and the Id* are found to diverge from each other roughly as much as do the draft and the fair copy of the "Demonological Neurosis." Besides further instances of stylistic retouching, significant variants in content can be discerned. To give just one example, where the fair copy often still refers to the "consciousness of guilt," the published version usually has "sense of guilt." This amendment may have been a last-minute reaction to an objection by Sándor Ferenczi, to whom Freud had sent the page proofs. On 18 March 1923, Ferenczi had drawn attention to "a minor inconsistency": "On page 4 you write (as often before) that 'a consciousness about which one knows nothing is [. . .] a good deal *more absurd* than something mental that is unconscious.' On page 13 you write 'notwithstanding all the phonetic contradiction of an *unconscious consciousness* of guilt.' It seems to me that you should tone down the judgment 'absurd' (in relation to ucs. knowledge) to some extent if you are expressing only formal reservations against the assumption of the unconscious consciousness of guilt. Otherwise you will be running the risk that people will turn your word against your term." Freud thanked him a few days later for his "critical comment, which [has] already had its effect."[28]

For all the differences between the two drafts here described in detail, they are both effectively *private* manuscripts, and the same applies to the three other documents mentioned at the beginning of this chapter. In each case, Freud completed the transition to the *public* text of the printed version only when he composed the fair copy.

---

[28]An echo of this delicate question of terminology can be found in the late work *An Outline of Psycho-Analysis*: "[. . .] the sense of guilt or consciousness of guilt, as it is called, though the patient does not feel it and is not aware of it" (1940a, p. 179f.).

8 FAIR COPIES

This process of stepping onto the public stage is already signaled by the graphic design of the opening of almost every fair copy, which, like the diagonal crossings out in the drafts, is effectively the distinguishing mark of the "fair copy" as a manuscript category. As if wishing to anticipate the eventual appearance of the printed page, the author inscribes the title ceremonially in big letters, sometimes underlining it; writes the word "von" [by] on the second line; and follows it on the third line by his name in the characteristic abbreviated form, "Sigm. Freud." He then draws a line across the entire width of the paper, causing the rubric to stand out neatly from the text proper.[1] Like the beginning, the end of the fair copy too is often graphically accentuated: a shorter horizontal line, sometimes adorned in the middle by dots above and below,[2] demonstrates that the author has finished; such fermatas can occasionally also be found at the end of the chapters of longer works. Freud developed this graphic presentation for his fair copies early on; the manuscripts dating from 1908, of "Charakter und Analerotik" ["Character and Anal Erotism"] and "Über infantile Sexualtheorien" ["On the Sexual Theories of Children"], already show some of the typical elements.[3]

As described earlier, Freud wrote on unusually large sheets of paper, sometimes on the front only but more commonly on both sides. According to information from Anna Freud, he had sheets custom-cut to a width of fifty centimeters and a height of forty centimeters. When folded once lengthwise, they could either be used as double pages or be separated to yield single sheets twenty-five centimeters wide. The majority of the fair copies are thus

[1]As examples, cf. facsimiles 8.1 and 8.2 of the first pages of the manuscripts of "Triebe und Triebschicksale" ["Instincts and their Vicissitudes"] and of "Das Unheimliche" ["The 'Uncanny'"].

[2]Cf. facsimile 8.3 of the last page of the "Notiz über den 'Wunderblock'" ["A Note upon the 'Mystic Writing-Pad'"].

[3]Although not strictly speaking fair copies, the even earlier manuscripts, such as that of the "Entwurf einer Psychologie" ["Project for a Scientific Psychology"], also illustrate Freud's esthetic sense of visual layout and accentuation of the written text.

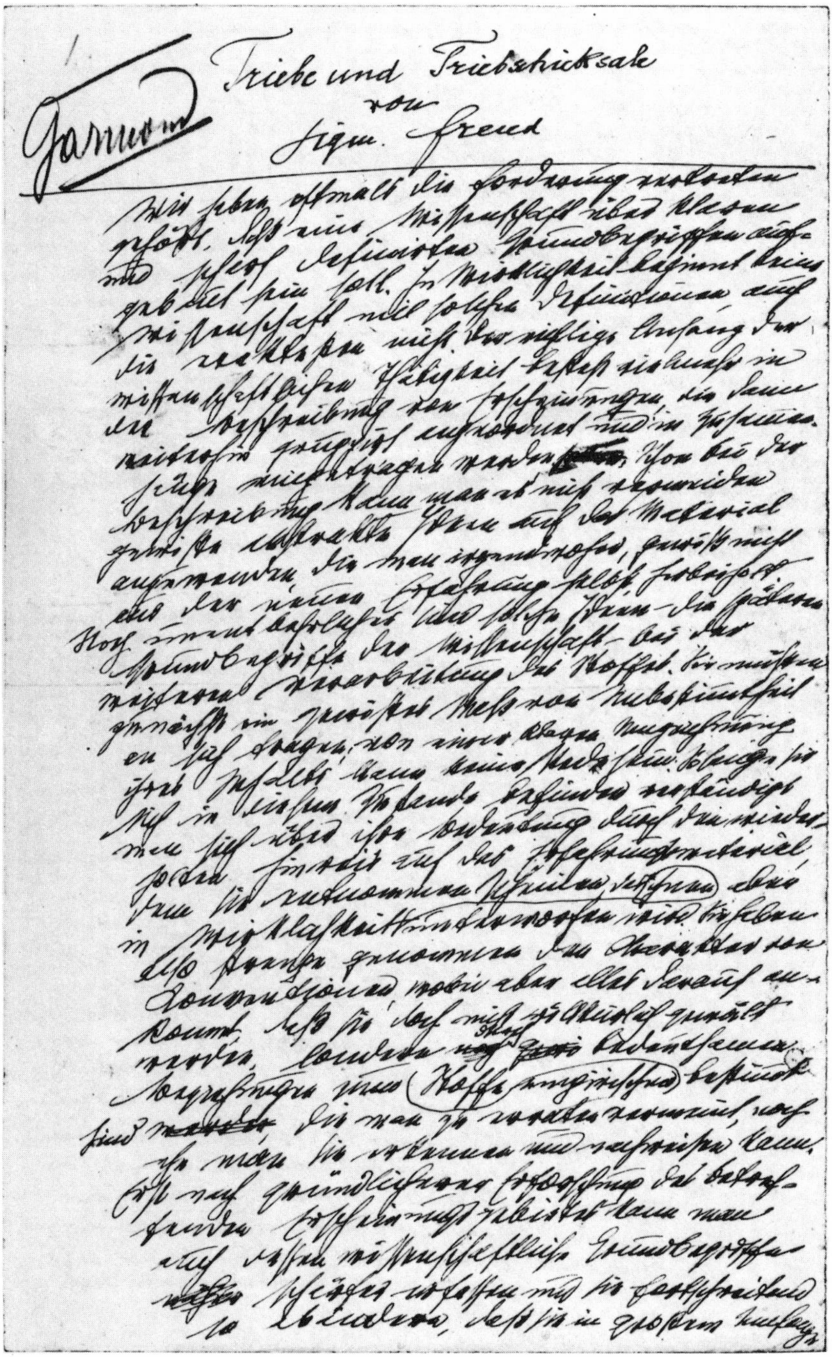

First page of the fair copy of "Triebe und Triebschicksale"] ["Instincts and their Vicissitudes"]. [8.1]

Das Unheimliche

von Sigm. Freud

First page of the fair copy of "Das Unheimliche" ["The 'Uncanny'"]. [8.2]

Last page of the fair copy of the "Notiz über den 'Wunderblock'" ["A Note upon the 'Mystic Writing-Pad'"].   [8.3]

preserved on these mighty substrates.[4] The material itself is almost always substantial ledger paper of uniform quality.[5]

Freud wrote with a fountain pen, in his later years occasionally with a massive, broad nib. As a rule he used German script, resorting to roman letters only exceptionally—for instance, to emphasize themes, titles, special terms, proper names, or foreign words. The distribution of the writing over the page remained unchanged for decades. Leafing through the pages of the fair copies, one is struck by the small number of corrections almost throughout. Like a robust spun web or loosely woven fabric, the writing—calm, generously sized, and sloping uniformly to the right—covers virtually the entire surface; the number of lines is all but identical on every page. On the left-hand side is a margin of slightly variable width but tending to widen toward the bottom, while the end of each line normally extends to the very edge of the paper. Where a word division is inappropriate, the line drops down a little, as if Freud wanted to continue down the right-hand edge for a bit so as to fit in the complete word after all.

The impression of a web or fabric presumably arises mainly from the interpenetration of descenders from one line with ascenders from the next; this gives the lines a loosely interlocking appearance, as if they were not clearly separated from each other by an interlinear space. This formal peculiarity of his handwriting too was typical of Freud from his youngest days. It characterizes the earliest surviving fair copy as it does the latest; indeed, the interlacing of the lines seems if anything to have become more pronounced with the passage of the decades. Anyone who goes through these many hundreds of pages today, coming for the first time face-to-face with the *Urtext* of such works as "Das Unbewusste" ["The Unconscious"], "Trauer und Melancholie" ["Mourning and Melancholia"], and "Die endliche und die unendliche Analyse" ["Analysis Terminable and Interminable"] cannot but be captivated by the classical beauty of these documents. The impression of regularity and relaxed severity that they convey must surely induce

[4]This also applies to some of the notes and to the drafts. Although the pieces of the Charcot translation are still written on small sheets, quite a few of the manuscripts from the Fliess period of the 1890s—e.g., that of "Die Ätiologie der Neurosen" ["The Etiology of the Neuroses"] (in 1985c, p. 39ff.)—are on the characteristic oversized paper (but not the main part of the manuscript of the "Entwurf einer Psychologie" ["Project for a Scientific Psychology"] of 1895, which Freud had in fact begun on a train journey). Later, too, he would occasionally, if extremely seldom, again use smaller paper: for instance, the brief study "Zwei Kinderlügen" ["Two Lies Told by Children"] is written on thin paper, presumably from a writing pad, while "Das Medusenhaupt" ["Medusa's Head"] is inscribed on both sides of a narrower sheet.

[5]For a realistic reproduction, cf. again the 1977 facsimile edition of the "Kästchenwahl" ["The Theme of the Three Caskets"].

an abrupt heightening of experience in the beholder. It is as if the puissant creativity of Freud's life were preserved in directly visible form in these sheets: "One of the very few ways in which life has been really thickened is by the great things that a few people have left."[6]

But harmony and immutability characterize not only the appearance of the handwriting. The author also retained throughout his life certain idiosyncrasies of spelling and punctuation in the composition of his fair copies. However, this was not a stylistic device to be defended against accepted usage at all costs, for these peculiarities have yielded to the customary forms by the stage of the first printing, the public text proper, the galleys of which would normally be read by Freud as well as by others.[7] In the manuscripts, punctuation marks are positioned singularly low relative to the base level of the line; it is not unusual for them to be omitted altogether, especially commas at the end of a line. He also often omits the two dots of the umlaut diacritic. Freud had a predilection for the official spellings of bygone days.[8] For example, words ending in "ieren" or "ierung" are almost always spelled without the "e" that was already customary in his day (for example, "isoliren" [isolate] or "Sublimirung" [sublimation]); while the obsolete "th" is found where initial "t" is now standard (for instance, "thun" [do], or "betheiligt" [involved]). Yet some orthographic peculiarities are Freud's own rather than manifestations of a reluctance to adopt the reforms of official spelling. This is true in particular of the conspicuous absence of the "h" normally used to indicate a long vowel in certain groups of words (for example, "Dreiza[h]l" [triad], "Totemma[h]lzeit" [totem meal], "Erzä[h]-lung" [story], "obwo[h]l" [although], or "Schuldgefü[h]l" [sense of guilt]); he knew that this was his personal custom because whenever he quoted other authors verbatim in his text he did not omit the "h" denoting a long vowel in the relevant word.

However, besides such features of timelessness, markers showing the passage of the years are to be found in the fair copies. Quite a few contain dates, from which the precise timing of the genetic process of the works concerned can be reconstructed: "Eine erfüllte Traumahnung" ["A Premonitory Dream Fulfilled"]—"10 Nov. 99"; "Zur Geschichte der psychoanalytischen Bewegung" ["On the History of the Psycho-Analytic

---

[6]Francis Bacon, as interviewed by David Sylvester (Sylvester, 1985, p. 89).

[7]Virtually the only exception is the word "anderseits" [on the other hand]; in the galleys of the *Selbstdarstellung* ["An Autobiographical Study"], Freud has changed the corrected spelling "andererseits" back to the original "anderseits."

[8]I wish to thank the Duden-Redaktion, Bibliographisches Institut, Mannheim, for information on spelling.

Movement"]—"Februar 1914."; "Psychoanalyse und Telepathie" ["Psycho-Analysis and Telepathy"]—"Gastein 4. [or 6.?] Aug. 21," begun on "2 Aug 21"; "Der Untergang des Ödipuskomplexes" ["The Dissolution of the Oedipus Complex"]—"21. 3. 24," begun on "2/3 24"; "Selbstdarstellung" ["An Autobiographical Study"]—"26. 7. 24."; "Die Zukunft einer Illusion" ["The Future of an Illusion"]—"15/9 [or 8?] 27"; "Neue Folge der Vorlesungen zur Einführung in die Psychoanalyse" ["New Introductory Lectures on Psycho-Analysis"]—"7/2 1932"; "Die endliche und die unendliche Analyse" ["Analysis Terminable and Interminable"]—"18/1 1937"; "Wenn Moses ein Ägypter war . . . " ["If Moses was an Egyptian . . . "]—"24/5 1937"; "Die Ichspaltung im Abwehrvorgang" ["Splitting of the Ego in the Process of Defense"]—"2/1 38," and so on.

For Freud the author, it was only in appearance that the solitude of writing had the character of a monologue. Even before his accession to fame, he imagined a constant dialogue with the reader; as we know, this molded the rhetorical structure of many of his texts. However, in setting down his fair copies, he had not only the reader in mind. He also had an empathic concern for the compositor who would be using his sheets as copy for typesetting. With the same courtesy and consideration that he displayed in trying to facilitate the reader's understanding of his arguments, he did his best to help the typesetter decipher his manuscript and spare him misunderstandings and ambiguities. This is evident from his manner of pagination, correction, and emphasis.

As a rule, the page numbers are written in large characters with a colored wax pencil in the top left-hand or right-hand corner of the sheet, after the full text has been written down; sometimes they encroach on the penned copy. The compositor can then easily identify the correct order of the pages even from a distance. Again, wherever Freud subsequently inserted an additional passage of any length, whether on a separate sheet or on the same page, he marked the position in the text where it was to go, usually conspicuously and also in color.

Shorter interpolations are seldom placed above or below the relevant line in the case of corrections and additions made at the time of writing; his idiosyncratic form of writing, described above, with interpenetrating descenders and ascenders, would after all have left Freud little room for them. He sometimes uses the blank left margin for a subsequent insertion. Wherever possible, however, he tried not to depart from the baseline, preferring instead to cross something out and to write the corrected or completed version immediately after. Here is another example: if he wished to qualify a noun already written with an attributive adjective, he would place it *after* the noun and mark the desired order of words with a line, as when correcting proofs—"der Mütter\narzisstischen" [of the mothers\narcissistic].[9] This preserves the unambiguous, clear *linearity* of the manuscript.

The typesetter was also to have no difficulty in recognizing paragraph divisions. For this reason, Freud consistently indents the first line of the new paragraph whenever the last line of its predecessor ends close to the right-hand edge of the page; otherwise he begins flush left. The location of footnotes, too, is made easily identifiable for the compositor. As a rule, the author places them, in his fair copies, not at the foot of the page or at the end of the manuscript but, to preclude errors, in the body of the text, immediately after the point marked with the sign x) to which the relevant note relates. However, the wording of the footnote is separated from that of the main text by horizontal lines extending across the full width of the paper. Anything that was to be set in widely spaced letters, italics, or small capitals—names, the titles of books or journals, foreign-language quotations, and so forth—was accentuated by Freud when he wrote down the manuscript, by the use of underlining or roman letters—and so exactly that, where necessary, he would switch from German to roman script in one and the same word.

That the fair copies actually served as copy for the typesetter is evident not only from the note often to be found on the first page of the manuscript, beside the rubric, informing the compositor how many proofs Freud required in each case. Some of the manuscripts are smudged with finger impressions from the typesetter's handling of lead type and composing sticks as well as marks that have left a visible record of breaks in the setting work.[10]

Other hands have also left traces in the fair copies. Editor's notes specify the font and type size (for example, "Garmond" or "Garamond," "Borgis," "Set in Petit") in which a text or a passage was to be set or where a new contribution by Freud was to appear in the relevant issue of a journal (for example, "f[or] Imago 1st position"). The fair copy of the fourth essay of *Totem and Taboo* bears the following note, prominent because written in huge letters in blue pencil, dated "5. VI. 13.": "Imago Number 4 August To be set up in type at once as quickly as possible and made up immediately after corr[ection]! D[r] Rank." Rather than reflecting a sudden access of impatience on the part of the editor, this is presumably an echo of the

---

[9]Cf. 1985a, pp. 50 and 51.

[10]In the later years, however, the fair copies seem no longer to have been used regularly as printer's copy. Some were typed out. Freud could then still enter the odd correction in these typescripts before they were forwarded to the publisher. This is true at any rate of the typed copies of "Die endliche und die unendliche Analyse" ["Analysis Terminable and Interminable"] and of "Konstruktionen in der Analyse" ["Constructions in Analysis"], both of which are preserved in the Sigmund Freud Collection.

author's own excitement and his urge to bring his new hypotheses, following their presentation and testing on the previous day in the Vienna Psychoanalytic Association, before the public without delay. Rank is sometimes addressed directly by Freud. The following brief message is written on the last page of the manuscript of "Erinnern, Wiederholen und Durcharbeiten" ["Remembering, Repeating and Working-Through"]: "Dear Herr Doktor [,] please include this essay in the sequence of the technical articles. I do not know what number this one will be." On the first page of the manuscript, Rank then inserted the following superior title in his own hand: "Weitere Ratschläge zur Technik der Psychoanalyse. II." ["Further Recommendations on the Technique of Psycho-Analysis. II."].

The odd discreet question mark or a marginal note of a manifest error has plainly not come from Freud's pen and indicates that, as described earlier, he occasionally submitted his fair copies to his most trusted associates for critical reading. Although he usually set out the bibliographic information in full himself, he sometimes gave only the title, with details such as place and year of publication, volume and page number, and so on, being completed by another hand; the handwriting of Anna Freud or Otto Rank can in some cases be identified in such additions.

Quotations, the results of literature searches, or reports of dreams supplied to Freud by third parties are also found physically inserted in the fair copies with a note of the source—as a piece of typescript or in the handwriting of the person concerned. For example, in the manuscript of "Eine Kindheitserinnerung aus 'Dichtung und Wahrheit'" ["A Childhood Recollection from *Dichtung und Wahrheit*"], the passage about Goethe's four siblings who died in childhood, in the handwriting of Hanns Sachs, is pasted in position, and the ensuing paragraph about Goethe's brother Hermann Jakob in that of Eduard Hitschmann; and the two observations about small children throwing objects out of the window, which Hermine von Hug-Hellmuth supplied to Freud on three handwritten pages, were also incorporated by him directly into his fair copy.

But however vividly a perusal of the fair copies brings back to life Freud's working scenery, with its dialogues and the interlocutors concerned, it is above all the variants contained in them that are relevant to the matters that occasioned my study of these sheets.

9 VARIANTS

Variants are defined in editorial theory as an author's revisions of his original choice of characters or other signs. Although each such revision occurs at a particular point in the text, its effect may extend beyond the localized sphere of a word, sentence, or paragraph and in some cases encompass the entire work. Consider a book entitled *Das Unbehagen in der Kultur* [*Civilization and its Discontents*], or *Das Glück und die Kultur* [*Happiness and Civilization*], or *Das Unglück in der Kultur* [*Unhappiness in Civilization*]: each possibility will evoke a distinct expectation in the reader who approaches the text and tinge his reading experience differently. Variants may be regarded as tokens of conscious, preconscious, or unconscious intentions on the part of the author.

As a rule, I became aware of the variants of Freud's texts mentioned in this chapter while comparing fair copies with their printed versions. They are presented as examples only and are representative neither of the scale nor of any particular typology of the changes introduced by the author at this final stage of his creative process. I repeat that I came across them in the course of more or less random sampling—more or less random because such searches so often prove to be motivated partly by one's own thematic interests and preconceived questions. Whereas some of the revisions described were already made by Freud in the relevant fair copies, others were clearly incorporated only during correction of the galley or page proofs. The point at which a given variant came about—whether in the fair copy, in one of the few surviving galleys, or not until the print stage—is specified only occasionally in the following. And I will not always conjecture on the reasons for the introduction of a variant; they will in any case often be manifest.

Let us first dispose of what might be described as a nonverbal type of variant, one that affects the text proper only indirectly and that is also very rare in the surviving manuscripts simply because Freud hardly ever used such means of presentation. These are two *graphic variants,* one of them not even from Freud's hand.

Accompanying the fair copy of the essay "The Moses of Michelangelo" is a drawing that modifies the posture of Michelangelo's statue and that Freud seems to have rejected; it is reproduced here smaller than actual size.[1]

---

[1]Conversely, the published four sketches (1914*b*, p. 226f., figs. 1 to 4) are not included with the pages of the manuscript.

Drawing for the study "The Moses of Michelangelo."   [Fig. 9.1]

This drawing, never published, shows more detail and therefore conveys a less sketchy impression than the illustrations familiar from the printed version; however, it is most probably by the same artist. We do not know why Freud excluded it from publication. Perhaps he was bothered by the fact that the entire figure of the colossus is depicted, from head to foot, and he may also have felt that the area of most interest to him, that of the tables/arm/chest/hand/beard—which is central to his interpretation—was not portrayed skillfully enough. As to the movement that Freud believed to have preceded the posture of the biblical hero recorded in the sculpture, the unpublished sketch could best be accommodated between Figure 1, with which we are familiar from the printed version (the portrayal of Moses sitting calmly), and Figure 2 (in which he is overcome by wrath and indignation). It might therefore be a demonstration of the following stage of Freud's reconstruction: "Suddenly the clamor [that is, the noise of the People of Israel dancing around the Golden Calf and rejecting monotheistic religion] strikes his ear; he turns his head and eyes in the direction from which the disturbance comes, sees the scene and takes it in."[2]

[2]Ibid., p. 225. *The Diary of Sigmund Freud 1929–1939* (1976m, p. 146) contains another

The second graphic variant is to be found in the fair copy of the *New Introductory Lectures on Psycho-Analysis,* in Lecture 31, "The Dissection of the Psychical Personality." Whereas the structure of the psyche is illustrated in the printed version[3] by just one drawing, the manuscript contains five sketches elaborated to different extents, here again reproduced smaller than actual size, only the last of which Freud retained and included in the printed version; he had already deleted its four precursors in the fair copy. He was manifestly not content until he had the idea of making a clear visual distinction between central concepts of his two successive topographical models—unconscious/preconscious, on the one hand, and id/ego/superego, on the other—by orienting the relevant inscriptions horizontally in the former case and vertically in the latter (see facsimile 9.1, p. 156).[4]

The *stylistic-rhetorical variants* are numerous. They are certainly never confined to the formal dimension of Freud's prose but always affect its semantic aspect too. The avoidance of word repetitions is merely the simplest process in this quest—which is probably in most cases preconscious[5] and therefore rapidly completed—for the sentence in which ultimately not a single element is replaceable, and every word is necessary and correctly positioned. This exactitude of expression, coupled with euphony in both consonance and dissonance and sensitive abatement or acceleration of the pace of the text, in the end gives rise to the unmistakable individuality and captivating presence of nearly all Freud's writings. Robert Coles recalls that Anna Freud had repeatedly stressed in interviews with him "how important writing was to her father—not only the ideas formulated, but also the process of giving the words a proper and inviting shape."[6] It is of course

---

Moses drawing not published by Freud. It exhibits the same technique as the one reproduced here but shows the figure in the upright posture of Michelangelo's sculpture. Freud may have asked the artist he had entrusted with the illustration of his hypothesis to prepare two sets of drawings: a first batch portraying the complete figure in detail, which includes the present example, and then a second depicting the colossus in sketchy, outline form, down to the knee only, which he selected for publication.

[3] 1933a, p. 78.

[4] [*Translator's note*: This should be compared with the drawing reproduced on page 78 of S. E. 22. Legend: W-Bw = Pcpt.-Cs.; Überich = Superego; Es = Id; Ich = Ego; vorbewußt = Preconscious; unbewußt = Unconscious; Vdg or Verdrängt = Repressed.]

[5] That is to say, it is always close to consciousness. Where the texts of others were being assessed, such aspects manifestly played a central part. This is not only evident from the letters to his various correspondents, but is also confirmed by the *Minutes of the Vienna Psychoanalytic Society*: again and again, Freud's discussion contributions begin with detailed formal criticism and comments on shortcomings of presentation, lack of consideration for the listener or reader, etc., but also, on occasion, with explicit praise for a rhetorically successful presentation.

[6] Coles, 1992, p. xxiiif.

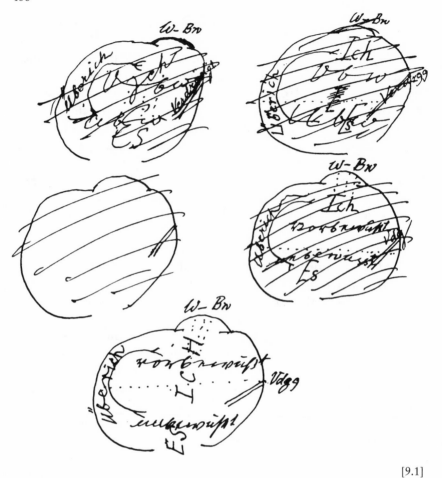

[9.1]

almost impossible to convey the subtle effects of such variants by a few short extracts; changes in the pace of the text, in particular, become evident only when alternative versions of relatively extensive passages are examined side by side. I shall nevertheless present three examples from the fair copy of the essay "Das Motiv der Kästchenwahl" ["The Theme of the Three Caskets"].

Only the avoidance of word repetitions, which seems to have been de rigueur for Freud, except where he used them as a deliberate device, is comparatively easy to illustrate. Whenever a repetition—in the following example, that of the word "dargestellt" [represented]—loomed in the process of setting down his thoughts, as he ran ahead of himself in his trial formulations, he would interrupt the momentum of his writing, in effect break into the flow of his words, and correct it forthwith:

Die drei Frauen, von	The three women, of whom the
denen die dritte die vorzüglichste ist, sind wol als	third is the most excellent one, must surely be regarded
irgendwie gleichartig aufzufassen, wenn sie	as in some way alike if they are repre[7] *portrayed* as
als Schwestern ~~darge~~ *vorgeführt* werden. Es soll uns	sisters. We must not be led astray by the fact that
nicht irre machen, wenn es bei Lear die drei Töchter	the Lear's choice is between three daughters. This may
des Wälenden sind. Das bedeutet vielleicht	mean nothing more than that he has to be *represented* as
nichts anderes, als dass Lear als alter Mann	an old man. An old man cannot very well choose
dargestellt werden soll. Den alten Mann kann	between three women in any other way. Thus they
man nicht leicht anders zwischen drei Frauen	become his daughters.
wälen lassen; darum werden diese zu seinen	

Töchtern.

The second example demonstrates not only the correction of a further repetition but also how Freud felt his way toward the correct, most forceful position for a phrase with particularly dense content:

Die schwerste Aufgabe ist dabei	The most difficult task thus
dem glücklichen dritten Freier zugefallen; was er zur	falls to the share of the fortunate third suitor; what he
Verherrlichung des Bleis gegen Gold und Silber sagen	finds to say in glorification of lead as against gold and

[7][*Translator's note*: The italics for "vorgeführt" and "dargestellt" are mine. Strachey has translated both words by "represented." To illustrate the point, I have altered Strachey's wording slightly.]

kann, ist wenig und klingt gezwungen. Stünden wir

in der psychoanalytischen Praxis vor solcher ~~Motivirung~~ Rede.,

so würden wir/geheim gehaltene Motive]hinter

der unbefriedigenden Begründung wittern.[8]

silver is little and has a forced ring. If in psychoanalytic

practice we were confronted with such a ~~motivation~~ speech, we

should suspect that[,] there were | concealed motives |

behind the unsatisfying reasons produced[,]

The third example illustrates for the reader Freud's endeavor to point up and to impart rhythm. He replaces the neutral, as it were modest, word "Schilderungen" [depictions] by the presumptuous "Anpreisungen" [laudations]. By adding the phrase "der Dritten" [of the third], which is not essential for understanding, he focuses attention even more inescapably on Cordelia. The substitution of three words, "erkennen und belohnen" [recognized and rewarded], for the single word "würdigen" [acknowledge] in effect unfolds the individual layers of meaning of this verb, while intensifying the text by slowing its pace; at the same time it gives rise to the syllabic consonance of "erkennen" and "verkennen" [recognize/does not recognize], while "verkennen," for its part, shares another consonance with "verstossen" [disown]:[9]

Der alte König Lear beschliesst noch bei Leb-

zeiten sein Reich unter seine drei Töchter

zu verteilen, je nach Massgabe der Liebe, die

sie für ihn äussern. Die beiden älteren,

Goneril und Regan erschöpfen sich in Beteuer-

The old King Lear resolves to divide his kingdom

while he is still alive among his three daughters,

in proportion to the amount of love that

each of them expresses for him. The two elder ones,

Goneril and Regan, exhaust themselves in asseverations

[8][*Translator's note*: The change of word order is perhaps less significant in English than in German, where it lays additional stress on the concealed motives. Strachey's wording has again been altered slightly.]

[9][*Translator's note*: To illustrate the point, it has again been necessary to modify Strachey's wording.]

Anpreis

ungen und S̶c̶h̶i̶l̶d̶e̶r̶ungen ihrer Liebe,
   die dritte

Cordelia weigert sich dessen. Er hätte
   diese

               der Dritten
unscheinbare wortlose Liebe w̶ü̶r̶d̶i̶g̶e̶n̶
       erkennen und belohnen

sollen, aber er verkennt sie, verstösst

Cordelia und teilt das Reich unter die

beiden anderen zu seinem und zu aller
   Unheil.

lauda

and d̶e̶p̶ictions of their love for him;
   the third,

Cordelia, refuses to do so. He should
   have

a̶c̶k̶n̶o̶w̶l̶e̶d̶g̶e̶d̶
recognized and rewarded
             of the third
     this unassuming, speechless love

but he does not recognize it. He
   disowns

Cordelia, and divides the kingdom
   between the

other two, to his own and the general
   ruin.

The third example shows how fluid is the transition between the stylistic-rhetorical variants and the next category, the *clarifying variants.* The reasons for revision are usually obvious here. Where Freud introduces variants of this kind, he is attempting to describe an observation, a hypothesis, or a theory in more detail and even more clearly as well as to specify and differentiate them. Note that this need not necessarily involve any diminution of multivocality: where the subject of the description so requires, the corrective intervention may even consist in a deliberate reinforcement of ambiguity. We may discern in such alterations marks of the author's effort to reproduce in language the characteristic multiple layering and overdetermination of psychic phenomena.

Yet the consistent aim of clarifying variants is to reduce the risk of misunderstandings. At the end of his preface to the *New Introductory Lectures,* for example, Freud notes that the public accepts as self-evident the limitations of the achievements of every field of scientific work—except psychology. The formulation of the relevant text in the fair copy, in which it had not actually been intended as a preface, is still somewhat misleading: "every unsolved problem, every admitted uncertainty is made into a reproach against it, and our ignorance is ultimately misused in order to belittle our knowledge." The printed version, however, is shorter and more succinct: "every unsolved problem, every admitted uncertainty is made into a reproach against it."[10]

[10]1933*a,* p. 6.

Freud occasionally also uses clarifying variants to inhibit his tendency all too readily to disregard his own terminological definitions. In his introduction to the anthology *Zur Psychoanalyse der Kriegsneurosen* [The Psycho-Analysis of the War Neuroses], at the end of which he refers to the contrast between and the reconcilability of the two nosological entities of traumatic neurosis, on the one hand, and transference neurosis, on the other, the manuscript originally read: "after all, we have a perfect right to describe repression, which lies at the basis of every neurosis, as an elementary traumatic neurosis." This was already corrected in the fair copy to the more exact formulation of the printed text, which tones down the original confusing equation of a defense mechanism with a syndrome: "after all, we have a perfect right to describe repression, which lies at the basis of every neurosis, as a reaction to a trauma—as an elementary traumatic neurosis."[11]

Clarifying variants can enhance the aptness of metaphors and similes. For example, in the fourth section of his late work "Analysis Terminable and Interminable," Freud turns to the question of the preventive treatment of drive conflicts that are not manifest, which he then answers in the negative, using the following simile: "We know, for instance, that a patient who has recovered from scarlet fever is immune to a return of the same illness; yet it never occurs to a doctor to take a healthy person who may possibly fall ill of scarlet fever and infect him with scarlet fever in order to make him immune to it. The protective measure must not produce the same situation of danger as is produced by the illness itself, but only something very much slighter, as is the case with vaccination against smallpox and many other similar procedures."[12] That is how the published version reads. Instead of scarlet fever, however, the fair copy refers to "typhus abdominalis," "typhoid fever," and "typhoid bacilli." Freud may have had two reasons for introducing this variant, which makes the simile more specific (the revision was, as it happens, already included in the typed copy of the manuscript): first, because the immunity following the contraction of typhoid fever is only partial, whereas after scarlet fever it is solid, provided that the infecting pathogen produces the same toxin; and second, because at the time of the genesis of "Analysis Terminable and Interminable," a typhoid vaccine existed, albeit not a very effective one, so that the situation was analogous to that of smallpox vaccination—the simile would therefore have been somewhat lame—whereas all attempts to develop a vaccine for scarlet fever had failed.[13]

[11] 1919*d*, p. 210.

[12] 1937*c*, p. 232.

[13] I am indebted to the virologist Professor Hans J. Eggers, of Cologne, for this information.

A clarifying variant may also consist in dropping a sentence that could not be made more specific at the time of writing or in the relevant context. For instance, in the fourth chapter of *Beyond the Pleasure Principle,* Freud subjects the Kantian theorem "that time and space are necessary forms of thought" to what he himself admits is a cursory psychoanalytic discussion.[14] He in fact deals here only with the category of time, which he contrasts with the "timelessness" of the unconscious, emphasizing that our abstract conception of time can therefore have been derived solely from the method of working of the system *Cs.* He admits that his remarks sound "very obscure" and that he must limit himself to hints. The manuscript of the first version[15] includes a further sentence at this point, which Freud suppressed in the printed version: "The other abstraction which can be linked to the functioning of Cs, however, is not space but material, substance." This sentence, incidentally, is still in the printer's copy of *Beyond the Pleasure Principle,* a typescript of the first version with handwritten corrections and additions—but here it has already been resolutely deleted in blue pencil.

Another form of clarifying variant comprises additions that occurred to Freud only after completion of the fair copy, at the time of correction of the galley or page proofs, with the aim of more precise specification and pointing up of the text. An example is the striking last sentence of the printed version of "The Infantile Genital Organization," which does not appear in the manuscript: "The vagina is now valued as a place of shelter for the penis; it enters into the heritage of the womb."[16]

For a final instance of this category, let us consider a clarifying variant drawn, so to speak, from the heartland of psychoanalytic theorization. It is to be found in the case history of the "Wolf Man," and a rather more extensive account of its context is called for in order to make the reason for the revision comprehensible. The passage concerned is a note to the last chapter, toward the end of which Freud mentions two fundamental problems the case material induces him to reflect upon. The first is the question of nonexperiential, "phylogenetically inherited schemata, which, like the categories of philosophy, are concerned with the business of 'placing' the impressions derived from actual experience."[17] The second, which is related to the first, is developed by Freud directly on the basis of the clinical

---

[14]1920g, p. 28.
[15]On this point, cf. the next chapter, "First Versions."
[16]1923e, p. 145.
[17]1918b, p. 119.

details, in fact from the example of how his patient, whom he treated as a young adult, had subsequently worked over an observation of parental intercourse that was assigned to his second year of life and had been reactivated at the age of four. The question was whether "some sort of hardly definable knowledge, something, as it were, preparatory to an understanding," might have been at work in the child at the time; if the psyche contained organizing factors analogous to the instincts of animals, these would be "the nucleus of the unconscious, a primitive kind of mental activity, which would later be dethroned and overlaid by human reason [. . .]. The significance of the traumas of early childhood would lie in their contributing material to this unconscious which would save it from being worn away by the subsequent course of development."[18] At the point where Freud discusses the patient's response to the reactivation of the primal scene when he was four years old, the manuscript includes the following note: "I may disregard the fact that it was not possible to put this behavior into words until twenty years afterwards;[19] for all the effects that we have traced back to the scene had already been manifested in the form of symptoms, obsessions, etc., in the patient's childhood and long before the analysis. Of course, the above remarks are valid only subject to the condition of the reality of this scene as opposed to the assumption of its fantasized nature." This last sentence has been deleted in blue pencil and replaced by the following radical variant, which eventually found its way into the printed version: "It is [. . .] a matter of indifference in this connection whether we choose to regard it as a primal *scene* or as a primal *fantasy*."[20]

[9.2]

[Continuation on a new page:]

[18]Ibid., p. 120.
[19]That is, during the treatment with Freud.
[20]1918*b*, p. 120, note 1.

[9.3]

At first sight, this is pure contradiction. It could be fully resolved only by detailed consideration of certain facts and developments, of which I can give but a broad outline. Freud set down this, the most comprehensive of his case histories, late in the fall of 1914, that is, not long after the completion of *Totem and Taboo*. It was originally intended for publication in 1915. However, he held the manuscript over because, soon after finishing it, he felt "cast into serious doubts," as he confessed to Ferenczi on 9 November 1914. These doubts presumably had to do mainly with the subject of the *reality* of the traumatic childhood experiences or, in other words, with the question of whether their reproduction was a matter of memories, on the one hand, or of fantasies or displacement combinations, on the other. Once again, therefore, we see the emergence of that most fundamental of questions as to the causative factors in the etiology of the neuroses, which we have already encountered in the chapter on the notes[21] and which Freud referred to in his account of the case of the "Wolf Man" as "the most delicate question in the whole domain of psychoanalysis."[22]

In the theoretical exploration of this rich clinical material, he seems, to judge from the original formulation of the manuscript quoted above, to have started from a realistic conception of what has come to be known as the *primal scene*—that is, observation of parental intercourse. One of the factors that then presumably kindled his skepticism was the precocity of that observation—and now the argument elaborated in *Totem and Taboo* may once again have pushed its way to the forefront of his reflections.[23] Step by step, there then emerged the theory of the *primal fantasies,* those few, typical, so to speak autonomous phantasmatic configurations, scenarios, precisely the phylogenetic schemata that structure human mental life independently of personal experience and that—as if running on a different causative track from individual vicissitudes, themselves equally influen-

[21]On pages 99 and 122ff. above.

[22]1918*b*, p. 103, note 1.

[23]The reader is reminded that, shortly after completing the first draft of his "Wolf Man" case history, Freud composed the twelfth metapsychological paper, in which he explicitly took up and pursued certain hypotheses from *Totem and Taboo*, such as the construction of the murder of the primal father and the theory of phylogenetic inheritance (1985*a*; cf. also Grubrich-Simitis, 1987, p. 90ff., and 1988, p. 22f.).

tial—can determine behavior, thus potentially generating conflict and giving rise to illness. From this point of view, the actual observation of the primal scene can have the same pathological consequences as its fantasization. At any rate, Freud was only now able further to elaborate the specific and complex psychoanalytic concept of fantasy—or of psychic reality proper—and thereafter to present it to the public in works that appeared during the First World War—in particular, in the twenty-third of the *Introductory Lectures on Psycho-Analysis.*

When he finally decided to publish "From the History of an Infantile Neurosis," he incorporated the theoretical advances achieved in the interim in two fairly long interpolations,[24] which he flagged as later additions, in one case including a specific reference to *Totem and Taboo*.[25] Apart from this, as he stresses at the beginning of the case history, "no alterations of any importance have been made in the text of the first draft."[26] He plainly did not consider it worth mentioning the clarifying variant quoted, which is at first sight confusing in its contradictoriness. Incidentally, further clarifying variants, on the question of the reality of the primal scene, added subsequently and also not labeled, can be found in the manuscript too; their detailed reconstruction will one day afford a clearer view of the work's chronological stratification, of the phases in the development of the concept of primal fantasies, and indirectly no doubt also of the notion of trauma, in the context of Freud's multidimensional etiological ideas.

Another type of variant, the *structuring variant,* calls for only a brief mention. By this means, Freud breaks up his texts for the eye and increases their transparency. The insertion of additional subtitles or roman numerals gives rise to structured blocks that make it easier for the reader to follow the steps and caesuras of Freud's process thinking. Examples of such subsequent efforts at organization can be found in many of the fair copies—for example, that of *The Question of Lay Analysis* and of *The Future of an Illusion.* The manuscript of *Inhibitions, Symptoms and Anxiety,* too, clearly displays the author's concern to master the centrifugal tendencies of this text's abundance of material by the multiple corrections made to its division into sections and subsections.

Another highly conspicuous type of variant encountered in sifting through the autographs are the *title variants.* As a rule, these may have arisen when Freud had finished the relevant fair copy and, looking back over it, considered that the initial heading was no longer appropriate. The "Five Lectures

[24]1918*b*, p. 57ff. and p. 95ff.
[25]Ibid., p. 60.
[26]Ibid., p. 7, note 1.

on Psycho-Analysis" (the American lectures), whose German title, *Über Psychoanalyse,* literally means "On Psychoanalysis," were originally entitled "Über die Entstehung und Entwicklung der Psychoanalyse" ["On the Genesis and Development of Psychoanalysis"], a formulation that he perhaps ultimately found too cumbersome and historicizing. In the fair copy, the original title of the first of the "Contributions to the Psychology of Love" was "Über einen häufigen Typus der Objektwal beim Manne" ["On a Frequent Type of Choice of Object made by Men"], before Freud substituted "besonderen" [special] for the adjective "häufigen" [frequent], probably to avoid misleading statistical implications. Incidentally, we know too of a title variant for the appreciably later third contribution on the psychology of love, one that, however, seems exceptionally to have been rejected *before* the commencement of the fair copy and that survives only in a letter. On 24 September 1917, Freud wrote to Sándor Ferenczi: "I am at present composing a third contribution on the psychology of love: The Taboo of Virginity and Sexual Bondage." Even before he received the paper for reading—at the time it was presumably still at the draft stage—Ferenczi replied on 10 October: "We[27] have agreed to ask you to delete from the title of your new work 'The Taboo of Virginity' the second element: 'And Sexual Bondage.' In our opinion it sounds better without it." And that is indeed what happened.

A part of the paper on technique "Zur Einleitung der Behandlung" ["On Beginning the Treatment"] was also originally intended to have a more extended title: "I. Zur Einleitung der Behandlung.—Die Frage der ersten Mittheilungen—die Dynamik der Heilung" ["I. On Beginning the Treatment.—The Question of the First Communications—the Dynamics of the Cure"].[28] "Über Triebumsetzungen, insbesondere der Analerotik" ["On Transformations of Instinct as Exemplified in Anal Erotism"] originally had the laconic title "Über die Wandlungen der Analerotik" ["On the Transformations of Anal Erotism"]. The *Introductory Lectures on Psycho-Analysis* seem to have received most of their individual titles only after the fair copy was finished: at any rate, in the manuscript only lectures XVI to XXVIII, apart from the numbering, have the headings familiar to us from the printed version; these are the predominantly theoretical lectures of part III, the "General Theory of the Neuroses," which Freud wrote down before delivering them, unlike those of part II.[29] The first title of the "Wolf Man" case history was "Aus der Geschichte einer kindlichen Zwangsneurose"

[27]He and Otto Rank.

[28]At any rate, this is the title of the section of the manuscript containing the second part of the paper. When first published in 1913, it actually appeared in two installments in the *Internationale Zeitschrift für ärztliche Psychoanalyse* (vol. 1, nos. 1 and 2); the second installment has the fuller title in the first edition too.

[29]Cf. Jones, 1955, p. 245.

["From the History of a Childhood Obsessional Neurosis"]. While still at the fair copy stage, Freud altered "Über einige Mechanismen der Neurosenbildung (Eifersucht—Homosexualität—Paranoia)" ["Some Mechanisms of the Formation of Neuroses (Jealousy—Homosexuality—Paranoia)" to "Über einige neurotische Mechanismen bei Eifersucht, Paranoia und Homosexualität" ["Some Neurotic Mechanisms in Jealousy, Paranoia and Homosexuality"], manifestly to obviate the misunderstanding that the three types of phenomena were all being described as neuroses. In the original title "Bemerkungen zur Technik der Traumdeutung" ["Remarks on the Technique of Dream-Interpretation"], "Technik" ["Technique"] was replaced by the words "Theorie und Praxis" ["Theory and Practice"] for the definitive heading of the printed version because the original was felt to be too narrow in relation to the content of the text. Freud must have had precisely the opposite reason for substituting the title "Kurzer Abriss der Psychoanalyse" ["A Short Account of Psycho-Analysis"] at the galley or page proof stage for the original ambitious formulation "Die Geschichte der Psychoanalyse" ["The History of Psychoanalysis"]; he no doubt also wished to preclude confusion with his major work on this subject, "Zur Geschichte der psychoanalytischen Bewegung" ["On the History of the Psycho-Analytic Movement"].

Sometimes the creative process may have assumed a life of its own while a given fair copy was still gestating, or at any rate have taken a different turn from that forecast by the author on the basis of the draft. As we know, in "Die Verneinung" ["Negation"], Freud examines in highly condensed sentences "the origin of an intellectual function from the interplay of the primary instinctual impulses"[30] and finds that a repressed ideational content can make its way into consciousness on condition that the subject can negate it; negation is therefore a kind of lifting of repression, but without acceptance of the repressed. In the fair copy, this short, compact text was initially entitled "Verneinung und Verleugnung" ["Negation and Disavowal"]. Did the author wish, when he began to set down his work, to distinguish between negation and disavowal as forms of defense? The word "Verleugnung" [disavowal] never actually appears in the text of the printed version, but only "Verurteilung" [repudiation]. At this point we may mention the title variant of another short, metapsychologically important paper, which again deals with a specific defense: significantly, "Die Ichspaltung im Abwehrvorgang" ["Splitting of the Ego in the Process of Defense"] was originally entitled "Die Ichspaltung als Abwehrmechanismus" ["Splitting of the Ego as a Mechanism of Defense"].

[30]1925*h*, p. 239.

[9.4]

A title variant is one of the indications of the extent to which Freud was at the mercy of the intrinsic dynamic of the creative process when he wrote *Hemmung, Symptom und Angst* [*Inhibitions, Symptoms and Anxiety*].[31] The study was originally to be called simply "Hemmung und Symptom" ["Inhibition and Symptom"]; by his completion of the title formulation, the author subsequently allowed for the fact that the work ultimately owes its status to the revision of the theory of anxiety undertaken therein.

Two of the major works on the theory of civilization were also intended to have different titles when Freud began to set them down. The important critique of religion, *Die Zukunft einer Illusion* [*The Future of an Illusion*] was originally called "Die Zukunft unserer Illusionen" ["The Future of Our Illusions"]. Freud corrected the original wording because he plainly did not want to identify even rhetorically with the faithful.[32]

[9.5]

In the case of *Das Unbehagen in der Kultur* [*Civilization and its Discontents*], the two variant titles quoted at the beginning of this chapter have been preserved. On the first page of the manuscript, Freud at first wrote *"Das Glück und die Kultur"* ["Happiness and Civilization"] but then

---

[31][*Translator's note*: The pluralization of "Inhibitions" and "Symptoms" is Strachey's.]
[32]A similar distancing function was, incidentally, performed by a textual variant in the fair copy of the third essay of *Moses and Monotheism*, in which the following wording originally appeared in the section entitled "The People of Israel:" "At the same time they are inspired by a peculiar confidence in life[,] such as is derived from the secret ownership of some precious possession, a kind of optimism or trust in God [oder Gottvertrauen]." Still at the fair copy stage, Freud replaced the words "oder Gottvertrauen" [or trust in God] by the following clause, preceded by a semicolon: "Fromme würden es Gottvertrauen nennen" [pious people would call it trust in God]. [*Translator's note*: The clause is preceded by a colon in the English translation (1939*a*, p. 105).]

crossed out this line and replaced it with *"Das Unglück in der Kultur"* ["Unhappiness in Civilization"].[33] The definitive title seems to have been adopted only in the phase between the composition of the fair copy and going to press. Freud may have felt the word "Unglück" [unhappiness] to be too dramatic, too clamorous, for that more silent, nagging sense of affliction fueled by renunciation of drives, which he wished to describe and explain, and which is indeed rendered much more accurately by "Unbehagen" [discontent].

There are also a number of lesser title variants: "Über die Genese eines Falles von weiblicher Homosexualität" ["The Genesis of a Case of Female Homosexuality"] versus "Über die Psychogenese eines Falles von weiblicher Homosexualität" ["The Psychogenesis of a Case of Female Homosexuality"]; "Der Wunderblock" ["The 'Mystic Writing-Pad'"] versus "Notiz über den Wunderblock" ["A Note upon the 'Mystic Writing-Pad'"]; the subtitle of "'Ein Kind wird geschlagen'" ["'A Child is Being Beaten'"] in the fair copy originally read "Beitrag zur Entstehung der sexuellen Perversionen" ["A Contribution to the Genesis of the Sexual Perversions"]; in "Über fausse reconnaissance ('déjà raconté') während der psychoanalytischen Arbeit" ["Fausse Reconnaissance ('déjà raconté') in Psycho-Analytic Treatment"], Freud added the parenthesis later; and in the paper "Die infantile Genitalorganisation (Eine Einschaltung in die Sexualtheorie)" ["The Infantile Genital Organization (An Interpolation into the Theory of Sexuality)"], the subtitle in parentheses was initially intended as the main title but was then presumably felt by the author to be too nonspecific; and, to judge from the appearance of the manuscript, the same applies to "Die Disposition zur Zwangsneurose (Ein Beitrag zum Problem der Neurosenwahl)" ["The Disposition to Obsessional Neurosis (A Contribution to the Problem of Choice of Neurosis)"]. The manuscripts also contain many variants on the level of subtitles.

Even an unsystematic perusal of the fair copies again and again reveals variants which—more or less obviously—owe their existence to conflictual motives, increased emotional involvement, and, in particular, the effect of

---

[33]The Sigmund Freud Collection includes a handwritten list, entitled "Überschriften" [Headings], in which Freud evidently sketched out titles and subtitles for the first four of the total of eight chapters of *Civilization and its Discontents*, although he did not use them as such in the eventual printed version. We find formulations reminiscent of the titles he had originally considered for his book: "Das Streben nach dem Glück" [The Striving for Happiness], "Die Quellen des Leidens" [The Sources of Suffering], "Glücksverlust bei Triebbeherrschung" [Loss of Happiness from the Control of Instinct], "Das Glück in der Liebe" [Happiness in Love], and "Die Kultur als Leidensquelle" [Civilization as a Source of Suffering]—but not the word "Unbehagen" [Discontent or Malaise].

ambivalence. They may sometimes assume the abrupt character of para-praxes. I should therefore like to call them *emotive variants*.

These occur most frequently in relation to descriptions of persons. For instance, in the fair copy of the first prefatory note to the essay "Moses, sein Volk und die monotheistische Religion" ["Moses, his People and Monotheist Religion"], Freud described Bernard Shaw in a note as a "brilliant dilettante," a characterization that he omitted from the printed version. In the fair copy of "On the History of the Psycho-Analytic Movement," he describes that enemy of psychoanalysis, Alfred Hoche, as "Der unsaubere Geist Hoche" [The filthy spirit Hoche], whereas the printed version has "Der böse Geist Hoche" [That evil genius, Hoche];[34] in this case, after reading the manuscript, Karl Abraham put the following to Freud in a letter of 9 March 1914: "Might the adjective you assign to Hoche not lead to disagreeable consequences?"[35] The response, by return of mail, was: "Instead of the 'filthy' spirit of A. Hoche I shall insert 'evil' spirit."[36]

Where these emotive variants concern Freud's relatively close colleagues, or even the closest, they may range from comparatively minor revisions based on conscious consideration to far-reaching alterations, behind which we may suspect the weight of complex motives, some of them preconscious and unconscious. When Freud set down his tribute to Ernest Jones on the latter's fiftieth birthday, he referred to him in the last sentence as "young and strong, combative and loyal." The printed version, however, reads "zealous and energetic, combative and devoted to the cause."[37] The fact that only one of the four epithets remained may be a case of Freud's subsequently stopping in his tracks and telling himself to be more objective: a fifty-year-old is not young, except from the point of view of an appreciably older person; "strong" might have sounded too physical for him, and "loyal" excessively oriented toward his own—Freud's—person.

If "On the History of the Psycho-Analytic Movement" is characterized by a polemical, affective tone, and not only in relation to Alfred Hoche, this has to do with the occasion of its composition: by writing this work, Freud was coming to terms with the secessions of Alfred Adler and C. G. Jung. It was directed especially against Jung, and the accumulation of emotive variants is hardly surprising in this context. Let us consider two of them.

In the printed version, Freud ends the passage in which he discusses Jung's views of schizophrenia—stating that, in 1908, Jung had preferred the toxic to the libido theory at the Salzburg Congress—with the following

---

[34]1914*d*, p. 45. [*Translator's note*: Strachey has changed "spirit" ("Geist") to "genius."]
[35]1965*a*, p. 166.
[36]Ibid., p. 170.
[37]1929*a*, p. 250.

sentence: "Later on (1912) he came to grief on this same point, by making too much of the material which he had previously refused to employ."[38] In the manuscript, there is a period after "grief" ["gescheitert"], followed by a passage that Freud omitted from the published version although it is not deleted in the manuscript: "When he for his part ultimately ventured to subject schizophrenia to the libido theory, he deviated in the opposite direction and modified[39] the concept of libido to such an extent that his libido theory has nothing other than the name in common with that developed hitherto. But even the name is illegitimate, as there was no need to use the word 'libido' for the principle by which he wished to elucidate schizophrenia dynamically. This appropriation of the name, however minor it might appear as a sign, was[40] an emanation of that character trait in Jung which rendered it impossible to maintain the working relationship with him, of his tendency inconsiderately to thrust aside an uncomfortable other." In the actual, theoretical discussion of Jung's contribution, in the final part of "On the History of the Psycho-Analytic Movement," there is a slip of the pen in the fair copy. In the sentence "The total incompatibility of this new movement with psychoanalysis shows itself too, of course, in Jung's treatment of repression,"[41] Freud originally wrote not "Verdrängung" [repression], but "Übertragung" [transference]. This word occurred to him in consequence of the criticism of Jung's therapeutic technique that he had voiced in the previous paragraph, but he now "undid" it with vehement short oblique strokes of the pen and replaced it with "Verdrängung" [repression].

Sometimes an emotive variant may consist of just one word. At the end of "The Dissolution of the Oedipus Complex," which dates from 1924, Freud mentions "Otto Rank's interesting study, *The Trauma of Birth*,"[42] which had appeared in the same year. Instead of "interessanter" [interesting], the manuscript has "faszinirender" [fascinating]. This change of a single word documents a change in Freud's attitude that took place within a few months at the end of 1923 and the beginning of 1924. On first acquaintance, he does indeed seem to have been fascinated by Rank's concept of the trauma of birth—this being not least an indication of the attraction that trauma theories of the development of neurosis could still exert over him— but then he sensed a claim to absoluteness, fearing, as he put it in a letter

[38]1914d, p. 29.

[39]Freud corrected the original "verflüchtigte" [literally, volatilized or evaporated] to "veränderte" [changed].

[40]"War" [was] corrected from "ist" [is].

[41]1914d, p. 64.

[42]1924d, p. 179.

to Ferenczi on 26 March 1924, "that our elaborate etiological structure [might] be superseded by the crude trauma of birth." To Rank himself, Freud had already written on 26 November 1923, in connection with an ironic comment on the former's interpretation of one of Freud's dreams: "[. . .] that you are the dreaded David, who will bring about the devaluation of my work with his trauma of birth."[43] Freud already had no illusions and realized that a pure trauma theory of the etiology of the neuroses sounded much more agreeable and probable and would therefore be more acceptable to the public than the theory of instinctual drives, let alone his far more complex etiological hypothesis implicating both drive and trauma aspects.

Traces of ambivalence—of unmitigated affection and the highest esteem, on the one hand, and disappointed alienation and repudiatory criticism, on the other—are betrayed by, for example, the manuscript of Freud's obituary for Sándor Ferenczi. It contains a number of variants, some of which have only a clarifying purpose and need not be mentioned here. However, emotive variants abound in the concluding passage, in which Freud describes Ferenczi's late technical innovations and notes critically that "the need to cure and to help had become paramount in him." This reads as follows in the printed version: "He had probably set himself aims which, with our therapeutic means, are altogether out of reach to-day. From unexhausted springs of emotion the conviction was borne in upon him that one could effect far more with one's patients if one gave them enough of the love which they had longed for as children."[44] These two sentences at first read somewhat differently in the fair copy: "He had probably set himself aims[45] which, with our therapeutic means, are as far as possible [möglichst] out of reach today. From unexhausted springs of his childhood emotional life, the conviction was borne in upon him that one could effect far more with one's patients if one gave them enough of the love which they had always longed for."

The word "möglichst" [as far as possible], which is heavily crossed out and almost illegible in the manuscript, sounds oddly ambiguous, as if a compromise had arisen in Freud between two different statements: first, the indication that it was not possible to achieve such aims with the instruments currently available—that is, the manifest message that Freud retained in the printed version—and, second, the almost invocatory adumbration of a latent preference that he suppressed in the published text and that could be expanded roughly as follows: one should as far as possible avoid setting

[43]From a transcription made available by Sigmund Freud Copyrights.
[44]1933c, p. 229.
[45]Corrected from: "endeavored to achieve more than."

oneself such aims from the outset because anyone who does so is bound to come into contact with the earliest preverbal, presymbolic phases of formation of the psychic structure. There is good reason to believe that Freud would always have preferred to avoid concerning himself with this archaic dimension of the psyche, not only owing to his skepticism about the depth of focus of psychoanalytic theory and therapeutic technique at the time, but also no doubt because, as a result of his own pregenital traumatization, alluded to in the chapter on his writing,[46] he would have felt too disturbed himself by such work. In addition to Ferenczi's glaring exaggerations, this personal sensitivity may have contributed to the alienation between the two friends and also to the partial failure of Ferenczi's analysis with Freud. There are further echoes of this tragic nonattunement in the other variants of these two sentences: in the final version, Freud withdrew the reference to Ferenczi's infantile emotional life as the source of his late work, perhaps because he recalled while setting down his text that, as recorded in the correspondence, Ferenczi had once vehemently resisted such an interpretation. The printed version's restriction to childhood of the statement about patients' longing for love gives the impression of a vestigial defensive movement on Freud's part toward the deceased; after all, he knew that the adult analysand Ferenczi's longing for love that had been directed toward his own person had remained unfulfilled—and he may probably also have sensed that one element in his friend's late technical experiments was the continued acting out of unresolved aspects of his own analysis.[47]

Years later, the conflict with Ferenczi found expression indirectly in an emotive variant to be found in the manuscript of Freud's late paper "Analysis Terminable and Interminable." We know that in this text Freud returns anonymously to Ferenczi's charge that he, Freud, had not taken account of the negative transference in the analysis with him. As Freud now argues defensively, there had been at the time no sign of such a manifestation; he adds: "furthermore, [. . .] not every good relation between an analyst and his subject during and after analysis was to be regarded as a transference; there were also friendly relations which were based on reality and which proved to be viable."[48] Instead of "during and after," Freud had at first written "before and during" in the fair copy—a slip of the pen that no doubt betrays the insight gained in the interim that an unconditional and undistorted analytic relationship cannot develop from a precious, inspiring friendship and an indispensable, intimate working partnership.

Emotive variants are also to be found in connection with those of his

[46]P. 78f.
[47]Cf. Grunberger, 1980, and Grubrich-Simitis, 1986b.
[48]1937c, p. 222.

own works, themes, and theses that were for Freud of preeminent, albeit sometimes concealed, autobiographical significance. As stressed earlier, *Totem and Taboo,* for instance, was one of his favorite works, in particular the fourth essay, "The Return of Totemism in Childhood," which contains the speculation on the murder of the primal father in the prehistoric family and on the consequences of this crime for the development of civilization. This hypothesis, which, I repeat, was intended at the same time to mediate in the form of a neo-Lamarckian construction between the drive and trauma models of the etiology of the neuroses, does indeed constitute an intellectual magnetic field in the oeuvre.[49] Freud not only continued it in the twelfth metapsychological paper in 1915 but returned to it yet again, as if succumbing to its attraction on one last occasion, in that work of his old age *Moses and Monotheism.*[50]

Throughout his life, however, Freud remained dubious as to whether his theory of the murder of the primal father and the constitution of the archaic heritage should be assigned any reality value. This vacillation is revealed by a number of emotive variants observable already in the fair copy of "The Return of Totemism in Childhood." Where the printed version refers to "that great primeval tragedy,"[51] the fair copy originally read as follows, before the author deleted and replaced the second adjective: "that great mythological tragedy." He thus seems to have clearly recognized, even if he was unwilling to admit it to himself, what Claude Lévi-Strauss has recently noted again: "With *Totem and Taboo* Freud constructed a myth, and a very beautiful myth too. But like all myths, it doesn't tell us how things really happened. It tells us how men need to imagine things happened so as to try to overcome contradictions."[52]

Freud's skepticism about the reality content of his phylogenetic construction may also have been responsible for a variant to be found in the manuscript of *The Future of an Illusion.* In the fourth chapter of this work, Freud again turns to the connection between totemism and the later god religions and to the roots of the "most fundamental moral restrictions"[53] in totemism. The relevant passage is followed in the fair copy by the subsidiary clause: "so that the religious assertion of the divine origin of cultural institutions makes good historical sense." This was already crossed out by the author in red pencil in the manuscript and replaced by the more cautious formulation we know from the printed version: "Whether or not you accept

[49]See pp. 118–25 above.
[50]1939*a,* p. 80ff.; see also below, p. 201f.
[51]1912–13*a,* p. 156.
[52]Lévi-Strauss and Eribon, 1988, p. 150.
[53]1927*c,* p. 23.

the conclusions of *Totem and Taboo,* I hope you will admit that a number of very remarkable, disconnected facts are brought together in it into a consistent whole."

It is as if he had in the end wanted again and again to convince himself of the scientific character of this consistent whole and had succeeded in doing so. The programmatic note toward the end of *Totem and Taboo* in which he defiantly claims a "central part"[54] for the psychoanalytic contribution to the elucidation of the origins of religion and society, as it were asserting its priority in the synthesis of the findings and theories accruing from other disciplines, was manifestly added to the fair copy later on a separate sheet. Two years later, in "On the History of the Psycho-Analytic Movement," Freud returns once more to *Totem and Taboo,* concluding his reference to his contribution to the theory of civilization with the skeptical sentence: "It is no doubt too early to decide how far the conclusions thus reached will be able to withstand criticism."[55] That is the reading of the printed version. The fair copy at this point has an emotive variant in the form of an independent phrase, which Freud then suppressed: "but I can surely dismiss as harmless nonsense objections such as those I have heard leveled at me that wild horses do not behave, under analogous conditions of family formation, in the same way as primal man according to my assumption."

It proved impossible in the long term to cast aside doubts at least as to the mechanisms he postulated for the handing down of memory traces of the archaic heritage. They found expression in his old age in a parapraxis in the draft of the third Moses essay, where he writes that "this situation [is] not strictly proven," but "that in any case" [ohnehin]—instead of "without it" [ohne ihn]—"we can explain nothing [in] group psychology." The fundamental criticism of *Totem and Taboo* voiced in the 1920s by the psychoanalytically oriented ethnologist Alfred L. Kroeber[56] did perhaps have some influence on Freud after all. Yet a willful variant can still be found in the third Moses essay, written in his old age. In the printed version of the section "The Great Man," he has the following to say about the murder of Moses committed by the Israelites: "And if, this being so, they killed their great man one day, they were only repeating a misdeed which in ancient times had been committed, as prescribed by law, against the Divine King and which, as we know, went back to a still more ancient prototype."[57] Instead of "as we know," the manuscript originally had a more cautious "perhaps," although

[54]1912–13*a*, p. 157, note 2.
[55]1914*d*, p. 37.
[56]Kroeber, 1920.
[57]That is, precisely, the murder of the primal father. For the quotation, see 1939*a*, p. 110.

this had already been the subject of a defiant, affirmative correction by the author at the same stage.

We cannot consider in detail here how far the essay on Michelangelo's statue of Moses has deep autobiographical significance, owing its genesis both to Freud's penetrating identification with the biblical figure and to the crisis into which he had been plunged by the secession of C. G. Jung.[58] At any rate, when Freud published the text in 1914, he dared to do so only anonymously at first. Until now it had merely been conjectured that the editorial note accompanying this contribution on its first publication in the journal *Imago* had come from Freud's pen. It reads: "Although this paper does not, strictly speaking, conform to the conditions under which contributions are accepted for publication in this Journal, the editors have decided to print it, since the author, who is personally known to them, moves in psychoanalytic circles, and since his mode of thought has in point of fact a certain resemblance to the methodology of psychoanalysis."[59] The fair copy confirms this presumption of Freud's authorship; the note features right at the beginning, identified as a footnote in Freud's usual style, separated with lines from the rubric and from the beginning of the text.

[9.6]

The ambivalence and the urge to declare himself the author after all have found expression in a number of emotive variants. Before Freud corrected it for the printed version, the sentence read as follows in the manuscript: "Although this is not strictly speaking a psychoanalytic contribution, the editors have decided to print it since its author, who is personally known to them, is close to our science, and since his mode of thought has in point of fact a certain resemblance to the technique of psychoanalysis."

[58]Cf. Grubrich-Simitis, 1991, p. 47ff.
[59]1914*b*, p. 211, note 1.

The detailed description of the tables/arm/breast/hand/beard part of the sculpture—which, as mentioned earlier,[60] is central to Freud's interpretation—contains an abundance of variants in the manuscript. To conclude, the reader's attention is drawn to a discrepancy toward the end of the essay. Freud reports on W. Watkiss Lloyd's study of Michelangelo's statue of Moses, which he had read late on—with mixed feelings because this author had evidently anticipated some of his own hypotheses. The printed version reads as follows: "I once more had an opportunity of experiencing in myself what unworthy and puerile motives enter into our thoughts and acts even in a serious cause."[61] In the manuscript, this is expressed even more pointedly: "what an admixture of unworthy, because selfish and puerile, motives enter into our thoughts and acts even in a serious cause, and are perhaps even indispensable to them." This sounds like an exegesis of the fine aphorism quoted in the chapter on the notes, "Great deeds are the preserve of those who can do no other" or of the entry on Champollion, also reproduced there.

Another of Freud's affectively charged favorite topics was, as we know, lay analysis. Through the admission of persons with a nonmedical background to training and practice, Freud hoped to ensure that in the future psychoanalysis would not be reduced to a medical discipline, a specialized method under the umbrella of psychiatry, but would instead be able to develop without compromise its full potential as a human science. His 1926 paper *The Question of Lay Analysis* triggered an international discussion among colleagues and pupils in which blatant differences of opinion were expressed openly for the first time. A phalanx of opponents of lay analysis formed, especially in the English-speaking world.

With his "Postscript," composed in June 1927, Freud concluded the series of controversial position statements that complemented and summarized his principal arguments in defense of lay analysis. Comparison of the fair copy of the postscript with its printed version shows that the two texts correspond almost word for word—until the end of the penultimate paragraph, where the author turns to his American colleagues' "bluntest rejection of lay analysis" and proposes to say "a few words to them in reply." He notes that the reasons for their resistance are wholly practical—mainly the fact that lay analysts have done a great deal of damage in the United States; it was therefore felt that they had to be automatically excluded from any psychoanalytic activity. Freud's counterargument is that "[. . .] the question of lay analysis must not be decided on practical considerations alone,

[60]See above, p. 154.
[61]1914*b*, p. 234.

and local conditions in America cannot be the sole determining influence on our views."[62]

At this point—that is to say, between the penultimate and the last paragraphs of the printed version of the postscript—the manuscript includes an extensive emotive variant consisting of three whole pages. Freud omitted this passage from the printed version, although it is not deleted in the manuscript. Its beginning and end are, however, marked. Ernest Jones reports that Freud had left it to Max Eitingon's discretion whether to leave it out should he find it "not politic or dangerous; they might seize the excuse to secede." Eitingon had shown him, Jones, the text, and they had ultimately agreed that "it would be wiser to omit three sentences[63] when printing it, and this was done."[64]

Because the vehement passage touches at several points on subjects that are of the highest present-day relevance, it will now be quoted in full:

> However, the attitude of the Americans seems to lay itself open to criticism precisely from the viewpoint of expediency. Let us put to ourselves the question of the cause of the rampant growth of harmful lay analysis[65] specifically in America. So far as it is possible to judge from a distance, a large number of factors are here combined, whose relative importance I am, I must say, not in a position to determine. It must be assumed first of all that the medical analysts have had remarkably little success in gaining the respect of the public and in influencing its decisions. There may be various reasons for this: the huge size of the country, the lack of an all-embracing organization extending beyond the boundaries of a city, and in addition the Americans' horror of authority, their inclination to assert personal independence in the few fields which are not yet occupied by the implacable pressure of public opinion. The same American trait, transferred from political life into scientific activity, is shown in the analytical group itself by the provision that the person of the president must change annually, so that no real leadership can be formed, essential as it would surely be in such difficult matters. It is exhibited, too, in the attitude of scientific circles, which, for example, bring the same interest to bear on all variations of the doctrines called psychoanalytic, which then boast of this as proof of their openmindedness.[66] The skeptical European cannot suppress the

[62]1927a, p. 257f.

[63]*Sic*; in fact more than three pages.

[64]Jones, 1957, p. 317.

[65][By this somewhat misleading term, here and later on, Freud no doubt meant what he had previously been accustomed to call "wild" psychoanalysis (cf. 1910k).]

[66][*Translator's note*: This word is in English in the original.]

suspicion that this interest never penetrates very deeply, and that much reluctance and inability to make judgments lies concealed behind this impartiality.

From everything one hears, it would seem that whole sections of the population in America are falling victim to exploitation by swindling lay analysts, whereas they would be protected from this risk in Europe if only by their prejudices. I cannot say what feature of the American mentality is to blame for this[,] why it should be that persons whose highest ideal in life is, after all, efficiency, fitness for life, should omit to take the simplest precautions when appointing a helper for their psychic troubles. But justice demands that I do not pass over in silence what could be adduced in at least partial mitigation of the perpetrators' misdeeds. In rich America, where money is readily available for every extravagance, there is not yet any institution at which either doctors or nondoctors can be instructed in analysis. Impoverished Europe has already established three training institutions from private funds, in Berlin, Vienna, and London. There is therefore nothing left to the poor robbers but to gain the little bit of wisdom they cannot dispense with in their equipment from a miserable popularization of analysis which some countryman of theirs has cobbled together. The good books in English are, after all, too difficult for them, and the German ones inaccessible. After existing for years as pirates and acquiring some earnings, some of these people then come to Europe in a belated fit of conscience, as if to legitimize their relationship with psychoanalysis after the event, to make honest men of themselves and to learn something. Our American colleagues usually take it amiss that we do not turn these guests away.

However, they also reject those lay persons who have sought analysis at our training institutions without having previously misused analysis and harshly criticize the exiguity of the gain with which these people, who have been so eager to learn, return to America. If they are right, this is not our fault but a consequence of two familiar idiosyncrasies of the American character to which I need only allude. First, there is no denying the fact that the level of general education and intellectual receptiveness is much lower than in Europe even in the case of persons who have attended an American college. Anyone who disbelieves this or deems it a malicious aspersion can find the evidence for himself in the work of honest American observers, for example by reading the examples in <u>Martin</u>, The Behaviour of Crowds.[67] Second,

---

[67][Martin, 1920.]

ment. At any rate, he alludes in telling phrases to the substitution of mass culture for education, the repulsion of autonomous reason by the manipulation of opinion, the replacement of long-term internalization by instant imitation, and the contradiction between the general increase in the pace of life and its associated "urge to abbreviate," on the one hand, and the completely different "temporal conditions" of psychic processes "between the conscious and the unconscious," on the other.

Yet Freud, the pioneer, stupendously underestimated the true slowness of the pace of psychic growth processes, as he had previously the radioactivity of the transference; this is evident from the requirement that the standard psychoanalytic training curriculum last only two years. As to the length of the treatment, he had, of course, voiced reservations three years earlier about the suggestions for abbreviation and simplification that Ferenczi and Rank had put forward with reforming zeal in their book *The Development of Psycho-Analysis.*[72] Anyone who reflects on the current controversy raging in the German Psychoanalytical Association on the question of training analyses and therapeutic analyses will quickly realize, considering the positions of the advocates of these modifications, how relevant certain of the comments in the variant quoted are today: for example, the fascination of large numbers, the alleged openmindedness to variations of the standard procedure, the willingness to espouse the general urge to abbreviate, and the rapidity with which "every practical need creates for itself the corresponding ideology." Incidentally, a few years after composing the "Postscript" to *The Question of Lay Analysis,* Freud would not be dissuaded from putting before the public, albeit in somewhat different form, some of the ideas in the text suppressed by Eitingon and Jones.[73]

At the end of this chapter, brimming as it is with details, let me repeat that, in addition to the categories of variants here proposed, some of them overlapping—graphic, stylistic-rhetorical, clarifying, structuring, title, and emotive variants—further types of revision characteristic of Freud's method of work could certainly be adduced.

[72]Ferenczi and Rank, 1925. Cf. Grubrich-Simitis, 1986*b*, p. 262ff.
[73]1930*c*.

10 First Versions

The examples of revision described in the previous chapter concern the fine structure of Freud's prose. They relate to a limited area of the relevant works—an illustration, a word, a title, a sentence, a paragraph, or a sequence of paragraphs. However, the manuscripts also include what may be described as two large-scale variants, which, when compared with the fair copies eventually published, are more in the nature of alternative versions. They are evidently not drafts—that is, immediate predecessors of the text as published—because they do not exhibit the typical features of the drafts, namely, the diagonal crossings out and the telegraphic style. They in fact take the form of manifestly repudiated quasi–fair copies in their own right, of *first versions* ultimately rejected, at least in part, by the author. Such independent textual stages survive from *Jenseits des Lustprinzips* [*Beyond the Pleasure Principle*] and *Der Mann Moses und die monotheistische Religion* [*Moses and Monotheism*]. To give the reader an impression of the specific and complex relations of these first versions to the familiar printed texts of the works, a relatively detailed description of the circumstances of their genesis and of the structures of their form and content will be necessary.

Beyond the Pleasure Principle and the book on Moses are, as we know, among the most speculative of Freud's works. Both came into being in the midst of traumatic life events: *Beyond* after the horrors of the First World War, in the hardships of whose aftermath the author felt himself growing old, weighed down by the experience of the deaths of two much younger people who had been close to him, his daughter Sophie and his munificent friend Anton von Freund; and the Moses book under the terror of the Nazi persecution and in the face of his inexorable terminal illness. However, Freud dismissed the supposition that the ideas he pursued in *Beyond the Pleasure Principle* were a reaction to the loss of his daughter. Fritz Wittels had advanced this hypothesis in his biography of Freud, published in 1924, whose text he had given its protagonist to read already in 1923. Freud had answered with a fairly long list of corrections, which included the statement that he had written the work in 1919, "when my daughter was still in excellent health. She died in January, 1920."[1] As will be shown, Freud is here referring to the first version and is minimizing the significance of the

[1] 1987a, p. 287, note 1.

process of reworking to which he had subjected this version, presumably after the death of Sophie. He incidentally concludes his admonition to Fritz Wittels with the sentence: "What seems true is not always the truth"—a formulation similar to the one used later, not only in the first version of his Moses, but also in the published Moses book.[2]

Both works deal, in one form or another and more or less explicitly, with trauma and death and with the importance of traumatic factors in the etiology of neurosis. Both contain attempts by the author to confront his psychoanalytic insights and concepts with notions and principles from biology, the basic science of the mortal somatic substrate, to approach its "land of unlimited possibilities"[3]—as if Freud had had a presentiment of the immense advances which, barely ten years after his death, were to be inaugurated in this discipline through the penetration to the molecular level of the cell.

In their foreword of 1940 to the seventeenth volume of the *Gesammelte Werke*, which presents the "posthumous works," the editors had already drawn attention to "a first version of the 'Moses,' which [might] perhaps be brought before the public at a later date."[4] It was therefore known to have been preserved. Conversely, I came across the other first version unexpectedly during my studies at the Library of Congress.

Two versions of the manuscript of *Jenseits des Lustprinzips* [*Beyond the Pleasure Principle*] are kept there. The catalog refers to them as "Handwritten manuscript" and "Handwritten and typewritten manuscript, bound," respectively. The first version is indeed handwritten throughout, on the usual large double sheets. It comprises thirty-four pages and exhibits all the hallmarks of a fair copy—that is, the "ceremonial" typography of the title[5] and the accentuation of the end by a kind of fermata. The other version exists in the form of a book bound in boards. The boards themselves are covered with brown marbled paper, and their corners and the spine with light-colored forel. The light-brown endpapers match the tint of the binding material. The inscription on the spine—the author's surname and the title— is gold-blocked. This is plainly the manuscript that Freud gave to Max Eitingon and that Eitingon had had bound.[6] The inner book consists partly of handwritten and partly of typed pages, the latter with a large number of handwritten corrections and insertions on additional slips and sheets of paper. Comparison of the two versions with the printed text of *Beyond the*

[2]1939*a*, p. 17.
[3]1920*g*, p. 60.
[4]P. ix.
[5]Cf. facsimile 10.1.
[6]See above, p. 89f.

First page of the first version of *Jenseits des Lustprinzips* [*Beyond the Pleasure Principle*].
[10.1]

Pleasure Principle shows that the book was set from the bound version,[7] despite its patched-together appearance, which distinguishes it from the serene beauty of most of the other fair copies.

When Lou Andreas-Salomé inquired in the spring of 1919 about the fate of his seven as yet unpublished metapsychological papers, written during the war, Freud replied evasively on 2 April: "The systematic working through of material is not possible for me; the fragmentary nature of my experiences and the sporadic character of my insights do not permit it."[8] As long as he remained capable of work, however, he promised to supply further contributions; he was already working on the first of these—*Beyond the Pleasure Principle.* It is indeed an exquisitely metapsychological work, containing as it does an outline of the forthcoming structural model of the psyche, introducing the new dualism of instinctual drives (death drives versus life drives), offering the first full appreciation of human destructiveness in the form of an attempt to account theoretically for the all-pervasive clinical phenomenon of the compulsion to repeat, and seeking to track down the elementary tendencies active in mental life—*beyond* and independently of the pleasure principle hitherto postulated as the ultimate and sole prime mover. A thinker about origins par excellence, Freud had embarked upon speculations of an almost mystical, philosophical, and poetic kind which raised questions about the very beginnings of life: "The attributes of life were at some time evoked in inanimate matter by the action of a force of whose nature we can form no conception. [. . .] The tension which then arose in what had hitherto been an inanimate substance endeavored to cancel itself out. In this way the first instinct came into being: the instinct to return to the inanimate state."[9] Or, put differently: "'*the aim of all life is death,*' and, looking backwards, [. . .] '*inanimate things existed before living ones.*'"[10]

By March 1919 Freud had informed Ferenczi, whom he considered to be the most competent biologist among his pupils, of his imaginative excursions. At the beginning of May he reported the completion of a "draft," which he wanted to have copied for his friend. Yet on 10 July 1919 he

---

[7]However, the comparison is at first confusing because the handwritten pages 5 to 27 that follow the typed page 4 have inadvertently been inserted in the wrong place. They belong in a much later position, as they form the continuation of the handwritten pages 1 to 4, which have been incorporated correctly between the typed pages 39 and 40. This extensive block, totaling twenty-seven handwritten pages (although page 27 consists only of a strip of paper comprising a few lines) makes up chapter VI, the part of the text which—as will now be discussed—is missing in the first version.

[8]1966a, p. 95.

[9]1920g, p. 38.

[10] Ibid.

described himself, before the beginning of his vacation, as "very tired, or rather ill-tempered, eaten up by impotent rage"; he had, he said, decided to take *Beyond the Pleasure Principle* with him to the summer resort of Badgastein. However, by 21 July he was in more cheerful spirits and wrote from there to his daughter Anna that the manuscript was now thriving: "There is a great deal about death in it, but it is unfortunately difficult to say anything decisive about it without literature and without practical experience." All the same, he was soon able to act to mitigate the first of these deficiencies, as he reported to Anna how helpful it had been to him to read the works of Schopenhauer, which Rank had sent to him at his request. After the holidays, at the end of September, Ferenczi came to Vienna for a comprehensive exchange of ideas. The discussion manifestly centered on topics and specialized literature in the field of biology[11]—not only to provide a basis for Freud's speculations concerning *Beyond*, but also for further clarification of Ferenczi's own "metabiological" or "paleobiological" reflections.[12]

After this, the fate of the manuscript of *Beyond* is not mentioned for a while in the correspondence between the two men. It was only on 25 May 1920—earlier in the same year his daughter Sophie had died unexpectedly, as had Anton von Freund after a long and serious illness—that Freud reported that he was engaged on this work again. In this connection, he asked Ferenczi for the reference to a quotation on repression that he had found in an English book and that was attributed to Ferenczi. His friend not having supplied the required information, he sent him a reminder on 17 June: in June-July, he said, he wanted to "finish 'Beyond,' to which some strange continuations have accrued [. . .]. So you should verify your quotation, otherwise I cannot include it, which would be a pity." Finally, the following laconic comment is recorded on 18 July 1920: " 'Beyond' is finished; you did not help me to quote your statement."

Without further detailed studies—for example, of the varying colors of the ink in the handwritten corrections and additions in the bound copy—it is impossible to assign the two surviving manuscript versions of *Beyond the Pleasure Principle* to specific phases in the chronology of that text's genesis. All we can be sure of is that we have before us two manifestations of a work in progress, whose metamorphoses continued into the stages of galley and page proof correction. The process of transformation did not come to an end even with the first publication of the book in 1920: the author in fact

---

[11]Ferenczi subsequently wrote reviews for the *Internationale Zeitschrift für Psychoanalyse* of biological contributions by Julius Schaxel and Alexander Lipschütz, in which he explicitly mentions points of contact between psychoanalysis and biology (1920*a* and 1920*b*).

[12]On this subject, cf. Grubrich-Simitis, 1987, p. 92ff.

made further substantial changes in the three new editions of his work that appeared between 1921 and 1925.[13]

Let us therefore confine ourselves here to a comparison of the two manuscript versions. The typed parts of the bound copy prove, apart from minor variants, to be a typewritten copy of the thirty-four pages of the first manuscript, which is handwritten throughout. Freud subsequently made handwritten alterations and additions of variable magnitude to this typescript, in a reworking process that was no doubt multilayered and involved several phases. These emendations range from the addition or replacement of individual words, via the interpolation of supplementary paragraphs, sections, or notes, to the composition of an entirely new chapter, constitutive of the structure of the work.

To begin with, let us consider an example of the smallest scale of alterations: it is to be found in the second chapter, which commences with an account of the enigmatic, "dark and dismal subject of the traumatic neurosis"[14] but then breaks off seemingly abruptly and continues with the analysis of the child's "Gone/There" game. The passage concerned is Freud's famous and much-quoted child observation of his grandson Ernst, Sophie's son: the little boy repeatedly dropped a wooden reel with a piece of string tied round it over the edge of his curtained cot so that it disappeared from his field of view and then pulled it back up and hailed it with a joyful "Da" [there]. The action of throwing was accompanied by a long drawn out sound, which the mother and grandfather understood as signifying the German word "Fort" [gone]. Freud interpreted the entire process as an attempt by the one-and-a-half-year-old Ernst to convert the painful experience of being left alone by his mother into a game of actively making something vanish and then bringing it back, played with the object of mastering the situation and thereby making the passively borne temporary separations from his mother not only more tolerable but actually pleasurable. The phonetic transcription of the sound accompanying the throwing away of the reel is <u>oooo</u> in the first version and <u>ooooo</u> in the bound typescript; however, Freud later onomatopoeically extended the sequence of vowels in writing as follows: o-o-o-o.[15]

[13]Freud's persistent dissatisfaction with the terminology of his new classification of instinctual drives is manifested, for example, in the long note at the end of chapter VI (p. 60f. in the published text). This too is lacking in the bound manuscript version; the first part of this note seems to have been incorporated during correction of the galley proofs, while the second was an addition actually made only for the second edition of 1921.

[14]1920g, p. 14.

[15]Incidentally, Freud made another of these late additions to his child observation, presumably while correcting the galley or page proofs. The following note, contained in the first

In the very first chapter of *Beyond the Pleasure Principle*, Freud added three extensive paragraphs or sections in handwriting to the typed passage in the bound version. After an initial complaint that neither psychology nor philosophy has furnished any theory that might facilitate understanding of the sensations of pleasure and unpleasure, which are so important in mental life, he pays homage in these interpolations, as if settling a debt of gratitude, and in almost affectionate terms, to Gustav Theodor Fechner, that "investigator of [. . .] penetration," the founder of experimental esthesiophysiology, crediting him with "a view on the subject of pleasure and unpleasure which coincides in all essentials with the one that has been forced upon us by psychoanalytic work."[16] In the context of a further discussion of the principle of constancy—already featured in Freud's early works but developed to its culminating point and hedged with definitive reservations in *Beyond*— Freud demonstrates this intellectual kinship by two longish quotations from Fechner, which are indeed astonishingly metapsychological.

Here is another example of a major handwritten addition of this kind to the typed text of the bound version. At the end of the fourth chapter, the entire important penultimate paragraph,[17] in which Freud continues his discussion of dreams that conform not to the principle of wish fulfillment but to the compulsion to repeat, was inserted later. Again, everything after the first sentence of the final paragraph, as far as the end of the chapter— that is, the complicated discussion in terms of libido theory on why physical injuries or somatic diseases can sometimes relieve psychic suffering—also

---

edition, is lacking in both manuscript versions: "When this child was five and three-quarters, his mother died. Now that she was really 'gone' ('o-o-o'), the little boy showed no signs of grief. It is true that in the interval a second child had been born and had roused him to violent jealousy" (ibid., p. 16, note 1).

Even if Jacques Derrida's characteristic analytic approach of turning texts inward blurs the extralinguistic points of reference, he was apparently basing his interpretation of *Beyond the Pleasure Principle*, published in 1980, on a connection with the loss of Freud's daughter in relation not only to this note but to the work as a whole. In the second chapter in particular, which was no doubt written before the unforeseeable death of Sophie, he discerns self-referential features in the text, claiming that the dynamic of the "Fort/Da" game as well as the rhythms of the compulsion to repeat in general determined the respective incidence of movement and marking time in Freud's argument. Working through the loss of his daughter in a kind of semimourning, he was, Derrida claims, treating this text in the same way as his grandson had the reel of thread.

[16] 1920g, p. 8. Because this edition is readily accessible and the bound manuscript differs little from the published version, to facilitate location of the quoted passages here and subsequently, I give the page numbers not of the manuscript but of the work as reproduced in the *Standard Edition*.

[17] Ibid., p. 32f.

consists of a handwritten addition on a separate page, in lighter-colored ink than the passage mentioned before and therefore presumably originating from a different phase in the process of reworking.

These substantive additions, together with a number of others that cannot be cited individually here, would constitute sufficient justification in themselves for deeming the two surviving manuscripts to be separate versions of *Beyond the Pleasure Principle* rather than a draft and a fair copy. However, the cardinal difference between the two versions concerns the chapters: the handwritten manuscript has only six parts, marked with roman numerals, whereas the bound copy comprises seven. The figure "VI" in the typed text of the bound copy was subsequently altered by the author to "VII" after he had added a different sixth chapter on another twenty-seven handwritten pages. The addition constitutes by far the longest section of the whole book, making up almost a third of the total volume of the printed version of *Jenseits des Lustprinzips*.

In the list of corrections for Fritz Wittels, Freud is no doubt referring to this piece when he says that, by the time his daughter Sophie died, it "was finished, except for the discussion concerning the mortality or immortality of protozoa."[18] The reader of this passage cannot but find the author's characterization of its substance inappropriately laconic. In fact, it is the concept of the death drive itself which appears for the first time in this subsequently composed sixth part of *Beyond the Pleasure Principle*. The description of a new dualism of instinctual drives or the adumbration of instinctual tendencies striving toward a return to the state of inorganic lifelessness as well as the incorporation of the biological dimension are admittedly prepared for in earlier parts of the work (part IV and, in particular, part V)—that is, in passages included in the handwritten first version, composed before Sophie's death. However, the actual specification of the concept of the death drive was surely not completely independent of the experience of these losses. The reader may discern an echo of the two recent bereavements right at the beginning of the new chapter, where Freud returns to the assumption, discussed previously, that all living substance is bound to die from internal causes and considers that people—including poets—cling to this idea so tenaciously because it is comforting: "If we are to die ourselves, and first to lose in death those who are dearest to us, it is easier to submit to a remorseless law of nature, to the sublime Ἀνάγκη [necessity], than to a chance, which might perhaps have been escaped. It may be, however, that this belief in the internal necessity of dying is only another of those

[18] 1987a, p. 287, note 1.

illusions which we have created '*um die Schwere des Daseins zu ertragen*' ['to bear the burden of existence']."[19]

To test this "belief," actually in the hope—even if only rhetorical—of finding it refuted there, he then turns to biology. We shall no doubt be justified in presuming that Freud's discussion with Ferenczi on the specialized biological literature the previous fall left some traces here; for instance, among the authors now quoted is Alexander Lipschütz, one of whose works Ferenczi had reviewed at the time. Freud's account in fact centers on the hypotheses of August Weismann on the division of living substance into the mortal soma on the one hand and the potentially immortal germ cells on the other, in which Freud at first discerns a morphological correspondence with his new dynamic dualism of instinctual drives; however, on closer examination, he finds that this agreement breaks down because Weismann declares unicellular organisms to be to all intents and purposes immortal, natural death being a later acquisition of higher, multicellular organisms (whether composed of small or large numbers of cells) and not an attribute of *everything* living. Freud therefore goes on to consider other authors and controversial experiments on the alleged immortality of protozoa and ultimately reaches the following conclusion: "Thus our expectation that biology would flatly contradict the recognition of death instincts [drives] has not been fulfilled."[20]

Freud is then able to proceed, in a climax, to flesh out his concept of the death drive and to develop it into its final form, basing his argument now more on philosophy, on Schopenhauer and Plato. At the same time, this highly condensed text gains in perspective in relation to both the future and the past: on the one hand, libido theory is boldly applied to the interrelations between cells, giving rise in playful fashion to a kind of psychosomatic model of thought; and, on the other, the author looks back over the laborious development of his theory of instinctual drives, based on decades of clinical observation, and derives from it the logical justification for its present revision. The abundance of themes and the obscurity of the final pages defy summarization. Let us merely note that, in attempting the formidable task of adducing direct, graphic evidence of the working of the death drives, Freud introduces another innovative concept, that of *primary* masochism. Even if he concedes at the end that "the third step in the theory of the instincts [drives], which I have taken here, cannot lay claim to the same degree of certainty as the two earlier ones—the extension of the concept of sexuality and the hypothesis of narcissism"[21]—there can be no doubt that

[19] 1920g, p. 45.
[20] Ibid., p. 49.
[21] Ibid., p. 59.

this compact sixth chapter, subsequently inserted, constitutes the nucleus of *Beyond the Pleasure Principle.*

It is for this reason that the handwritten manuscript, in which this core section is lacking, cannot be deemed a "draft"; it is in reality an alternative first version, ultimately considered inadequate. Without wishing to anticipate the necessary detailed examination of the material, I think we may nevertheless suppose that this central text was not set down until some time between May and the late summer of 1920[22]—that is to say, *after* the two deaths; should this be confirmed, Fritz Wittels's hypothesis would not have been entirely wrong after all. At any rate, it was surely these twenty-seven important pages, described by Freud in his letter to Ferenczi of 17 June 1920 as "strange continuations," that had meanwhile been brought forth.

Moreover, they necessitated further changes to the final part of the book. The bound copy of the manuscript contains, as the foundation of the final part, a typed copy of what Freud had recorded in handwriting as part "VI" in the first version. He then deleted a number of passages in this typescript in red pencil. The same applies to a handwritten addition by which he had at first plainly wanted, in an initial process of revision, to enhance the specificity of the end of the typed text. In a more radical further step, he seems ultimately to have rejected the concluding lines of the first version altogether. He replaced them, on a separate page written in darker ink, by the long concluding paragraph familiar to us from the printed version.[23] This expresses the tenor of the deleted passage more clearly and comprehensively as well as enjoining patience and a willingness "to abandon a path that we have followed for a time, if it seems to be leading to no good end"; it closes with the telling lines from Rückert's German translation of the *Maqâmât* of al-Hariri: "Was man nicht erfliegen kann, muss man erhinken . . . Die Schrift sagt, es ist keine Sünde zu hinken" [What we cannot reach flying we must reach limping . . . The Book tells us it is no sin to limp].

In a number of respects this quotation is equally applicable to that magnificently singular work of Freud's old age, *Der Mann Moses und die mono-*

[22]Although Freud had written in the quoted letter to Ferenczi dated 18 July 1920: " 'Beyond' is finished [. . .]," this might have referred, typically for him, to the draft of this chapter—i.e., to the phase of conception. The archives of the Freud Museum in London contain some notes written on leaves from a Hungarian calendar which unmistakably record ideas and even detailed formulations from the sixth chapter, dated by Freud 15, 16, and 17 July but without specification of the year. It is unlikely that the notes were made in the previous year because, after all, as Freud told Wittels, the passage on the mortality and immortality of protozoa—which is the subject of these brief notations—was added only after Sophie's death.

[23]1920g, p. 63f.

theistische Religion [*Moses and Monotheism*][24] as well as to its first version, *Der Mann Moses* [The Man Moses] with its subtitle "Ein historischer Roman" [A Historical Novel].[25] Another of the surviving Moses manuscripts, the draft of parts of the third essay of the book, has already been mentioned in the chapter on the drafts.[26] In the appendix to *Freuds Moses-Studie als Tagtraum* [Freud's Study of Moses as a Daydream], I published the first coherent description of the three bundles into which the Moses manuscripts can be divided.[27] One of these bundles is precisely the so-called historical novel, the second example of a preserved alternative first version of one of Freud's published major works. Some dates and characteristic features will now be adduced to illustrate, first, the fact that it differs structurally from the first version of *Beyond the Pleasure Principle*, and, second, the nature of the relevant differences.

In 1933, Thomas Mann published *Die Geschichten Jaakobs* [*The Tales of Jacob*], the first part of his Joseph tetralogy. Although it was not until 1936, in the speech he delivered on Freud's eightieth birthday, that Mann explicitly stated that "that novel so kin to the Freudian world" was "a celebration of the meeting between the poetry and analysis,"[28] Freud will nevertheless have sensed this kinship as soon as he read that new work. This he did at a time when he himself was in a state of despondency, filled with helpless rage, and no longer wanting to write. The advance of Hitler, and not least the burning of his own books, had indescribably exacerbated the experience of his own powerlessness, old and ill with cancer as he was. There are a number of indications that Freud allowed himself to be inspired by Mann's novel to undertake a liberating excursion of his own into the realms of fantasy and to seek imaginative reinvigoration in remote epochs and distant regions. "Long-past ages," we read in the book on Moses, "have a great and often puzzling attraction for men's imagination. Whenever they are dissatisfied with their present surroundings—and this happens often enough—they turn back to the past and hope that they will now be able to prove the truth of the unextinguishable dream of a golden age."[29] Freud, who had always striven to rein in his own speculative tendency, may have seen the genre of the "historical novel" as a tempting compromise form in which he could at last give his ideas their head while nevertheless assuring himself here and there of a basis in reality.

[24]1939a.
[25]Cf. facsimile 10.2 of its first page.
[26]See above, beginning of chapter 7.
[27]Grubrich-Simitis, 1991, pp. 79–103; revised 1994 edition pp. 81–104.
[28]Mann, 1936, p. 427.
[29]1939a, p. 71.

9.8.1934

Der Mann Moses.
Ein historischer Roman.

First page of the first version of *Der Mann Moses*.

[10.2]

Contrary to his initial intention, however, Freud acted more like a conventional historian than a creative writer in his increasingly obsessive expeditions in the domain of the Mosaic tradition, as if the details of the life history of the founder of the religion recounted in the biblical text were in essence factually documented traces of real events and not for their part products of ancient creative reworkings, displacements, and condensations—although he himself again and again emphasizes precisely this interpretative character of the textual material, which itself challenges the reader to interpret it. The Bible narrative, he tells us, contains "precious and, indeed, invaluable historical data, which, however, have been distorted by the influence of powerful tendentious purposes and embellished by the products of poetic invention."[30] Again, he has the following to say about the results of such reworkings in the five books of Moses—nicely anticipating today's poststructuralist fashion of taking texts literally: "Thus almost everywhere noticeable gaps, disturbing repetitions and obvious contradictions have come about—indications which reveal things to us which it was not intended to communicate. In its implications the distortion of a text resembles a murder: the difficulty is not in perpetrating the deed, but in getting rid of its traces. We might well lend the word '*Entstellung*' [distortion] the double meaning to which it has a claim but of which today it makes no use. It should mean not only 'to change the appearance of something' but also 'to put something in another place, to displace.' Accordingly, in many instances of textual distortion, we may nevertheless count upon finding what has been suppressed and disavowed hidden away somewhere else, though changed and torn from its context."[31]

It should nevertheless be borne in mind that Freud, notwithstanding his modernity in the decrypting of such secret writing, remained identified with an academic tradition in which the blurring of differences between genres was deprecated. At any rate, Freud's distrust of the fictional and his inhibition about relinquishing scientific in favor of artistic discourse may well have motivated his eventual repudiation of the historical novel about the man Moses—that is, the first version. Yet he had attempted, right at the beginning of the manuscript, which is dated 9 August 1934, to distinguish between different meanings of the generic term "historical novel" and had defined how it was to be understood in the case of his own Moses experiment, in which, as we know, he took the liberty of declaring Moses to have been an Egyptian and of having him murdered by the Israelites. The relevant passage from the introduction will now be quoted because it will deter the reader from expecting anything novelistic in the popular sense of the word

[30]Ibid., p. 41.
[31]Ibid., p. 43.

from this first version of the Moses book; it also appears to confirm the presumed motives for its abandonment:[32]

> However, since I am neither a historical researcher nor an artist, if I introduce one of my works as a "historical novel," this name must admit of another use. I was educated to the meticulous observation of a certain field of phenomena, and for me poetic creation and invention are readily attended by the blemish of error. My immediate intention was to gain a knowledge of the person of Moses, but I also had the more distant objective of contributing in this way to the solution of a problem that is still current today, but can only be mentioned later. A character study must be based on reliable material, but nothing at our disposal concerning the man Moses can be counted reliable. It is a tradition from a single source, not confirmed from any other side, probably recorded in writing too late, in itself contradictory, no doubt reworked many times over and distorted by the influence of new tendencies, and intimately interwoven with the religious and national myths of a people. One would be justified in giving up the attempt as hopeless, if the grandeur of the figure did not countervail its remoteness and spur us to new efforts. One therefore endeavors to treat every one of the possibilities inherent in the material as a clue and to fill the gaps between one piece and the next, so to speak, by the law of least resistance—i.e., by giving preference to that assumption to which the greater probability may be ascribed. The yield accruing from this technique can also be regarded as a kind of "historical novel"; if it has any validity at all in terms of reality, then that validity is indeterminable, for mere probability, however great, does not coincide with the truth; the truth is often very improbable, and deductions and considerations are but a meager substitute for actual evidence.

No sooner had he decided on these principles and set down his historical novel in the light of them than he informed Arnold Zweig, at the end of September in the same year, that he wished to hide his new work away; not only was he dissatisfied with it, but he also feared that if it were published there might in particular be reprisals against psychoanalysis from the Catholic Church, from which, on the other hand, he hoped for protection from the Nazi persecution. To invalidate the political objections, Zweig advised Freud to have the work published privately, but the latter repeated in his

---

[32]This passage has been published before; it was first presented by Pier Cesare Bori (Freud, 1979j). A few lines from it are reproduced in facsimile 10.2 of the first page of the historical novel.

subsequent letters that the historical novel could not in fact stand up to his own criticism. He had been unable to avoid constructing "so imposing a statue on feet of clay, so that any fool could topple it."[33] On 13 February 1935, however, he nevertheless extended an invitation to Zweig: "When you next come to Vienna I shall be pleased for you to read the manuscript which has been laid aside so that you may confirm my judgment."[34]

Yet the subject of Moses is broached again and again in the ensuing period in the correspondence with Arnold Zweig. In his urge for verification, Freud eagerly seized on literature references supplied by that writer, who, having emigrated to Palestine, felt it incumbent on himself to undertake research on the spot and to consult specialists in the relevant disciplines. In this intensive exchange of ideas, which is documented in the correspondence, we can discern signals of the process of reworking to which Freud subjected the original conception of his Moses study in the years that followed, as the fruits of which, first, the two essays "Moses, an Egyptian" and "If Moses was an Egyptian . . . " were presented to the public separately in the journal *Imago* and then, in 1939, the book *Der Mann Moses und die monotheistische Religion* [*Moses and Monotheism*], now supplemented by the important third essay, was brought out by Allert de Lange, the Dutch publishing house that served the needs of German-speaking exiles. What has been preserved of the manuscript of the historical novel, once laid to rest, and in what respects does it differ from the printed Moses text with which we are familiar? Even if these questions can be answered here only in outline, the reader cannot be spared some rather dry comparisons in the following pages.

What survives of the first version is a manuscript comprising twenty-eight pages, followed on nine more pages[35] by a "Critical Appendix." An additional thirteen pages contain a separate manuscript, manifestly belonging to the historical novel, with "Notes," a "Key to the Notes,"[36] and a "List of the Main Works on which I have drawn." Finally, a plan of the contents of the first version is also preserved, although not in Freud's hand; the writing may be that of Anna Freud. The tabulation is as follows:

[33] 1968a, p. 99.

[34] Ibid., p. 102.

[35] Numbered 28a to i; a passage on the back of page 28i, amounting to only a few lines and with no other identification, also belongs here.

[36] This material may already be the result of an initial process of revision, which did not, however, involve massive changes but comprised only additions, for the manuscript of the historical novel itself already contains two annotations. In accordance with his usual practice in his fair copies, Freud included them directly in the run of the text, flagged as footnotes.

The Man Moses.
A Historical Novel.

a) Did Moses live?
b) The Origin of Moses.
c) The New Religion.
d) The Exodus from Egypt.
e) The Chosen People.
f) The Sign of the Covenant and the Name of God.
    Critical Appendix.

II: The People of Israel.

b) The Great Man.
c) The Advance in Intellectuality.
e) Renunciation of Drives

III. What is True in Religion.

b) The Tradition.
c) The Return of the Repressed.
d) The Historical Truth.
e) The Historical Development.

The manuscript of the historical novel itself comprises only sections a) to f) of the first group of headings in this table. The parts identified by roman numerals II and III are lacking in the collection of surviving manuscripts. Because the first part is not clearly marked in the contents list with a figure I and a title of its own, there is a strong presumption that Freud intended, in the very first phase of the work's genesis, to end it with the "Critical Appendix." Two formulations toward the end of the preserved manuscript appear to bear out this hypothesis. One of them reads: "At this point I can conclude what I announced as the historical novel about the man Moses."[37] The other, at the beginning of the "Critical Appendix," is as follows: "I did not know that it would be so difficult to compose a 'historical novel.' Now it is finished, my conscience enjoins me to apply the criterion of sober historiography to it."[38] The sixteen additional annotations in the "Notes" manuscript, except for the last, to which it is difficult to assign a place, also clearly belong to the surviving manuscript of the first version. However, the attempt to adduce scientific evidence for his material, adumbrated in the "Critical Appendix," seems to have led rapidly to the composi-

[37]Manuscript page 26.
[38]Manuscript page 28a.

tion of the additional second and third parts outlined in the table of contents—for, not long after starting to set down his manuscript, Freud informed Max Eitingon in a letter dated 27 October 1934 that the "Moses" was "finished": "It bears [. . .] the subtitle: 'A Historical Novel' "—and furthermore Freud means the *complete* text, because he continues: "The structure falls [. . .] into three parts, 1) The Man Moses, 2) The People of Israel, 3) What is True in Religion." Earlier still, on 30 September, he had told Arnold Zweig in the letter quoted earlier: "The material fits into three sections. The first part is like an interesting novel; the second is laborious and boring; the third is full of content and makes exacting reading."[39]

As to the relationship borne by the two parts of the first version that have *not* survived to the Moses book with which we are familiar,[40] we must confine ourselves to some conjectures, which result from a collation and comparison of parts of the two tables of contents:

Contents of part II and part III of the *first version*:	Contents of the second part of essay III in the *printed version*:
"II. The People of Israel.	"Summary and Recapitulation
b) The Great Man.	A. The People of Israel
c) The Advance in Intellectuality.	B. The Great Man
e) Renunciation of Drives	C. The Advance in Intellectuality
III. What is True in Religion.	D. Renunciation of Drives
b) The Tradition.	E. What is True in Religion
c) The Return of the Repressed.	F. The Return of the Repressed
d) The Historical Truth.	G. The Historical Truth
e) The Historical Development."	H. The Historical Development"

It is immediately obvious that the second part of the published third essay originated directly from the amalgamation of parts II and III of the first version. The fact that the manuscripts of the latter have not come down to us may be attributable to this late reworking, on which Freud, by his own account,[41] embarked only after his arrival in exile in London. At any rate, the structural differences between the two tables of contents are minimal. What still appear as titles of parts in the first version once again become headings of equal rank in the work as printed; this leveling is already prepared for in the contents list of the first version insofar as each part lacks a section a). Admittedly, the section "b) The Tradition" provided for in the plan of the third part of the first version has no direct equivalent in the book

[39]1968a, p. 91f.

[40]The fair copies of only the second and third of the book's essays have survived; that of the first is missing.

[41]1939a, p. 103.

as published.[42] Conversely, the section "Summary and Recapitulation" in the printed text will be sought in vain in the first version. There was in 1934 as yet no occasion for such an insertion, which has the character of a third prefatory note;[43] for Freud here refers to his emigration, which had since taken place, and to the traces—deficiencies and in particular repetitions—left behind in the text by the vicissitudes of its genesis.

If parts II and III of the first version have been incorporated in the second part of essay III in the printed version, it is reasonable to expect that the substance of the ideas of the surviving first part of the early version, described by the author as "like an interesting novel," will be found in the first and second essays and the first part of the third essay of the work as published. If we read the two versions one after another, this does indeed prove to be true on the macro level. However, it is not really possible to peruse the two texts in parallel in this way because—unlike the case of *Beyond the Pleasure Principle*—it cannot be said that the first version so to speak constitutes the foundation of the work as printed, the latter being composed, on the one hand, of unaltered or barely altered elements of the text of the first version and, on the other, of significant new blocks constitutive of the definitive shape of the work. In fact, the impression is gained from a reading of the two versions of Moses that the author, in the transition to the printed version of the Moses study, subjected his original historical novel to a process of intellectual and literary transformation, the pressure or temperature attained in which, as it were, brought about a change in the physical state of the text as a whole that extends to the most subtle microstructures of its ideas and language.

This metamorphosis was no doubt occasioned by Freud's insight that he was after all not a writer of literature and was unsuited to the composition of a historical novel—even according to his own restricted definition of this genre. At any rate, when he had finished his historical novel, that hermaphroditic creature that is in reality a kind of essay—Freud himself called it such[44]—he confessed to Max Eitingon: "I am no good at historical romances. Let us leave them to Thomas Mann."[45] What became of the first version after that process of reworking is admittedly still an essay, but one more closely related to the ductus of Freud's oeuvre than was the historical

[42]The first part of the third essay of the Moses book, which is not quoted here, does, however, include a passage "B. The Latency Period and Tradition."

[43]The third essay of the Moses book is introduced by two prefatory notes, one of them set down in Vienna before March 1938—i.e., before the *Anschluss*—and the other composed after arrival in exile in London in June 1938. The fair copies of both texts have survived.

[44]1968a, p. 92. [*Translator's note*: Freud's word "Essay"—German edition page 102—has unaccountably been rendered as "work" in the English version.]

[45]Quoted in Jones, 1957, p. 207.

novel. So the author no longer describes his new product as a "historical novel"; he now soberly refers to it merely as a "short paper," "an application of psychoanalysis."[46] Before drawing attention to some distinctions between the two physical states, I should like to emphasize that, for all the differences of form and content, a background of similarity remained—as it were the material, the subject matter submitted to psychoanalytic examination: Moses.

The historical novel is not only shorter than the corresponding section of the printed version;[47] it is also more supple, more intimate, and more poetic. At times it attains that lyric intensity and rapt contemplation which Freud extols in the hymns of the pharaoh Akhenaten, to whose spiritualized Aten religion he after all traced back Mosaic monotheism. He luxuriates almost throughout in the storytelling aspect, allowing it in many passages to meander back and forth in the manner of a daydream. Where the conceptions of other authors are introduced, they too tend to be reproduced narratively, woven casually into the dramaturgy of Freud's tale and of his reflections on it. This applies even to the "Critical Appendix," which, although it begins by expressing an objectivizing intention, immediately leads into a fascinating dialogue of *two* historical novels, Freud's and Hugo Gressmann's; Gressmann's treats in particular of the volcanic catastrophe in the Red Sea, allegedly the Gulf of Aqaba. Concerning at least the central part of Gressmann's account, Freud thought it to be "also nothing but a historical novel," "no more reliable than that constructed by ourselves." It was only in the subsequent process of revision which ultimately brought forth the printed version that he actually obeyed the call to order which he had addressed to himself. After further study of the relevant specialized literature, uninhibited flights of fancy began to yield to the rhetoric of relatively unadorned scientific discourse: linearity of structure,[48] the application of strict logic in his theorization, justification of the method used, attempts to persuade the reader by reason, and impartial, detailed acknowledgment of other authors' publications, whether they diverged from his views or tended to bear them out.

As it happens, these predominantly formal differences between the two versions also reflect a change in the author's intentions. As he states in the

[46]1939a, p. 10.

[47]In the remainder of this chapter, the terms "historical novel" and "first version" relate to the surviving part of the manuscript of the first version, whereas "printed text" means essentially essays I and II of the published Moses text ("Moses, an Egyptian" and "If Moses was an Egyptian . . . "). I shall not discuss in detail the repetition of the relevant material in the first section ("A. The Historical Premiss") of essay III of the Moses book.

[48]The oft-noted compositional fragility of the Moses book in fact concerns mainly the third essay, which is not discussed in detail here.

introductory passage quoted, his main objective in the historical novel was "to gain a knowledge of the person of Moses." He was fascinated by the grandeur of the figure. He wanted to throw light on its essential traits and motives in a character study: Moses' wrathful temper and his speech defect, that is, his being strangely slow of speech; his tendency toward the highest degree of intellectualization; his unconditional, haughty ambition to secure permanent prominence for the austere faith in a single god founded by the biblical hero in emulation of Akhenaten; and the imperious capacity, "after a disappointment and deprivation by a stroke of fate, immediately to reconstruct that which has been lost on new soil, by new means."[49] I cannot discuss here in more detail the work's latent autobiographical dimension of depth which makes of it the document of a personal crisis, but it will be obvious to the reader even without such a full treatment that Freud, himself an angry man with a speech impediment due to the operations on his palate, is in this work undertaking some further self-portrayal and self-analysis, while at the same time attempting to allay his concern that his own demanding doctrine, psychoanalysis, might be extinguished by the Nazi persecution. However, what he wished to acquaint himself with in the writing of the historical novel was no doubt something very private: a core area of his own ego ideal, his powerful identification with Moses, dating back to his reading of the Torah in early childhood.[50]

One of the effects of the objectivizing intention that ushered in the reworking process was to modify the subject of his investigation. In contrast to the historical novel, Freud wanted to furnish in the printed version not so much a colorful character study of the founder of a religion as a depersonified analysis of his lifework. In the author's own words, he was now mainly concerned with "the possible basis of a number of the characteristics and peculiarities of the laws and religion" that Moses the Egyptian had given to his chosen People of Israel as well as to arrive at new "considerations regarding the origin of monotheist religions in general."[51] For this reason, Freud, in the printed version, gives an even more comprehensive and more subtle description than in the historical novel of the magic polytheism of the traditional Egyptian religion, so as to make the sudden creation of Akhenaten's sun-god faith, the first full-fledged monotheism in the history of mankind, stand out with even greater radiance against this primitive background. The presumed murder of the founder of the religion by his people is not acknowledged as the culmination of the tragic biography of a hero. Instead, the main function of this hypothesis in the printed version is

[49]Manuscript page 20.
[50]For further details, cf. again Grubrich-Simitis, 1991.
[51]1939*a*, p. 16.

to allow Freud to develop fully the link, which was merely adumbrated in the "historical novel," with the phylogenetic theory formerly advanced in *Totem and Taboo*—in other words, the construction of the murder of the tyrannical primal father and the creation of a genetically transmitted "archaic heritage" in the psychic life of man could in this way once again be given adequate expression.

We thus reencounter here the intellectual magnetic field referred to several times in the foregoing pages—for Freud in this way, crossing not a few vertiginous bridges as he develops his ideas, believes that he has found an explanation in terms of both individual and group psychology for the unprecedented and manifestly undying power of monotheism, which is now the predominant object of his interest: in his view, it can be attributed to the fact that, in it, some primal trauma returns from repression, and the primal father is symbolically restored to his rights in the form of the *one* god. Only with this part of his argument does there appear the multidimensionality that was later to distinguish the third essay on Moses, of which there is no sign in at least the surviving part of the historical novel.

One of the effects of the shift in emphasis, outlined above, from the person of Moses onto his work during the course of the reworking may have been that, on the one hand, a number of elements of the historical novel went by the board, while, on the other, some completely new thematic strands were taken up. An example will be given of each type. Although the printed version at one point contains a reference to the breaking of the tables of the law and the furious indignation of Moses[52]—a situation on which Freud had dwelt in his interpretation of Michelangelo's statue of Moses, as mentioned in the chapter of the variants—he does not here refer to the earlier essay; a fine annotation on this subject from the historical novel, emphasizing the affective processes in Moses, was therefore lost.[53] Conversely, the author discusses the Levites at length in the printed version; this resulted in a passage that one would seek in vain in the historical novel. Now that Freud's interest was centered on Moses' life achievement, he came to attach greater significance to the persons who, originally recruited from the followers of the founder of the religion, had collectively ensured the posthumous permanence of the doctrine.

Yet precisely the section on the Levites shows that, on the latent level, Freud was now still concerned with a matter dear to his own heart: the destiny of his work. Exercised as he was by the question of whether and how psychoanalysis could withstand the Nazi persecution, the account of the fall

[52]Ibid., p. 48.

[53]Its German text is presented in Grubrich-Simitis, 1991, p. 87; revised 1994 edition p. 88f.

telepathic phenomena: whether there might be any connection between the prophecy of a fortune-teller, on the one hand, and the unconscious internal world of his client, on the other, such that the prophecy—by way of thought transmission of whatever kind—essentially comprises the revelation by the fortune-teller of a powerful wish on the part of the client himself, albeit one of which he is unconscious, its astonishing accuracy being derived from this feedback. Using the example of the fortune-teller, Freud is therefore here once again discussing his assumption, supported by many observations, "that everyone possesses in his own unconscious an instrument with which he can interpret the utterances of the unconscious in other people"[7]—that is to say, an archaic, phylogenetically early medium of understanding overlaid by the development of language, the modes of functioning of which are, however, admittedly enigmatic.

The correspondence between the two men shows that during their trip to America in 1909 Ferenczi had already informed Freud of his experiences with a Berlin fortune-teller. Partly fascinated and partly irritated, if not horrified, by these observations, soon to be supplemented by further experiments, they conducted an intensive exchange of views on the subject in their letters after their return. At its very beginning, Ferenczi outlined the tentative explanation that was subsequently incorporated in Freud's preliminary report as its central thesis: "Now, if I assume," he writes in his letter of 5 October 1909, "that she really possesses uncommon abilities, then this could perhaps be explained as a kind of 'mind reading,' as reading *my* thoughts. [Paragraph] The intensive self-analysis that I undertook immediately after the séance led me to this hypothesis. Most of her statements [. . .] correspond to trains of thought that I really produced, but partly also those which I could have repressed."[8]

On closer consideration, the subject appears from today's perspective to be not at all aberrant but in the highest degree relevant to our own time and still almost as obscure as it was then.[9] It confronts us again and again in the clinical situation, for example, when we observe the undeniably massive effect of processes of projective identification[10] and do not really know how

---

[7]1913*i*, p. 320; cf. also 1919*h*, p. 234, and 1933*a*, p. 54.

[8]1992*g*, p. 75f.

[9]However, modern baby researchers' studies on the earliest mother-child communication, or the work of Rainer Krause on unconscious regulating mechanisms of interaction, hold out the promise of progress in our knowledge of this field. Incidentally, Freud had the prescience to expect further discoveries from child analysis, particularly if mother and child were analyzed simultaneously (1933*a*, p. 56).

[10]The Freud-Ferenczi correspondence does indeed prove that, in connection with the subject of telepathy, the two investigators were at this time already directly engaged in the discovery of the psychic mechanism of projective identification—for example, when Ferenczi attempts, on 17 August 1910, to explain a case of thought transmission between analyst and

they are mediated or when we wonder about possible transmission routes on finding that extreme traumatization of parents can have a cumulatively traumatizing effect on the psychic development of their children, even if the traumatic experiences are *not* spoken of between the generations.[11]

At no time did Freud consider publishing the preliminary report, presumably not so much because he did not wish to place an even greater burden on psychoanalysis, which was still struggling for recognition after the First World War, with a contribution on a subject held to be disreputable by the scientific establishment of the time, but because he considered his reflections as such to be not very fruitful. Only a few elements of the manuscript of the lecture were taken up in later publications on related topics, sometimes in more concise form: for instance, in "Dreams and Telepathy," in the section on the occult significance of dreams in "Some Additional Notes on Dream-Interpretation as a Whole," and finally in the thirtieth of the *New Introductory Lectures*, "Dreams and Occultism." An extract from this lecture was reprinted in the *Almanach der Psychoanalyse* in 1934 under the title "Zum Problem der Telepathie" ["On the Problem of Telepathy"], immediately prompting Walter Benjamin, when he read it at the time, to emphasize the modernity of Freud's ideas against the background of his own studies on the mimetic faculty: "In the course of his reflections, Freud—in passing, as is his wont with the greatest ideas—establishes a connection between telepathy and language, by making the former the phylogenetic precursor of the latter as a medium of understanding—in explanation, he refers to insect communities."[12]

A parallel reading of the manuscript and the printed version of the preliminary report reveals—apart from minor discrepancies of spelling and punctuation, expansion of a small number of abbreviations, and so on—variants in the extensive vignettes in particular. In the first,[13] the editors have merely made some slight changes to help disguise the identity of the analysand. For example, the young man concerned was stated in the manuscript to be "from Nuremberg," whereas the published version gives Germany as his region of origin.

Such discrepancies are also to be found in the second vignette,[14] containing the prophecy of marriage and an abundance of children for one of Freud's later female patients, who ultimately remained childless. Here, how-

---

analysand, namely, between himself and a masochistic patient: "I *project* the stimulus words ucs. [unconsciously], he *introjects* them" (Ferenczi's emphasis) [1992g, p. 209].

[11]Cf. Grubrich-Simitis, 1981.

[12]From a letter to Gretel Adorno dated 9 October 1935 (Benjamin, 1980, p. 953).

[13]Printed version, 1941d, p. 181ff.

[14]Ibid., p. 185ff.

ever, the editors have also excluded a fairly long section of the manuscript from the printed text. It follows the presentation of this patient's anamnesis,[15] before Freud goes on to discuss the prophecy, which the analysand had once reported to him and which had induced him to include the vignette in the preliminary report. To facilitate understanding of this passage, which I believe to be hitherto unknown, I should like to precede it with some information about the patient, which can be reconstructed from, for example, the Freud-Jung correspondence. This patient had been suffering from severe obsessional symptoms for more than ten years; all treatment, some of it in institutions, had so far proved fruitless. When she consulted Freud at the end of 1908, he at once noted that she was "a very serious case of obsessional neurosis, improvement is bound to be very slow";[16] after several years of analysis, he seems to have given up even this feeble hope toward the end of 1911. The omitted passage reads as follows:

> When I heard her case history, I did not at first want to accept her into treatment; later I was sufficiently curious, ignorant and acquisitive to commence an untendentious analysis with her after all. The result was thoroughly negative, at least for her. Analysis is indebted to her for certain points. She presented me with the explanation of some lies told by children, and set me on the track of the disposition to obsessional neurosis. She was also the first occasion on which C. G. Jung betrayed his dubious character, for which his subsequent warped theories could not compensate me. While on vacation in Zurich, she once invited him over in order to make his acquaintance. He took this opportunity to express his surprise to her that she was able to endure an analysis with me lacking in warmth and sympathy, and recommended himself for a more lively treatment that would proceed at a higher temperature. When she warned him that she would have to report this statement to me, he took fright & asked her not to do so. The affectionate son's first, not yet sublimated, attempt to dispute the father's right to the female object had failed; the second followed two years later.[17]

This fragment casts light on a number of areas of Freud research and of the historiography of psychoanalysis. These include personal and biographical aspects. We immediately learn something of the candor with which

[15]On the basis of the text as reproduced in the printed version, this missing paragraph would belong on page 187, between "[. . .] to which her childlessness was due" and "On one occasion, [. . .]."

[16]1974a, p. 175.

[17]The reference to the second, sublimated, attempt at appropriation no doubt concerns psychoanalysis. [*Translator's note*: The noun "Psychoanalyse" has feminine gender in German.]

Freud confessed that curiosity, ignorance, and acquisitiveness were legitimate motives for exposing oneself to the process of an untendentious analysis with a severely disturbed human being, a therapeutic enterprise that does not leave the psychic substance even of the analyst unaffected. In the case of this patient, the curiosity incidentally centered on the fact that her obsessional neurosis had developed relatively suddenly out of a prior anxiety hysteria, which for its part had been the response to a traumatic experience; Freud presumed that the case might therefore perhaps "claim to be looked upon like a bilingual document and to show how an identical content could be expressed by the two neuroses in different languages"[18]—an expectation which, however, was not borne out during the course of the treatment.

The passage omitted from the printed version also documents a refreshing willingness to call a therapeutic failure such without any ifs and buts. Finally, it affords further evidence of the fact, which Freud never denied, that he was primarily a researcher and only secondarily a therapist and that he needed the work with his patients mainly in order to deepen his insights into the unconscious inner world and to allow him to develop psychoanalytic theories further. In a letter to Jung dated 17 December 1911, he writes quite bluntly, and to our present way of thinking all too apodictically in view of the relative brevity of the treatment, that the patient is now "beyond any possibility of therapy, but it is still her duty to sacrifice herself to science."[19] Freud may well have felt this unambiguous and no doubt also one-sided research orientation to be conflictual, and this may be one reason that Jung's attempt to entice his patient away occurred to him; furthermore, the interpretation of this interference using concepts from *Totem and Taboo* signals the autobiographical dimension, referred to earlier,[20] of the phylogenetic construction of the murder of the primal father as well as the nagging, easily activated, and still highly ambivalent memory of the once preferred disciple and the break with him.

However, light also falls on the process of research itself, in particular on Freud's specific approach to the abundance of material that accrued to him daily from his clinical work. For if we follow his clue that the patient presented him with the explanation of some lies told by children and set him on the track of the disposition to obsessional neurosis, and if we refer to the relevant papers, published as far back as in 1913—"Two Lies Told by Children," that short study of children lying for reasons of incestuous love,

[18]1913*i*, p. 319.
[19]1974*a*, p. 474.
[20]Cf. above, p. 125.

and "The Disposition to Obsessional Neurosis," the innovative theoretical paper that introduced the concept of the anal-sadistic phase—we are surprised to reencounter the same patient, whose picture is now unexpectedly completed in all its subtle detail like a coarse-grained image that suddenly snaps into much finer resolution.[21] Or, seen from a different perspective, the hitherto concealed passage reveals afresh the architecture of material spanning the oeuvre as a whole, as described in the chapter on the notes: three thematically unrelated texts from different periods share a clinical foundation in one and the same analysis.[22]

However, this technique of selective, single-aspect utilization of clinical material served another purpose as well. If Freud presented to the public only carefully isolated fragments of those "great art works of psychic nature,"[23] he could protect patients' identities better than by publishing compact and more or less complete case histories. This method of depiction can to some extent already be seen in *The Interpretation of Dreams*, in which he used it for self-disguise. Here, Freud analyzes his own major exemplary dreams not as a rule in one go, each in effect as a unity: rather, he spreads their interpretation throughout the book, taking up one element after another of the individual dreams, scattered in often widely separated passages, and then using them as appropriate to elucidate one or other of the mechanisms of dream formation. In this way the dreamer—namely, himself—can remain in the background or at least out of the focus of the reader's attention.[24]

Freud manifestly felt it incumbent on him thus to protect in particular the patients mentioned in the preliminary report, and this was surely a motivating factor in the decision not to publish it. After all, on 15 February 1925 he was still explicitly emphasizing: "[. . .] there is the insuperable obstacle of the limitation of medical discretion, which would be seriously impaired by publishing data from the life stories of two of my patients. It is the very sensation this publication would cause [owing to the scandalous subject of telepathy] that imposes reserve as a duty; distortions are not possible, nor would any sort of weakening help. If fate brings about the

---

[21]Cf. 1913g, p. 307f., and 1913i, p. 319f.

[22]Incidentally, the Freud-Binswanger correspondence (1992a, p. 148ff.) shows that this patient also plays a part in a fourth of Freud's works, namely, in the paper "An Evidential Dream," which also dates from 1913, although she appears here not primarily as a patient but as a clever interpreter of her nurse's dream, thereby stimulating Freud to penetrate more deeply into this dream interpretation. She had been in contact with Binswanger since 1915 and spent several periods as an inpatient at his Bellevue Sanatorium in Kreuzlingen in the ensuing years; as a result, the two doctors had occasion to correspond with each other about her many times.

[23]1974a, p. 238.

[24]Cf. Grubrich-Simitis, 1971, p. 328f.

death of the two people [. . .] before my own death, the obstacle would vanish."[25]

The editors of the *Gesammelte Werke* seem to have made these fundamental reservations of Freud's their own when they left out an even longer passage from the text of the preliminary report's manuscript. It belongs in the vignette, placed at the end "by way of appendix,"[26] on a patient in whose life Rafael Schermann, a graphologist renowned in Vienna at the time, had played a part. It was said of this miracle man that, given a sample of someone's handwriting, he could use it not only to read that person's character but also to make predictions "which later come true."[27] Freud's account in the manuscript begins with the exact date "In the y[ear] 1920," whereas the printed version has "A few years ago."[28] The next three sentences, in which Freud reports that a particularly likable young man had turned to him for help, substantially correspond to the published version; however, we learn in addition that the subject, who was involved "with one of the best known *demi-mondaines*,"[29] had been "about 35 y[ears]" old. Following the third sentence, in which Freud describes the success of the treatment—the analysand was set free from this entanglement and contracted a respectable marriage—that is, quite a bit before he first mentions Schermann's role in the patient's life—the following lengthy passage is to be found in the manuscript:

> His case is so interesting that I would crave your attention for it independently of occultism. A person of demonic passion and energy, irresistible to women, well-liked and esteemed among men, he enjoys the reputation of a brilliant financier, and rose during the war from the position of a subordinate official to rank and fortune. The youngest child of a very ordinary family[,] he developed an exceptionally powerful affection for his mother from infancy. His boyhood was unhappy; when he was 14 y[ears] old, one of his much older brothers married[,] and he transferred a passionate love to his young and beautiful sister-in-law, who at first treated him as a child. But he became more and more demanding as a lover, and, at the age of 17, unable to gain a hearing from his sister-in-law and having failed his examinations at business school—i.e., being spurned by both man and woman—he fired a bullet into his cardiac region and hovered for months between life and death. After this suicide attempt and the death of his mother which followed

---

[25]Cf. Jones, 1957, p. 420 [translation slightly modified].
[26]1941d, p. 181.
[27]Ibid., p. 191.
[28]Ibid.
[29]Ibid.

soon after[,] he ultimately succeeded in conquering his beloved, who was 6 y[ears] older than himself. He lived in this brother's house and became the second husband of the young woman, with whom he gradually displaced the first[,] the father of her children. So 10 y[ears] ago[,] when he was 25 y[ears] old, he began to chafe at the bit in this relationship, whereas she, the aging woman[,] clung to him more and more tenderly. Characteristically, the turning point resulted from jealousy, as he watched her feed her last boy, who, incidentally, was by her account his child, because this revived in him the repressed memory of the same situation with his own mother. He now took other women as mistresses, whom he soon discarded again, until he came upon that cocotte, in whose toils he became entangled. She was, as it happens, the official sweetheart of one of his friends, whom he therefore had to deceive. The whole time he continued his intimate relations with his sister-in-law, who was also the confidante of his love affairs, which caused her great suffering.

This highly specific, quasi-incestuous constellation, the novelettish description of which betrays Freud's delight in the unusual story of his patient's love, was excised by the editors in its entirety. They then also had to make drastic changes to the structure of the rest of the paragraph and of the next two paragraphs,[30] in which Freud discusses Schermann's prophecies of the behavior of the demimondaine. Phrases and whole sentences were added, relationships were retouched—for example, the sister-in-law appears in the more harmless guise of the "woman he had loved since his youth"—dates are glossed over, and so on.

Extensive variants of this kind raise two questions: why did the editors of the posthumous writings introduce these changes at all in the preparation of the printed version of the preliminary report, and why did they do so tacitly—that is, without informing the reader in detail in editorial commentaries? The "editors' foreword" to the seventeenth volume mentions only "a very few omissions."[31] Some will be quick to voice the stock suspicion that the editors wished, in obedience to their idealizing tendency, to conceal something felt to be detrimental to Freud. Because none of the editors is still alive, we can admittedly do no more than speculate on the true reasons, but they are likely to have been at once simpler and more complex.

As stated in part I, the relevant volume of the *Gesammelte Werke* in any case appeared with a meager editorial apparatus in adverse circumstances in the midst of the Second World War. Moreover, those who produced this

[30]1941*d*, pp. 191 and 192.
[31]P. viii.

complete edition of Freud, put together in exile in London, were unfamiliar with the rules of critical editing. When they came across the manuscript of the preliminary report among the few papers left behind after Freud's death, they seem to have asked themselves what the author himself would have altered had he after all prepared this manuscript for publication. From the vantage point of today, too, we may legitimately assume that Freud, in this hypothetical case, would not only have given the preliminary report an official title, but also would have allowed for the change in his intended public—and probably much more decisively than the editors did. The idea that he was now addressing himself no longer to the restricted group of his intimates but to a larger anonymous readership would no doubt have had as one of its consequences the deletion or at least abbreviation of the two passages quoted.

At any rate, Freud would have toned down the spontaneity appropriate to an exchange of ideas with friends, which characterizes the first piece in particular. The sentences about Jung, which if anything disturb the flow of his argument, would surely have been omitted. The account of the entice-ment episode seems to have had the sole function of indirectly reminding his friends of the conditions under which the committee was formed—that is, the secessions. The preliminary report even begins with an explicit mention of the attacks by Adler and Jung on psychoanalysis. In other words, Freud manifestly wished to take advantage of the rare opportunity of having all six members of the committee together in one place for the purpose of subtly reinforcing its coherence as a group. The use of figures of thought from *Totem and Taboo* may in addition have recalled to the memory of the six listeners that that book, like the committee itself, had come into being at the time of the dispute with Jung and that on one of its many levels of meaning it actually represented a mythologization of that historical conflict. Individual members of the committee may perhaps also have perceived the silent affin-ity for Jung, observable in the ironically equivocal formulation of the "affec-tionate" son and indeed in the choice of this particular subject, as occultism was after all one of Jung's hobbyhorses.[32] All these hints and allusions would have escaped the general reader or confused him, as signs that the author was digressing.

Again, in order not to give the impression of wandering from his sub-ject, Freud would no doubt also have omitted the other passage, the account of the life and loves of that patient "of demonic passion" for whom he wished to secure his friends' attention—as he himself emphasizes, *indepen-*

---

[32]The Freud-Ferenczi correspondence shows that Jung had indeed been initiated into the exchange of ideas on the subject of telepathy at an early date; this fact too had been unknown to the other members of the committee.

dently of occultism.[33] Yet considerations of discretion alone would have dictated its deletion, as the patient, in his mid-fifties in 1941, would still have been identifiable in Vienna from his striking biography. When Freud set down the text of the printed version of a part of his preliminary report in the form of the thirtieth of the *New Introductory Lectures* in 1932, he returned to this patient who so fascinated him.[34] On that occasion he introduced certain disguises to the story of his life, in particular playing down the delicacy of the constellation by substituting an unspecified "young woman" for the sister-in-law. In this way he prevented the reader from fully understanding that the family of origin was meant in the following sentence at the end of the vignette: "Incidentally, my patient succeeded, with the help of analysis, in finding an object for his love outside the magic circle in which he had been spellbound."[35] As we can now see, the editors of the *Gesammelte Werke*, in their introduction of variants into this text, took the author's *own* camouflaging measures as their guide, especially in their replacement of the sister-in-law by a "woman he had loved since his youth."

As a model for their editorial activity, they could also draw upon another example of the way Freud emended a part of the manuscript from the same context before publishing it in the thirtieth of the *New Introductory Lectures*. Toward the end of the second vignette, the following passage features in the preliminary report: "The two cases that I have reported to you are both concerned with unfulfilled prophecies. Observations of this kind, in my opinion, can provide the best material on the question of thought-transference [. . .]. I had also intended to bring you an example based on material of another kind—a case in which a patient of a special sort talked during one session of things which touched in the most remarkable way on an experience which I had had myself immediately before. But I can now give you visible proof of the fact that I discussed the subject of occultism under the pressure of the greatest resistance. When, while I was at Gastein, I looked out the notes which I had put together and brought with me for the purpose of this paper, the sheet on which I had noted down this last observation was not there [. . .]. Nothing can be done against such a clear resistance. I must ask you to excuse me for omitting this case, for I cannot make the loss good from memory."[36] On his return from the trip to the Harz, however, Freud did write up this example, under the title "Post-

[33]From our present-day vantage point, we may wonder whether Freud included this digression in the address to the members of the committee because he considered the patient's extraordinarily strong bond to the preoedipal mother of earliest infancy and the envy of the breast to be noteworthy and to merit discussion.

[34]1933*a*, p. 43ff.

[35]Ibid., p. 47.

[36]1941*d*, p. 190.

script," starting with the sentence: "Here is the report, omitted on account of resistance, of a case of thought induction from analytic practice."[37]

The editors of the *Gesammelte Werke* comment laconically in their preliminary note to "Psycho-Analysis and Telepathy": "It [the postscript] was included in the 'Lectures' and is therefore not reproduced here."[38] They are referring to the complicated vignette organized around the associative strings *Forsyth-Forsyte-foresight-Vorsicht* and *Freud-Freund*. Comparison of the seven-page manuscript with the printed version of the relevant text in the *New Introductory Lectures*[39] shows that Freud subjected the original wording to several stages of revision before integrating its content into the fair copy of the thirtieth lecture. I do not wish to discuss these numerous author's variants in detail here, in the chapter on editorial variants, but shall merely give a cursory description. Freud honed his style, shortened or varied his text for reasons of discretion, toned down some aspects and pointed others up; he clothed certain parts of his narrative in more luxuriant garb, updated it, and took account of the change of intended audience; and he attempted, with a modicum of success, to clarify the complicated sequence of events of the vignette by changing the order of its elements, and so on. Many of the interventions are reminiscent of the metamorphoses to which Freud customarily subjected his texts during the transition from draft to fair copy—that is, from their private to their public wording.

We do not know whether the editors reconstructed this process of transformation at the time. There is, however, no doubt that Freud, in preparing the text of the postscript for publication in the *New Introductory Lectures* at the beginning of the 1930s, revised it on the whole more rigorously than the editors, about a decade later, did the preliminary report for publication in the context of the *Schriften aus dem Nachlass 1892–1938* [the collection of posthumous writings from the period 1892–1938]. They plainly attempted to incorporate the manuscript of the preliminary report in the canon of the works that Freud had himself conveyed to the press. Working so to speak in his place, they endeavored to apply his criteria at least in the matter of protecting patients' privacy.

Among the late texts dating from 1938, the posthumous printed version of the short innovative paper "Die Ichspaltung im Abwehrvorgang" ["Splitting of the Ego in the Process of Defense"], which deals with alterations of the ego and in particular the formation of that "rift in the ego which never

---

[37]In the Sigmund Freud Collection, the manuscript is currently (i.e., in early 1992, at the time of my last visit to the Library of Congress) included among the texts dating from 1933 [1932], following the manuscript of the obituary of Sándor Ferenczi.

[38]1941*d*, p. 26 [in G. W. 17].

[39]1933*a*, pp. 48–54.

heals but which increases as time goes on,"[40] exhibits only a few variants from the manuscript. In the second sentence of the manuscript, set down, according to the date written on it, on 2 January 1938, the editors have overlooked a "doch" [after all] and omitted it from the published text: in his opening sentence Freud notes an uncertainty, that of not knowing whether what he has to say should be regarded as "something long familiar and obvious or as something entirely new and puzzling"; this he then qualifies with the somewhat defiant statement: "But I am *after all*[41] inclined to think the latter." The printed version of the paper ends with a line of dots, suggesting to the reader that it was unfinished. By contrast, the manuscript—which consists of a double sheet divided into four pages of writing—ends at the foot of the fourth page, literally filling the space down to the last millimeter, so that Freud had to place the final period *underneath* the last letter. There are no further dots; neither, however, is there any sign of the fermata with which he was accustomed to mark the end of his manuscripts, at least in the case of the fair copies. The course of his argument does not preclude the possibility that the manuscript originally consisted of more than four pages; if so, the remainder is lost.

The changes made by the editors of the seventeenth volume of the *Gesammelte Werke* to the longest and most important of the works left behind after Freud's death, the *Abriss der Psychoanalyse* [*An Outline of Psycho-Analysis*], are much more far-reaching. In a brief preliminary note they comment only that this contribution must be deemed "unfinished" and that in particular the third chapter has been "set down in the form of catchwords using many abbreviations" and had been "expanded into full sentences" by the editors.[42] They also do not conceal the fact that they were responsible for the addition of the title of the first part, "Die Natur des Psychischen,"[43] in fact using a formulation from "Some Elementary Lessons in Psycho-Analysis," the text of which they evidently saw as a later version of the *Outline*.[44] In reality, however, many more changes to the original wording were made tacitly.

In terms of the characteristic stages of the genesis of Freud's texts—

[40]1940e [1938], p. 276.

[41]My emphasis. (P. 275.)

[42]1940a [1938], p. 64 [in G. W. 17].

[43][*Translator's note*: Strachey's title in the *Standard Edition* is "The Mind and its Workings"—1940a (1938), p. 139.]

[44]Incidentally, the text of the editorial commentary corresponds substantially to the preliminary note by the editors (p. 5) that introduced the first publication of the *Abriss* in the *Internationale Zeitschrift für Psychoanalyse und Imago* (1940, vol. 25, pp. 7–67). At one point (p. 21), the editors have here even added extensive excerpts from the "Elementary Lessons" as a note.

First page of the *Abriss der Psychoanalyse* [*An Outline of Psycho-Analysis*]. [11.2]

notes, drafts, fair copies—the general tendency of the editors' activity could be described as follows: without so declaring and probably also without realizing it, they were attempting to make a fair copy from a draft. At the time, it seems to have been completely unknown that Freud's fair copies stemmed from earlier stages already fixed in writing. Indeed, in his editor's note to the reproduction of the *Outline* in the *Standard Edition*, James Strachey wrote as late as in 1964: "The manuscript of this whole work is written out in an unusually abbreviated form."[45] This assessment is valid only on the assumption that it was a fair copy; the many abbreviations are in fact by no means unusual for the manuscript of a draft. Examination of the manuscript proves beyond a shadow of a doubt that only the draft of the *Abriss der Psychoanalyse* [*An Outline of Psycho-Analysis*] has survived. Freud did not live to compose the fair copy—that is, to expand the formulation to the stage of a text ready for setting. At any rate, the sheets do not bear the hallmark of other draft manuscripts, the successive diagonal crossings out made paragraph by paragraph by the author, to indicate how far he had advanced, following the consistent thread of the draft, in the production of the fair copy.

But it is also conceivable that he never intended the work for publication. According to the date written on the first sheet, the draft of the *Outline* was begun on "22/7";[46] the author is said to have stopped writing at the beginning of September 1938, when he had to undergo another operation on his jaw. In a letter to his daughter Anna dated 3 August 1938, he had given a kind of interim account of his progress in writing: "My vacation work is proving to be an entertaining occupation. It has already grown to a length of 26 pages, and will be divided into three parts. General aspects— the practical task—the theoretical yield. I am still maintaining the fiction that it does not need to be printed."

The draftlike character of the entire manuscript, which ultimately comprised sixty-six pages,[47] is manifest; however, passages that are almost fully written out stand alongside more or less drastically abbreviated ones. Where Freud is substantially breaking new ground and reporting his latest discoveries, as in the eighth chapter, which once again deals with the relationship of the ego to the outside world, with the splitting of the ego, disavowal, and fetishism, the sentences tend to be more complete, whereas

[45]Strachey, 1964b, p. 141f.

[46]Cf. facsimile 11.2 and fig. 11.1, which, according to Ernst Freud, shows Freud in the act of writing the *Abriss* [*Outline*]. At this time, Freud was still working at his temporary London residence, 39 Elsworthy Road, while waiting to move into the house at 20 Maresfield Gardens.

[47]Pages 5 to 14 are missing from the manuscript, which consists of double-size sheets comprising four pages covered with writing. However, these pages are included in a microfilm of the manuscripts prepared in London while Anna Freud was still alive.

Freud writing the *Abriss* [*Outline*] in 1938.　　　　[11.1]

abbreviations clearly predominate where his argument is proceeding along familiar lines.

The editors' assertion that the *Abriss* [*Outline*] remained "unfinished" is accurate only in the sense that Freud never reached the stage of composing the fair copy. As to the draft itself, the manuscript does not show any sign of an intention on Freud's part to continue it. It ends with the last six lines at the top of the sixty-sixth page and does not exhibit the dashes incorporated by the editors into the printed version, which suggest that he did so intend. My view is that the manuscript that has come down to us comprises the *complete* draft of the *Outline*—with a beginning, middle, and end. Neither the brevity of the final, ninth chapter nor the conciseness of the third part argues against this conception; both characteristics may have misled the editors into assuming that the manuscript was incomplete—yet the first three chapters are almost as short as the last, and the second part, like the third, comprises only two chapters.

As to the introduction of variants, massive interventions on the part of the editors are already evident in the structure of the opening passage. When the work was first published in 1940 in the combined periodical *Internationale Zeitschrift für Psychoanalyse und Imago*, brought out in exile in London, the editors—predominantly the persons who also edited the *Gesammelte Werke*—declared these lines to be a "Vorwort" ["Preface"], although there is no indication in the manuscript that the author intended them as such. On the other hand, again on the first page of the manuscript, they omitted a kind of subtitle that Freud included after the first paragraph of the first chapter: "Zwei Voraussetz[un]gen" ["Two Conditions"]. When the *Abriss* was reprinted a year later in the seventeenth volume of the *Gesammelte Werke*, the passage marked "Vorwort" ["Preface"] was dropped without any reason being given—perhaps because it had not been specifically mentioned in the table of contents of the *Zeitschrift*.[48]

To provide the reader with a graphic impression of the original diction of the *Outline* and to illustrate the nature of the alterations introduced at the various stages of editing, both versions of the relevant passage are reproduced below. First, the manuscript:

Dieses kleine Buch—Schrift—will die	This little book—work—is intended to bring together the
Lehrsätze der ΨA in knappster—gedrängt-	tenets of ΨA in [the] briefest—most concise

---

[48]P. 7. It was made available again in the G. W. *Nachtragsband* [supplementary volume] in 1987 (p. 749 [*S. E.* 23, p. 144]), albeit in the "preface" version of the first publication: because the supplementary volume had not been conceived as part of a historical-critical edition, I had not at the time consulted the manuscript of the *Abriss*.

ester—Form u in entschiedendster gleichsam dogmatisch Fassung zusam̃enstellen, zum Ausdruck bringen.
—form & in the most unequivocal as it were dogmatically terms.

Catechism zu verwerfen, weil Form von Frage u Antwort hat.
Catechism to be rejected because has form of question & answer.

Glauben zu fordern u Uberzeug[un]gen zu wecken, liegt nicht in seiner Absicht selbstverständlich begreiflicher Weise
Intention not to compel belief & arouse conviction naturally understandably

Die Behaupt[un]gen—Aufstellungen— der ΨA
The assertions—teachings—of ΨA

ruhen auf einer unabsehbaren Fülle von
are based on an incalculable number of

Beobachtungen (u Erfahrungen), und nur
observations (& experiences), and only someone

wer diese Beobacht[un]g an sich u anderen
who has repeated these observation[s] on himself & others

wiederholt, hat den Weg zu einem eigenen Urteil eingeschlagen.
is in a position to arrive at a judgment of his own upon it.

The passage as first published in 1940 reads as follows:[49]

Preface

The aim of this brief work is to bring together the tenets of psychoanalysis and to state them, as it were, dogmatically—in the most concise form and in the most unequivocal terms. Its intention is naturally not to compel belief or to arouse conviction.

The teachings of psychoanalysis are based on an incalculable number of observations and experiences, and only someone who has repeated those observations on himself and on others is in a position to arrive at a judgment of his own upon it.

As a comparison of the two texts shows, the editors have by no means confined themselves to the expansion of abbreviations and the completion of punctuation. All the tentative gropings of the original wording—in particular, the trying out of synonyms—have been sacrificed to rigorous editorial smoothing. To judge from other Freud texts of which the fair copies have been preserved, the author would no doubt have wished to incorporate one or another combination of words with similar meanings—for example, "in [the] briefest—most concise—form"—in the final version of the *Out-*

[49]P. 8 (of the first edition) [*S. E.* 23, p. 144].

line. The omission of the two lines "Catechism to be rejected because has form of question & answer," deleted without comment from the opening passage, almost gives rise to a lacuna in Freud's argument. His declared aim of bringing together the tenets of psychoanalysis, "as it were, dogmatically," for a moment led him by association close to the sphere of instruction in religious belief—specifically, of the instruction manual of the Christian religion, in which the material is presented in the form of alternating questions and answers. But by stressing the empirical provenance of psychoanalytic theories he turns away abruptly from this analogy in his next step. The deletion of the allusion to the catechism removes a link in the chain of comparison. We may recall an earlier recourse to this simile at the end of *Beyond the Pleasure Principle*: "Only believers, who demand that science shall be a substitute for the catechism they have given up, will blame an investigator for developing or even transforming his views."[50]

In my essay on Freud's study of Moses,[51] I attempted to justify the assumption that one of the reasons Freud wrote the two texts conceived as summae of his life's work, the *Outline* and the "Elementary Lessons," may have been his penetrating identification with Moses and his concern that psychoanalysis might not survive the Nazi persecution. As he worked on *Moses and Monotheism*, a sequence of essays that stems from the same late period of his creativity, he may again have turned to the study of the Torah. In the "Israelitische Bibel," the Jewish Bible used by Freud as a child, the exegete Ludwig Philippson describes in his concluding commentary on the Fifth Book of Moses how the founder of the religion set about "a final powerful inculcation of the Law" before his death. "The scattered doctrine and laws had to be gathered into a clear, concise, summary presentation"— so Philippson too used a sequence of synonyms. Parallel formulations to the expressions used by the Bible commentator can be found in the opening passage of the "Elementary Lessons";[52] and a perusal of the manuscript shows that this is also true of the *Outline*. Of course, Freud at once distances himself emphatically from the religious analogy in both cases.

The editors' approach to the opening section of the *Abriss* is paradigmatic of the editorial style applied to the entire text and in particular to the abbreviated passages. The characteristic features of trial thinking and formulating—that is, of a draft—have substantially disappeared in the process of retouching: strings of synonyms have been curtailed, at first sight confusing parentheses deleted, and telling question marks expunged, although the author manifestly used them to record his doubts. Some of the editorial

[50]1920g, p. 64.
[51]Grubrich-Simitis, 1991, p. 72f.; revised 1994 edition p. 73f.
[52]Ibid.

omissions produce the effect of abstraction. For instance, the following passage appears in the manuscript of the second chapter, on the theory of instinctual drives: "In biological functions the two basic drives operate against each other or combine with each other. Thus, the act of eating is a destruction of the object with the final aim of incorporating it, including cannibalism, and the sexual act is an act of aggression with the purpose of the most intimate union."[53] In the printed version,[54] the parenthetic phrase "including cannibalism" is missing, although it illustrates for the reader in concrete, so to speak bloodcurdling, terms the combination of the two instinctual drives. However, the capacity the aged author still had for amazed enthusiasm is sometimes also robbed of its spontaneous expression. In the fourth chapter, on psychical qualities, the beginning of the second paragraph reads as follows in the manuscript: "Den Ausgang für diese Untersuch[un]g giebt die einzig dastehende, jeder Erklär[un]g u Beschreib[un]g trotzende Tatsache des Bewusstseins, unvergleichliche" ["The starting-point for this investigation is provided by the unique fact which defies all explanation or description—the fact of consciousness, without parallel"]. The word "unvergleichliche" ["without parallel"], which is given exclamatory status by its eccentric position, is overzealously integrated in the printed version, the synonymous formulation at the same time being eliminated: "Den Ausgang für diese Untersuchung gibt die unvergleichliche, jeder Erklärung und Beschreibung trotzende Tatsache des Bewusstseins" ["The starting-point for this investigation is provided by a fact without parallel, which defies all explanation or description—the fact of consciousness"].[55] The traces of Freud's self-correction have also been obliterated—as when he catches himself in the act of a parapraxis: for instance, more than once he wrote "Ich" ["ego"] instead of "Es" ["id"].

Besides such smoothing operations, the editors made certain structuring interventions: they started new paragraphs where these are manifestly not marked in the manuscript; they altered the positions not only of words but also of phrases and sentences; they completed or varied the punctuation; and they relegated some passages to a subordinate rank by having them printed as footnotes, although the author had included them in the run of the text.

All these variants were no doubt introduced with the intention of enhancing the readability of the *Outline* or of making it readable in the first place. The latter consideration applies in particular to the first three paragraphs of the third chapter, on the development of the sexual function,

[53]Page 5.
[54]1940*a*, p. 149.
[55]Ibid., p. 157.

which are recorded only in the form of a small number of isolated word fragments. These contractions would surely have sufficed the author as signposts for the formulation of the fair copy; however, they are too demanding for the expansion capacity of anyone not unusually familiar with Freud's thought. Incidentally, the first sentence of the third chapter reads as follows in the manuscript: "The first erotogenic zone to make libidinal demands on the mind is the mouth." Freud deleted it and did not return to this subject until the fourth paragraph of the chapter. He therefore in effect interrupted himself and placed the three introductory paragraphs before this statement. One reason he noted them with such extreme conciseness may have been that he wanted to return as quickly as possible to the train of thought that was his main concern.

All in all, there can be little doubt that, in the course of their work and in particular in the filling of gaps, the editors did their best to follow Freud's stipulations faithfully and to limit the risk of misinterpretations.[56] Indeed, these cannot be ruled out, especially in passages that admit of more than one reading. Perhaps the main shortcoming to be entered on the debit side of the emended version is that it tends to obscure the relationship, alluded to above, between Freud's essays on Moses on the one hand and the late writings of 1938 on the other.

As stated, in "Splitting of the Ego in the Process of Defense," Freud held his comments on the problem of traumatic alterations of the ego to be "something entirely new and puzzling" rather than "something long familiar and obvious."[57] At the end of the thematically related eighth chapter of the *Outline*, on the other hand, he expresses a view that has manifestly changed in the interim: "The facts of this splitting of the ego, which we have just described, are neither so new nor so strange as they may at first appear."[58] In the following sentences of this final paragraph of the chapter, he draws these phenomena closer to the general characteristics of neurosis, thereby blurring the differences, accentuated in the earlier study, between neurotic and psychotic defenses.

In chapter 10, "First Versions," I indicated how my earlier study of the Moses manuscripts[59] led me to the reconstruction that this book had its origins in a severe inner crisis triggered by the Nazi persecution. I argued

[56]This quite apart from the fact that there were occasional inadvertent omissions, misreadings, and erroneous, unnecessary, overpedantic, or otherwise willful corrections and/or additions.

[57]1940e [1938], p. 275.

[58]1940a, p. 204. The manuscript incidentally shows that Freud originally wanted to begin the final chapter, "The Internal World," with this sentence, but then deleted the chapter heading and repeated it only at the end of that paragraph.

[59]Grubrich-Simitis, 1991.

that the experience of helpless dependence and of the threat of death had touched upon an early infantile trauma[60] in Freud and set in train a regressive process. During the course of this late period of distress, which Freud succeeded in overcoming through self-analysis and by virtue of the saving emigration, he had for the first time gained deep insights into archaic forms of defense; the self-curative effects of this creativity were comparable in their drama with the young Freud's crisis at the end of the previous century that had occasioned the beginning of his self-analysis and accelerated the discovery of unconscious psychic processes. At any rate, the late findings on traumatic alterations of the ego and the defensive process of splitting make up the substance of the truly innovative passages in the works dating from 1938.

The manuscript of the last few paragraphs of the eighth chapter of the *Outline* in particular still seems to betray, in many a slip of the pen, something of the effort, confusion, not to say terror of that consuming process of self-exploration. For instance, the split is explained as follows in the published version: "Two psychical attitudes have been formed instead of a single one—one, the normal one, which takes account of reality, and another which under the influence of the instincts detaches the ego from reality. The two exist alongside of each other. The issue depends on their relative strength. If the second ["die letztere"] is or becomes the stronger, the necessary precondition for a psychosis is present. If the relation is reversed, then there is an apparent cure of the delusional disorder."[61] In the penultimate sentence, the manuscript has the clearly legible words "die erstere" [the first] instead of "die letztere" [the second], a slip that Freud neither noticed nor corrected.

After his last operation, Freud began on "20/X. 38" to set down "Some Elementary Lessons in Psycho-Analysis." He wrote only the title in English, as if he now wished to address himself to readers in the country where he had found asylum. The manuscript is written on both sides of two double sheets, the pages of which Freud numbered in blue pencil. Although some of the ideas from the *Outline* recur in its seven pages, it is not possible to claim them as a second version of that work. Certain structural resemblances— the concise and summary character of both texts—can indeed not be overlooked. Unlike the *Outline*, however, Freud left this, the last of all his works, in fully formulated sentences. Although a centered horizontal line appears at the foot of the seventh page of the manuscript,[62] there is reason to believe that he did not stop at this point because he had come to the end, but that he

[60]As briefly outlined above on page 78.
[61]1940*a*, p. 202.
[62]Cf. facsimile 11.3.

Last page of "Some Elementary Lessons in Psycho-Analysis."   [11.3]

broke off intentionally and definitively—literally drawing the final stroke beneath his monumental lifework as an author in the fatigue of approaching death, even if the clarity and freedom of his argument betray nothing of his physical affliction. The eighth page, which remained blank, had been numbered in advance. In any case, the beginning of the "Elementary Lessons," with its detailed discussion of the advantages and disadvantages of the genetic and dogmatic methods respectively of portraying a field of knowledge, would lead us to expect a much more comprehensive study.

This fragment survives in effect as copy ready for the typesetter, and for this reason the variants introduced by the editors are, not surprisingly, far less numerous and drastic than in the *Outline*. They are confined to some adjustments of spelling, punctuation, and paragraphing. There are also a few conspicuous errors of transcription. The two most prominent of these are as follows: where the published version[63] has "Moralbesetzungen" [moral cathexes], the manuscript reads "Voraussetzungen" [conditions]; and "Erklärung" [explanation] in the former is "Entscheidung" [decision] in the latter. Otherwise, the manuscript nowhere departs essentially from the familiar printed version.

---

[63]1940*b* [1938], pp. 282 and 284, respectively.

12 UNPUBLISHED MATERIAL

It is clear from the account given so far that Freud was really not one of those authors who produced work to be put away in a drawer for posterity. He wrote with the aim of immediate publication. This means that all the unpublished material mentioned or quoted in chapters 6 to 11 was not intended for publication. Indeed, among the manuscripts belonging to the context of Freud's oeuvre, there are only a small number of brief documents a reading of which arouses the impression that he wrote them with the clear intention of bringing them before the public, but that this intention was frustrated, in each case for unknown reasons.

These items include first of all[1] a manifestly unpublished appreciation of Max Eitingon, whose context is uncertain:

> The present text, which reports on the foundation and achievements of the Berlin Psychoanalytic Policlinic, also has another, more intimate purpose. It is intended as a tribute to Dr Max Eitingon, the current President of the "International Psychoanalytical Association," who established this institute some years ago from his own resources and has since maintained and directed it by his own efforts. The occasion for this tribute was the circumstance that Eitingon, in the 50th year of his life, has attained the pinnacle of human existence; the decisive factor in his friends' choice of such a publication was the consideration that the modesty of this reserved man would have rejected any other celebration. Eitingon, although thoroughly versed in psychoanalysis, an experienced therapist and a thinker of certain judgment, has denied himself—and us—the possibility of enriching the analytic literature through his contributions, but he has other, hardly less important

---

[1] In the original German edition of this book the first piece mentioned was the manuscript of a two-page "Bibliography" with commentary, in which Freud, also listing translations of his writings, records with tangible pride the fact that his work has now achieved world renown. This bibliography, which extends as far as 1923, at first seemed to be unpublished, and I presented some considerations on the place to which it should be assigned. When I recently succeeded in obtaining a copy of the first edition of the "Selbstdarstellung" [An Auto-biographical Study], which appeared in the series Die Medizin der Gegenwart in Selbstdarstellungen ["Contemporary Medicine in Self-Portrayals"], edited by L. R. Grote (Leipzig: Verlag Felix Meiner, 1925), this list was in fact found to be reproduced at the end of Freud's "Selbstdarstellung" (page 52). Although it was never reprinted in the many subsequent editions of this work, it can now therefore no longer be counted among the "unpublished material."

achievements to his credit. As Uhland wrote in his poem "König Karls Meerfahrt" ["The Voyage of King Charles"]:

> 'Der König Karl am Steuer sass;
> Der hat kein Wort gesprochen,
> Er lenkt das Schiff mit festem Mass,
> Bis sich der Sturm gebrochen.'[2]

It did not seem essential for outsiders to learn of this activity on Eitingon's part; but once at least we must express a public word of thanks to him.

Sigm. Freud

Eitingon was born in 1881. This means that the article, which was explicitly intended as a public tribute and hence for publication, must have been composed about 1930/31. This in turn suggests that it might be Freud's contribution to the commemorative publication dedicated to Eitingon entitled *Zehn Jahre Berliner Psychoanalytisches Institut (Poliklinik und Lehranstalt)* [Ten Years of the Berlin Psychoanalytic Institute (Policlinic and Training Institution)], edited by the German Psychoanalytic Society and published in 1930 by the Internationaler Psychoanalytischer Verlag in Vienna. Now this Festschrift does indeed contain a preface by Freud.[3] However, the emphasis is different: it is the institute rather than the figure of Eitingon that is its principal subject. Yet some of the formulations in the text quoted above also appear verbatim in the published "Preface." Could it be that Eitingon got wind of the projected more intimate appreciation and thwarted it before it reached the stage of publication? At any rate, the fact that his fiftieth birthday came only in 1931 is not inconsistent with this attempt to place the article: when the tribute appeared, its subject was in the fiftieth year of his life. The matter may one day be clarified when more of the correspondences have been disclosed.[4]

But the most important of the documents which remained unpublished although intended by the author for publication is a manuscript from the context of *The Question of Lay Analysis*. This is not the long passage, quoted and discussed in the chapter on the variants, from the Postscript ["Nachtwort"] to *The Question of Lay Analysis* dating from 1927, in which Freud vents his opinions on the situation of lay analysis in the United States and which was ultimately suppressed for tactical reasons. Although

---

[2][Translation: King Charles sat at the helm, / Saying not a word; / He steered the ship with measure firm, / Till the breaking of the storm.]

[3]1930*b*.

[4]The "Kürzeste Chronik" contains the following entry dated 4 November 1929: "Preface for Eitingon" (1976*m*, p. 2 of the complete publication [English text]).

the one-and-a-half-page manuscript has a very similar title, "Nachschrift zur Frage der Laienanalyse" ["Postscript to the Question of Lay Analysis"], the second line of the title mentions the date "(1935)." The relevant bundle of documents includes two further pages; under the heading "Noten zur Laienanalyse" ["Notes for Lay Analysis"], Freud set down the text of a total of seven footnotes, their position indicated in each case by a page number and a sentence or phrase in English.

A perusal of the first English-language edition of the work on lay analysis—*The Problem of Lay-Analyses*—published by Brentano in New York in 1927, confirms unequivocally that Freud's indications of the location of the footnotes relate to this edition. The wording of the postscript itself, too, bears out the assumption that these are author's additions for a planned reissue of the first American edition. The latter also contains, in effect as the second part of the book, the first English translation of the *"Selbstdarstellung"* [*An Autobiographical Study*], although this is not mentioned on the jacket, cover, or title page.

In 1935, the New York publishing house W. W. Norton, which had evidently acquired the rights in the interim, seems to have planned an updated new edition, intended to be issued, probably in compliance with a wish expressed by the author, in two separate volumes. The original combination of the works had not in fact been to Freud's liking. Norton may have invited him to write new postscripts for both *The Question of Lay Analysis* and *An Autobiographical Study* as well as a set of additional annotations to incorporate the latest research into the texts. So it was that the new English version of the *"Selbstdarstellung"* appeared in 1935 under the title *Autobiography*, accompanied by a "Postscript 1935" and additional notes, in the form, as the publisher's imprint has it, of a "New, revised and enlarged edition." The German text of the updates was published only *after* the English version. Freud expressly returned in the 1935 postscript to his criticism of the earlier Brentano anthology: "It [the *"Selbstdarstellung"*] first appeared in America in 1927 (published by Brentano) under the title of *An Autobiographical Study*, but it was injudiciously brought out in the same volume as another essay of mine which gave its title, *The Problem of Lay-Analyses*, to the whole book and so obscured the present work."[5] However, the new edition of the work on lay analysis was not in fact published in 1935, for unknown reasons. It was only in 1950, after the Second World War and more than ten years after Freud's death, that W. W. Norton brought out the work in a new translation under the title *The Question of Lay Analysis*, albeit without the substantial additions com-

[5] 1935*a*, p. 71.

posed by Freud in 1935; perhaps the new generation of staff at the publishing house were unaware of their existence. At any rate, the relevant sheets remained unnoticed among Freud's manuscripts for decades.

The postscript is translated below; as we read it, we would do well to bear in mind the far-reaching changes that had taken place since the first publication of the American edition: Hitler's seizure of power, the world economic crisis, and so on:

> This essay was composed in 1926 and presented to American readers in 1927 (by the publishing house of <u>Brentano</u>). When the question of its reissue recently arose, I carefully reviewed it and found that it can remain as it is; that it neither needs nor can tolerate drastic alterations. The kindly disposed reader will have to delete certain details as no longer relevant to the present time. An adaptation to the conditions prevailing in the German Reich is no longer desirable here in Austria; the expectation, never, of course, meant entirely seriously, that American generosity would solve the problem of spiritual care along psychoanalytic lines could not survive the decline of American prosperity. Apart from this, I felt that a small number of notes would suffice to bring the portrayal up to the level of our present-day insight.
>
> The essay "The Question of Lay Analysis" was a true *pièce d'occasion*. It had happened in Vienna that one of our colleagues, a capable and trustworthy man, not a doctor, but D^r phil., was falsely accused by a psychopathic patient of having claimed for himself a medical qualification in order to secure him, the patient, for treatment. The Austrian law on quackery is strict; we were afraid that this incident would provide the authorities with an occasion for prohibiting without reservation the practice of analysis by lay people. The "Impartial Person" of my little book really did exist and is still alive today. He is an influential member of our educational establishment,[6] for whom I prepared a report on the matter with which we are concerned. I do not know whether my arguments made much impression; at any rate, lay analysis was not then banned in Austria.
>
> The essay which issued from this report did not meet with a friendly fate. It is one of the few of my writings which did not run to a second edition in German, which have seldom been translated, and which are hardly ever quoted. I consider this treatment to have been unfair. The work is good and perfectly well deserves the appreciative judgment pronounced on it by my late friend Ferenczi in his "Introduction." But I had once again taken up arms against a prejudice, I had strongly con-

[6][*Obersanitätsrat* Durig.]

demned the behavior of the medical profession, to which I myself have belonged for over fifty years, and that could not—at least at first—have any other consequence.

In the second paragraph, then, Freud informs the American reader of the circumstances of the genesis of his study on lay analysis, the "Causa Reik," as he had already done in his 1927 postscript[7]—which was not included in the American edition.

The final paragraph sounds like a plea, penned in a combination of pique and defiance, for the status of the essay and presumably also for his own favorable position on lay analysis, in which he felt at the time that his only unconditional supporter was Ferenczi. In the latter's introduction[8] to the first American edition, the reprinting of which in the second Freud no doubt took for granted when he wrote his "Postscript," Ferenczi does indeed present an enthusiastic defense of lay analysis, precisely in the context of a portrayal, brimming over with ideas and still worth reading today, of the wide-ranging future fields of application of psychoanalysis in "criminal therapy," pedagogy, anthropology, sociology, history, and so on. Ferenczi also emphasizes that the essay on lay analysis contains much more than the title promises, namely, an introduction, as succinct as it is lucid, to psychoanalysis as such; if someone were to ask him which book to read in order to become acquainted in easily comprehensible form with the essentials of psychoanalysis, he would without a second thought commend the work on lay analysis to that person.[9] He goes on to praise Freud's extraordinary skill in presenting his teaching in popular terms; this he attributes to the specific Freudian method of plumbing the minds of others by talking to them in their own language. Again, the text of this introduction, set down by Ferenczi in New York in September 1927 during his sojourn in the United States, proves how unjustified was Freud's assumption that that country had alienated Ferenczi from him at this time.[10] Despite the actual, tragic alienation in the last few years before Ferenczi's death, Freud now, in his 1935 postscript, expressly refers to him in retrospect as his "friend." It was certainly politics rather than chance that dictated the substitution in the 1950 Norton edition

[7]1927a, p. 251.

[8]Ferenczi, 1927.

[9]Thinking along lines very similar to those of Ferenczi, Anna Freud wrote to me decades later, on 8 October 1975, when we were considering how to structure the *Werkausgabe in zwei Bänden* (see above, last third of chapter 3): "What if we were to put the 'Question of Lay Analysis' at the beginning as an introduction and then present the subjects in the order in which they appear in the essay on lay analysis? In teaching students, I have always found that this work of my father's is the best introduction to psychoanalysis, even more effective than the Introductory Lectures."

[10]See above, end of chapter 9.

of a dry foreword by Ernest Jones for Ferenczi's inspired introduction; Jones was indeed not among the convinced champions of lay analysis.[11]

The annotations with which Freud wanted to update his essay on lay analysis in 1935 are also presented to the reader in full below. The first note belongs to the third chapter, in which the author attempts to explain to the "Impartial Person," his imaginary interlocutor, the genesis of neurotic suffering, the dynamic of the interplay of forces between the ego and the id, and shows that the infantile ego, when confronted with an instinctual demand from the id which it cannot yet control and noticing a looming "traumatic situation, a collision with the external world," treats the instinctual demand as an external danger and turns away from it in the act of repression, as it were making an attempt at flight. To the sentence "The ego, as we put it, institutes a *repression* of these instinctual impulses,"[12] Freud wished to add the following metapsychological note, introducing an element of differentiation and so to speak postulating an internal antagonism between instinctual drive and ego:

> The theory of psychoanalysis, to which I must draw the reader's attention. The portrayal in the text recognizes as a motive for repression only the case in which the satisfaction of the drive is dangerous and would lead to a "collision with the external world." The question is, however, whether this is the sole, or only in fact the original, condition of a repression. Whether repression, this attempt by the ego to flee from the drive, does not in fact occur every time every time[13] the instinctual demand, by virtue of its intensity, exceeds the capacity of the ego to master it, in which case consideration of the danger threatening from the external world would be irrelevant. The question has not yet been decided, and the relations between the two possible motives for repression not yet clarified.

Freud's late exploration of the primary mother dimension and of the complicated process of female sexual development—that is, the gradual self-correction of his assignment of a privileged place to the male principle—is reflected in the second note, which he wanted to add in the fourth

---

[11]The objection that Ferenczi's introduction ends with a few brief references to *An Autobiographical Study*, which is also reproduced in the Brentano edition, could easily have been met by omitting the relevant passage. Perhaps the only idea surviving from Ferenczi's introduction is the subtitle added by the Norton editors on their own initiative to the essay on lay analysis: *An Introduction to Psychoanalysis*.

[12]1926e, p. 203. [*Translator's note*: This and subsequent references to this work are to the *Standard Edition*, not to the version published by Brentano.]

[13]The German word "jedesmal" [every time] appears twice in the manuscript.

chapter to his earlier statement that the first object of a boy's love was his mother and of a girl's her father:[14]

> Our investigations have since taught us that the mother is the first love object for the girl too. She later succeeds, by a long detour, in placing the father in the position of the mother.[15]

Freud seems to have been unable to resist the temptation to add a polemical note against Alfred Adler and his school in the fifth chapter. This was admittedly not without reason. Since the mid-1920s, Adler had been giving lectures and talks in the United States; in stark contrast to Freudian psychoanalysis, his teaching was the object of great public esteem in the New World in the mid-1930s. At the time, some of Adler's books even appeared in English first, and the former adherent and later dissident had taken up permanent residence in New York in 1935. At the point in the text where Freud discusses the gain from illness, the possibility of using the latter to gloss over "incompetence in one's profession or in competition with other people, while in the family it can serve as a means of extorting from the other members sacrifices and proofs of their love or for imposing one's will upon them,"[16] he intended to insert the following note:

> This is the aspect which so-called individual psychology has detached from the structure of psychoanalysis and made popular by inappropriate generalization.

On the first appearance of the term "Über-Ich" [superego], also in the fifth chapter[17]—rendered as "Super-Ego" in A. P. Maerker-Branden's translation for the Brentano edition[18]—Freud wanted to add a footnote which is of particular interest in view of the criticism that has been leveled at James Strachey's translation of Freud, although it cannot be adduced as an un-

---

[14]1926e, p. 212.

[15]At least according to Otto Rank's minutes of the meeting of the Vienna Psychoanalytic Society of 10 November 1909, Freud does seem to have taken this view at a very early stage, almost twenty years before he composed the essay on lay analysis. Freud is said to have observed, in his comment on a paper by Isidor Sadger that contained what amounted to a precocious reference to narcissism: "In general, man has two primary sexual objects, [. . .]. These two sexual objects are for every individual the woman (the mother, nurse, etc.) and his or her own person" (Nunberg and Federn, 1967, p. 312 [translation slightly modified]; cf. May-Tolzmann, 1991).

[16]1926e, p. 222. [*Translator's note*: Strachey's translation—"while in the family it can serve as a means for sacrificing the other members and extorting proofs of their love or for imposing one's will upon them"—is here in error.]

[17]Ibid., p. 223.

[18]P. 124 in that edition.

equivocal espousal by Freud of the cause of a non-Latinized rendering of his terminology;[19] all the same, the difference between the vital original word, embedded as it is in the vernacular, and the much more static scientific translation seems to him to be worth commenting on:

It has become customary in the English psychoanalytic literature to replace the English pronouns "I" and "It" by the Latin ones "Ego" and "Id." In German we say: Ich, Es and Uberich.

[12.1]

One of the matters with which Freud acquaints the "Impartial Person" in the fifth chapter is the phenomenon and theory of transference; this he does by way of a graphic portrayal of transference love, the storms of which, he tells us, had long ago caused the unnamed Josef Breuer to abandon the treatment of his patient "Anna O.," and which ever since consistently arose in analyses, threatening their success—for "it extinguishes interest in the treatment and in recovery" and replaces "one form of illness with another."[20] At this point Freud wanted to insert a note explaining the reason for the sexual emphasis of his first theory of instinctual drives and incorporating his late full recognition of human aggression. This annotation may be interpreted indirectly as a sign that Freud found it difficult to perceive the manifestations of negative transference, even if it was in the guise of passionate transference love, so that a second step was necessary before he could succeed, on the level of theory too, in recognizing the instinctual factors that underlay it. Indeed, he was thereby opening up the path along which modern theorists of destructive narcissism can still proceed today:

[19]Since the publication of the correspondence between James and Alix Strachey, we know that neither of them was happy with this choice of words, which resulted from a decision by Ernest Jones, who insisted on standardization of the English Freudian terminology; cf. James Strachey's letter of 9 October 1924 and Alix Strachey's of 10 January 1925 (Strachey and Strachey, 1986, p. 83 and p. 176; cf. also Steiner, 1991, p. 376).
[20]1926e, p. 228.

[12.2]

This character of the transference in analytic treatment[21] was the main reason for assigning a prominent, perhaps a specific, role in the etiology of the neuroses to the erotic impulses. However, the general question arises whether the destructive (or aggressive) impulses might not justifiably claim the same status in every respect. The presentation given in the text takes account only of the erotic drives, in accordance with an older version of the theory.

Toward the end of the fifth chapter of Freud's essay on lay analysis, the "Impartial Person" asks where one can learn to practice analysis, and Freud replies in the first edition of Die Frage der Laienanalyse with a reference to the two institutes which existed at the time, in Berlin and Vienna, and to the training center about to be opened in London.[22] In 1935, he wanted to supplement this information with the following annotation:

The number of training institutions has been substantially increased and the arrangements for instruction in psychoanalysis have been greatly improved since the above was written.

In the seventh and last chapter, in connection with diagnostic considerations and with differential diagnosis in particular, Freud turns again to maturation-related feebleness of the ego during childhood, which has the later consequence of a disposition to neurotic illness. He considers this infantile feebleness of the ego to be one of the "normal" causes. The extraordinary burden on childhood is imposed by the fact that "we have in a few

[21][I.e., transference love.]
[22]1926e, p. 228.

years to cover the enormous developmental distance between stone-age primitives and partakers in civilization, and, at the same time and in particular, to fend off the instinctual impulses of the early sexual period."[23] Here again, he felt it necessary in 1935 to draw attention to the progress in research on aggression made in the intervening period. He also linked this idea with his theory of civilization:

> We should add here: the task of taming man's innate, constitutional tendency to aggression, which is, of course, incompatible with the preservation of human society. It cannot be doubted that our civilization is based on the suppression of drives; the question is whether it is structured more at the expense of the erotic than of the destructive drives.

If the additional texts written in 1935 for the essay on lay analysis—the postscript with its accompanying notes—are compared with those composed at the same time for *An Autobiographical Study*, which are justifiably held in high esteem and often quoted in the secondary literature, it must be admitted that they are inferior in status to the latter addenda, which show even greater personal involvement. The latter are, after all, something unique: the continuation of Freud's quasi-autobiography. The additions to *The Question of Lay Analysis* nevertheless deserve to be appended to that work in the future. In particular, some of the notes contain hitherto neglected, substantial comments by Freud on the further development of central aspects of his doctrine, such as the theory of instinctual drives and the concept of repression; some of these passages sound like variations on themes struck up in the supplementary material for *An Autobiographical Study*.

Let us end this first tour of the landscape of Freud's manuscripts in this relatively unspectacular textual region. I would rather not, at this point, invite the reader as it were to climb with me onto an eminence in order to retrace the route we have traveled from a distant perspective. It will have become clear even without such a bird's-eye view that not a few sections of our path have been traversed by the shortest diagonal, while vast areas have not been touched upon even tangentially. By summarizations and conclusions of various kinds concerning the presumed form and results of a future critical edition of Freud, something like a map projection will be attempted in the final part of this book.

[23]Ibid., p. 241.

Part Three

Sketch for a Future Critical Edition

An ideal, no doubt. But an ideal

which can and must be realized.

—"Postscript to *The Question
of Lay Analysis*"

13 OBSERVATIONS: ON EDITING IN GENERAL

Those wishing to bring out a historical-critical edition of Freud's oeuvre in the future will not start from scratch. Their work not only will continue the line of editions published so far, as described in part I of this book, but also will take its place within a second tradition, that of established editorial practice. This second tradition is far older than the brief history of psychoanalysis. The need to preserve the legacy of great authors from oblivion and distortion or to restore it to its authentic form, as well as the exercise of textual criticism, dates from the Alexandrian period and probably owes its existence to the dawning realization at that time that the texts handed down to posterity embody the memory of mankind. Yet the modern concept of historical-critical editions and the establishment of editorial theory as a science in its own right are considered to date only from the nineteenth century, an age pervaded by a fundamental current of historicism; however, other contributory elements are the historicizing philology of the Renaissance humanists and the linguistic achievements of seventeenth- and eighteenth-century biblical criticism.

In the German-speaking world, the editorial culture has since been nurtured and further developed mainly by the disciplines of philology and literary scholarship, on the one hand, and philosophy, on the other, following in the footsteps of such savants as Karl Lachmann and Wilhelm Dilthey. If we recommend to the editors of a future critical edition of Freud that they take advantage of this wealth of experience, that is not to argue in favor of the blurring of the distinction between genres that is commonplace today. It is not a matter of equating, in terms of content and form, the three sciences that are emphatically language-oriented—philology, philosophy, and psychoanalysis—but merely of advising these editors to acquaint themselves with the proven rules for the handing down of texts and to keep abreast of the debate on editorial methodology.[1] Again, the organizational forms that

---

[1] To judge from his preface to the *Standard Edition*, James Strachey (1966a), an autodidact of the editorial craft, responsible for the most comprehensive critical edition of Freud to date, evidently did not engage in an ongoing working dialogue with an experienced editor active in a different field, although he did make sure that he was thoroughly acquainted with the relevant standards. Had he done so, he might perhaps have seen the relationship between interpretation and documentation in the editorial introductions and notes as a problem and

have been found appropriate in the context of long-term editorial projects in the fields of literary scholarship and philosophy could serve as models in the search for a suitable institutional framework for the elaboration of a new complete edition of Freud. This also applies to the use of electronic data processing, which is now well established in editorial practice, whereby such tasks as collation can be simplified and accelerated. Among the editors of the works of philosophical authors in particular, a kind of forum of experts already exists in Germany in the "Arbeitsgemeinschaft philosophischer Editionen" [Philosophical editions study group]. An *Internationales Jahrbuch für Editionswissenschaft* [International yearbook of editorial theory][2] was founded under the title *editio* in 1987, in which editorial activity not only in the German-speaking countries but also in other linguistic areas and other disciplines is reported and discussed. As a further manifestation of the increasing awareness of the function and effect of editing, a number of colloquia on the subject have been held in the past few years.

Nevertheless, standard definitions of basic concepts, even as regards a typology of editions, do not yet seem to exist. As indicated in part I of this book, three types are as a rule distinguished: reading editions, critical editions, and historical-critical editions. These will now be described in rather more detail.

Reading editions are those that serve simply to present and disseminate a text, with little or no commentary. First publications commonly belong to this type, as do new editions of older texts that are not provided with a substantial editorial apparatus. Reading editions keep the author in the public mind, promote the right kind of awareness and popularization of his work, and perform a legitimate function essential to its continued impact.

Critical editions, sometimes also called *study* or *textbook editions,* on the other hand, do not confine themselves to merely reproducing the text. Their editors claim that, by making it accessible and commenting on it, they are contributing to science. Their aim is not only to offer texts to the interested individual reader but also to supply a foundation for teaching and research. Editorial forewords, introductions, afterwords, and appendixes are therefore added, giving bibliographic details, setting forth the rules applied in the constitution of the text, sketching the history of the relevant

---

possibly have withdrawn certain subjective assessments of the status of particular texts (such as the "Project for a Scientific Psychology") or of formal merits or deficiencies. He does not in fact always remain faithful to the principle enunciated in the preface of abstaining from the expression of his own views and of enabling the reader to encounter Freud's writings virtually uninfluenced.

[2]Cf. Woesler, 1987ff.

work's genesis, and so on; editorial notes draw attention to parallel passages in other works by the same author and to changes in his concepts and theories, explain historical, literary, and other allusions, give the appropriate references for quotations, and so on. Bibliographies, lists of abbreviations, glossaries, name and subject indexes, and the like are provided to facilitate the use of critical editions for scientific purposes. Critical editions may exist of individual works of an author, major sections of his oeuvre or his entire writings, individual correspondences, anthologies of letters, or the totality of letters left behind after his death.

Just as the boundaries between reading and critical editions are fluid, so, too, are those between critical and historical-critical editions. Characteristic features of *historical-critical editions* are the transparent application of the historical-critical method and the aspiration to completeness. Their editors wish to issue the entirety of the texts bequeathed by an author, whether or not they were published during his lifetime. This includes all works, taking account of the manuscripts and the alternative formulations recorded therein as well as of amendments made by the author for the first and subsequent editions—that is, of all manuscript and print variants—and also all letters, translations, diaries, summaries of lectures, minutes of discussions, and other testimonies to the author's life from his literary remains. The texts are constituted by a process of independent research based on critical scrutiny of all the material preserved. The structure of the editorial apparatus roughly corresponds to that of critical editions. With the aim of providing the maximum possible historical documentation, some editors demand the consideration or even the reproduction of statements by contemporaries on the work and person of the author. It is evident from this brief characterization that historical-critical editions are in every respect demanding and costly, dedicated to the requirements of research. The general reading public may, of course, also benefit from them insofar as the research results accruing from the editorial work—for example, in the form of corrected transcriptions—may feed through to the reading editions and critical editions of individual works or parts of works by the author concerned.

However, the fact that there are no standardized catalogs of rules to be observed in order for an edition to be deemed "critical" or "historical-critical" is a consequence not only of the situation of editorial theory but also of the great diversity of the oeuvres and literary remains of individual authors. There are admittedly genealogies, so-called stemmata of editions; for example, the paradigm represented by Wilhelm Dilthey's *Akademie-ausgabe* of Kant's *Gesammelte Schriften* [Collected writings], dating from the end of the nineteenth century, crucially influenced the form assumed by the historical-critical editions of the three great idealist philosophers Hegel, Schelling, and Fichte, which were not begun until some fifty years later. However, each critical or historical-critical edition owes its fundamental specificity to the flexible adaptation of the editorial method to the peculiarities of the texts to be edited.

The more extensive and complex the unpublished material that is preserved in the literary remains or that appeared posthumously in distorted form, the more important the results of such editorial work, compared with the reading editions previously published, will normally be: they may complement or even drastically modify the hitherto prevailing image of the author. Indeed, the ratio of published to unpublished material throws light on how the author concerned worked, on his handling of the conflicts involved in the transition from the privacy of the manuscript which can still be changed to the public form of the definitive printed version—that is, on his attitude toward separation from his own productions.

Let us consider the example of Husserl, whose literary remains, saved from the Nazis and taken to Belgium, far exceed in quantity the volume of material published during his lifetime; mostly recorded in the Gabelsberg system of shorthand, they show the great phenomenologist immersed in unremitting descriptive approximations to what he has seen, in search of an unambiguous relationship between words and things, engaged in a permanent dialogue with his own writings, one that is only gradually becoming audible through the editorial work of the Husserl archives: "Read, improve, and copy the old manuscripts over and over again."[3]

Then there is Leibniz, who also published only a negligibly small proportion of his manuscripts. These have come down to us in an extensive literary estate that also includes more than fifteen thousand letters. Leibniz, on account of his timidity and excessive self-criticism, evidently never showed anyone precisely what was most important to him, and at most communicated it to others orally. The countless excerpts, drafts, preliminary versions, and corrected fair copies have for decades confronted the editors with transcription problems of the utmost difficulty and, in particular, with dating puzzles that they are attempting to resolve by such techniques as watermark analysis and the methods of statistical linguistics. With the appearance of the successive volumes of the historical-critical edition of Leibniz, we are afforded a prospect of the stages of the incessant, self-surpassing creative process in the author and of his position within the communication system that linked European scholars of the seventeenth and early eighteenth centuries. Both the figure and the oeuvre of Leibniz will

[3]Husserl, 1984 [1906], p. 447; cf. IJsseling, 1987.

retrospectively take on clearer contours through the many texts made available for the first time; until now, because so few completed works reached the public during his lifetime, his ideas have had to be deduced more from their refractions in the writings of his contemporaries.[4]

Another example is Kafka. Everyone knows the extent to which he concealed his activity as an author during his lifetime. It was the administrator of his estate, Max Brod, who, by bringing out provisional editions after his death, revealed him as the paradigmatic writer of the twentieth century; Kafka himself had released only a very few stories for publication. Working from a textual structure—drafts, fragments, diary entries, and so forth—set down in notebooks and on loose sheets, littered with words and phrases written in the opposite direction to the main text and with veritable tangles of corrections, the producers of the historical-critical edition of Kafka must edit both the printed material—that is, what Kafka himself published—and the unpublished manuscripts intended by him to be burned, while doing equal justice to Kafka's contradictory attitude to both textual modalities. For when this writer decided to prepare a work for printing, he would isolate segments from the uninterrupted flow of the pen reflected in his manuscripts and assemble them into higher-order configurations.[5]

Recent changes in editorial style seem particularly well suited to such authors and such literary remains. In the past the emphasis was laid on the last editions supervised by the author himself—texts elaborated by him to the print-ready stage and, where possible, of which he oversaw the entire production process, including his own galley and page proof corrections and even his alterations and additions for subsequent editions. The editors' ideal was to preserve the oeuvre in or restore it to its definitive printed form. Today, however, editorial attention tends to be focused on the manuscripts. This implies a tendency to relativize the classical concept of an "oeuvre." Two new critical editions that have been particularly well received in the last few years by the public at large as well as among specialists surely owe their outstanding results partly to this change of editorial perspective: the Nietzsche edition of Mazzino Montinari and Giorgio Colli, and D. E. Sattler's and Wolfram Groddeck's edition of Hölderlin.

The complete, strictly chronological reproduction of Nietzsche's manuscript books dating from the last twenty years of his work, including all their excerpts, reading notes, concealed quotations, and sudden expositions of his own ideas, has put an end to decades of polemics about the authenticity of the work posthumously published under the title *Der Wille zur Macht*

---

[4]Cf. Schepers, 1987.
[5]Cf. Kittler and Neumann, 1982.

[*The Will to Power*], a work that had such momentous consequences for the reception of Nietzsche. It was proved once and for all to be a compilation invented by the first editors—that is to say, it was banished from the scene.[6]

The declared aim of D. E. Sattler is to permit the reconstruction of the creative process in Hölderlin, of "the movement of the text towards itself."[7] The fragmentary nature of the text is taken by the editor not as a sign of failure on the part of the poet but as the triumph of the tragic, deliberately pursued by him to the point of the shattering of form. The Frankfurt edition of Hölderlin presents in facsimile all the writings that have come down to us—an innovation which discloses the basis of the edition to the reader. The sibylline Homburg folio book constitutes an extreme case. A look at these pages, which are reproduced unemended, that is to say, simply in the form of facsimiles and typographically faithful transcriptions, is enough to convince the reader that what has hitherto been regarded as Hölderlin's late work is indeed barely any more than a product of his former editors and that these enigmatic manuscripts essentially defy any emendation having the aim of conferring upon them, through the extraction and montage of segments, the unequivocality and linearity of conventional textual coherence.

These brief descriptions suffice to indicate that editors of such authors, such literary remains, are bound to be working in hazardous regions. However, even the developments that have taken place in editorial theory in the wake of structuralism and poststructuralism, as outlined above, risk the danger of imposing excessive strains on the editors: "For editing in the modern sense is on the track of the imponderable gestures and postures of inspiration which cannot be conveyed in printer's type."[8] The question is whether such an ambition, if taken to its deconstructivist extreme, might not lead to hubris on the part of the editors and to a violent and impermissible disintegration of texts, merely because their alleged deeper truth and authenticity are thought to have been discovered in the earliest phases of their genesis, the preservation of which is declared to take priority. Such an attack on the integrity of an oeuvre may also be a manifestation of the editors' unconscious envy of the superior creative power of great authors.

[6]Cf. Montinari, 1980.
[7]1984, p. 11.
[8]Kittler and Neumann, 1982, p. 82.

14 Suggestions: On Principles of a New Freud Edition

Let us consider Freud and his oeuvre against the background of these general observations on editing. One's spontaneous inclination might be to assume that the modern method, which privileges the earliest forms of the texts, would be particularly appropriate for the writings of the thinker who himself chose the genetic approach when he sought to expose the unconscious infantile wishes and fundamental early psychic structures that lay behind the messages of adults' symptoms, dreams, or parapraxes dating from later in their life history. However, this is tenable only for the aspect of Freud as a psychologist confronted with mental conflicts, and not for the attitude of Freud as a writer toward his own work. As described in detail in part II of this book, he was a different kind of author from those mentioned in the previous chapter, and his literary remains are quite distinct from the material they left behind.

There were admittedly phases in Freud's early career when, as documented in the letters to his fiancée, he was plagued by intense self-doubt. Yet a radiant self-assurance developed as a countervailing tendency during the same period. "If the energy I feel within myself remains with me," he wrote at the age of twenty-nine to Martha Bernays, "we may yet leave behind us some traces of our complicated existence."[1] Perhaps from the time of *On Aphasia*—that is, the beginning of the 1890s—but certainly from the writing and publication of *The Interpretation of Dreams*, Freud was perfectly aware of his outstanding stature both intellectually and as a writer. Writing had assumed pride of place among his forms of expression, and from then on he wrote with the immediate objective of publication, almost always passing quickly from the intimacy of the manuscript to the public status of the printed version.[2]

In contrast to, for example, Ferdinand de Saussure, whose *Cours de linguistique générale* began to exert its influence on our century in 1916 through the medium of oral communication—as reconstructed after his death from notes taken at his Geneva lectures—Freud did not rely on posthumous discovery or immortalization by literary executors who would

---

[1] 1960*a*, p. 170 [translation slightly modified].

[2] However, a comment quoted in the chapter on the notes (p. 108 above) shows that this step was occasionally conflictual.

determine the form in which his work was to be made known or handed down. What was to be presented to the public and when and how were matters to be decided by no one but himself, down to the smallest details of galley and page proof correction and of the notes in which he would not uncommonly record the latest advances and discoveries from edition to edition. As Walter Muschg put it in 1930, he had indeed, by the long-term success of his publication policy, "founded an intellectual great power of the age."[3] "There are no works of Freud already forgotten during his lifetime."[4]

Yet it seems that for him only what existed in the medium of print possessed the dignity of a work. He sometimes quickly lost interest in manuscripts that he had originally intended to publish but whose publication had to be postponed for external reasons. I have already mentioned the most momentous example: when, during the First World War, he composed the twelve metapsychological papers, in effect a fundamental synthesis of his theoretical views, and the publisher Hugo Heller was unable to bring them out immediately in monograph form, Freud presented the first five in the *Internationale Zeitschrift für ärztliche Psychoanalyse* in 1915 and 1917.[5] Once the war was over, he could have published the project as a whole, but the seven unpublished texts were by then plainly no longer consistent with the developments in his theoretical thinking that had since taken place. He rejected these papers and even presumably destroyed them; at any rate, they are now deemed lost. Although they were surely hardly less important than, for instance, "The Unconscious" or "Mourning and Melancholia," they seemed to the author not to be worth keeping. It apparently never occurred to him that later editors might one day wish to integrate them into his oeuvre as transitional documents that could provide information on the history of his work.

As we have seen, comparatively few as yet unpublished manuscripts were found among Freud's papers after his death in London in 1939. The bulk of the unpublished material is without question constituted by the letters. Estimated to amount to between ten thousand and fifteen thousand documents,[6] they represent one of the most voluminous surviving epistolary collections ever to have been left behind by an author.

These initial characterizations indicate that Freud's work does not confront its editors with deciphering or dating problems of the same order of

[3]Muschg, 1975 [1930], p. 5.

[4]Ibid., p. 65. This of course applies to the period *before* the violent interruption of their influence caused by the Nazis. But it can now again be asserted that there are at any rate no forgotten psychoanalytic works by Freud.

[5]1915c, 1915d, 1915e, 1916–17f, and 1916–17g.

[6]Cf. Eissler, 1980, p. 105.

magnitude as, say, the Leibniz papers, the Husserl manuscripts, or the late Hölderlin material; neither does it leave them such wide scope to indulge their process-related curiosity and delight in emendation as do the literary remains of Nietzsche or Kafka. Almost all of Freud's texts have to be edited from the printed versions, and major difficulties of authorization[7] and text constitution are by and large not to be expected. After all, he made his wishes as an author very clear and placed his work before us with such distinct contours and in such finished form that we cannot but respect them.

However, even the most painstaking study of the methods developed by editorial theorists[8] will not spare the editors of a new Freud edition the task of gradually elaborating specific rules of their own, optimally matched to the subtleties of the oeuvre, in their practical day-by-day grappling with the texts. Although I have certainly given an unprecedentedly detailed description in this book of the configuration and modality of preservation of the work in manuscripts and printed texts, our knowledge is insufficient, even with these additions, to anticipate the future process of editorial reflection, which will inevitably involve many trial-and-error loops. So when I gave notice of making a map projection at the close of part II, at the end of that first peregrination through the landscape of Freud's manuscripts, even that aspiration may have sounded too ambitious. This simile was in fact used merely to denote the intention of incorporating the hitherto unknown material within the outlines of a new critical edition.

The following discussion of some guiding principles for this major project is merely tentative in character; it is not much more than a sequence of suggestions. I shall begin by describing the attitude which in my view could make it easier for the editor to perform his task. After this, against the background of the material described in part II—that is, again on the level of examples and without laying claim to completeness—I should like to discuss some principles for the presentation of selected areas of the oeuvre. Then comes an outline for the editor's commentary, as it were the editorial system of coordinates, which is intended to allow the reader to place a given Freudian text in its context. The chapter ends with some considerations on institutional requirements and on the element of time in the genesis of historical-critical editions.

---

[7]Problems of location and attribution may arise at most in regard to the early writings, particularly the numerous shorter reviews (cf. Fichtner, 1987); however, a fair proportion of these questions may be deemed already answered. As to the later works, further discussion may perhaps be necessary about Freud's contribution (1966*b*) to William C. Bullitt's book on President Wilson (cf. Freud's letter to Marie Bonaparte of 7 December 1933, quoted in Schur, 1972, p. 449, and Peter Gay's account, 1988, p. 553ff.).

[8]Cf., for example, Jacobs, 1987; Martens, 1971; Scheibe, 1971.

As to the attitude of the editor to his work, let us summarize it by a number of negative recommendations.

He should *not* forget that any editorial activity is bound to be of its time, for all its aspirations to so-called objective methods. He should therefore *not* on any account allow the editorial work to be governed by one of today's popular intellectual trends because this could expose the edition to the risk of being rapidly set aside as outmoded once the relevant tendency abates.

The same applies to certain editorial preferences based on such currents; the editor should therefore *not* surrender uncritically to these. For example, if the editorial apparatus of a new edition were to emphasize or even concentrate solely on the linguistic aspects of Freud's oeuvre, this would seem hardly less arbitrary than James Strachey's much-criticized accentuation of the scientistic "Project for a Scientific Psychology."

A stereotyped predilection for a particular stage in the process of genesis of the text could prove similarly one-sided—if, through idolization of the early forms, the text to be edited were constituted, for example, from the drafts or fair copies, faithfully reproducing their spelling and punctuation, while the authorized first printed versions or the last editions supervised by the author were dismissed. The editor should therefore *not* practice historicization of the texts, as it were retrogressing behind Freud's own intentions.

He should *not* lose sight of the editor's position in the field of tension between editorial theory and hermeneutics. Of course, there is bound to be an element of interpretation in even the most discreet of editorial work—in the decisions on the constitution of the text or the assembly of material for the edition, in the way the dynamics of textual development are interpreted, in the structuring of the editorial commentary, and so forth. Yet he should *not* depart from the principle that the business of the editor as such is not interpretation but the disclosure of the documentary foundations, the presentation of the material for productive reading, for interpretation by others. In other words, he should *not* give rein to his inclination to offer extensive textual interpretations and evaluations of his own.

On another level, such restraint would have the following implications. The editor should *not* aspire to correct the text but should enable it to reveal itself in its authenticity. He should *not* suppress anything that is unclear, tentative, halting, unsound, or even downright erroneous. But on the other hand, he should *not* break up felicitous, polished formulations or disturb their readability—for instance by the forced synoptic presentation of independent textual stages or the exaggerated use of sigla. He should enable the oeuvre to speak for itself and *not* allow his own voice to intrude excessively.

As an overriding principle, he should *not* indulge in editorial maximalism or perfectionism. If he deems readability a worthwhile objective even for a large-scale critical edition, this is no more inconsistent with a scientific aspiration than the considered attitude that not every line Freud ever wrote—on a visiting card, a complimentary copy, an order form—need be reproduced in slavish subjection to a hypertrophied demand for completeness. An editorial apparatus brimming over with a show of superior knowledge in the field of philology or even of analysis could alienate the reader from Freud's text, as could a huge number of volumes, perhaps running into three figures, which would at any rate be prohibitively expensive. However, the exercise of such proportion by no means implies that the intention to present the oeuvre in its totality would have to be abandoned.

Just as D. W. Winnicott's principle of the "good-enough"[9] is applied to the facilitating mother-child relationship or to the therapeutic alliance of analyst and analysand, so it could, albeit figuratively, be used with regard to the editor's attitude to the text entrusted to him (or to its author and reader, as the case may be): "good-enough" in the sense of better than perfect because it connotes a more living, more unobtrusive reaction, one that has greater empathy with the gestures and needs of the object. This parallel among the three modalities of relating can, of course, refer only to a situation in which the person concerned makes himself or herself available in a caring manner and adopts that characteristic optimal distance that allows empathy. The text (or its author or reader) no more belongs to the editor than the child does to the mother or the analysand to the analyst. He or she does not determine it, does not place it in the service of his or her own drive-related or excessively narcissistic needs but makes it easier for it, so to speak, to be itself.

At this point the reader may be reminded of the epigraph at the beginning of this book. Although the subject of Jean Starobinski's essay, as emphasized in the introduction, is the work of the interpreter, whom he enjoins to respect the recalcitrant materiality of the text, he describes the elements of the editor's attitude outlined above in the most precise terms. Let me therefore repeat at least a part of the epigraph here: "Our prime concern must therefore be to guarantee the maximum of presence and independence for the object of our study [that is, the text to be interpreted], so that its own existence is consolidated and it can offer itself to us with all the hallmarks of autonomy. It must be able to assert its difference and maintain its distance. The object of my attention is not within myself; it lies before me, and I would do well not to appropriate it from the aspect which my desire confers upon it [. . .], but to allow it to deploy all its properties and particular determinations."

[9]Winnicott, for instance, 1960, p. 145f.

It is not possible at this juncture to suggest an overall structure for a new critical edition of Freud. All the different types of material that have come down to us should obviously be included: at any rate, all the works, including all the so-called preanalytic early writings, notices and reviews, translations (including his own additional forewords and annotations), the notes, and in addition the letters, the diarylike personal jottings,[10] records of oral communications,[11] and so on. For several reasons, however, of which I shall mention two, it would be premature to go into more detail.

If the edition is to be organized essentially on chronological lines, no definite statement is possible, for example, about the sequence of the various sections as long as it remains unclear whether those parts of the Sigmund Freud Collection in the Library of Congress that are still restricted contain further manuscripts that ought to be included in the new edition. This seems probable, at least in the case of the notes: we may yet discover some that go back to the very beginnings of Freud's scientific career, the dating of which would thus suggest that the section with the notes should precede that which presents the early writings.

Another field that is still substantially unclear comprises the letters. If the definition of the criteria applicable to historical-critical editions set out in the previous chapter were followed, the aspiration to completeness would entail the integration of all of Freud's letters in the new edition and, in the case of the correspondences vital to the understanding of the oeuvre, presumably also the letters of the addressees, such as Karl Abraham, Sándor Ferenczi, and C. G. Jung. The surviving letters have so far not even been fully cataloged; many of these documents in the Sigmund Freud Collection are restricted; and previously unknown examples continue to turn

---

[10]For example, the slim "Geheim-Chronik" [secret chronicle] kept jointly with his fiancée from 1883 to 1886; the "Reisejournal" [travel diary], also comprising only a few pages, on the beginning of the voyage to America in 1909 with Ferenczi and Jung; the entries in "Prochaskas Familien-Kalender"; the "Kürzeste Chronik"; the surviving late pages of the index of letters; the "Chronologie"-bibliography of the oeuvre; comments on translations of his own writings and on portrayals of his work and his person by third parties; etc. This personal sphere would no doubt also include Freud's various wills—for example, that of 31 January 1919, with which, having "regard to the extraordinary deterioration of our financial position due to the consequences of the war," he superseded his previous will and which ends with characteristic laconicism: "As much as possible is to be saved on the cost of my interment: the cheapest category, no speeches at the graveside, and announcement after the event. I promise not to be offended by the omission of every 'piety.' If convenient and inexpensive: cremation. Should I be 'famous' at the time of my death—one never knows—that is not to make any difference."

[11]For instance, the discussion contributions at meetings of the Gesellschaft der Ärzte [Society of Physicians] in Vienna, the Wiener medizinischer Klub [Vienna Medical Club], the Verein für Psychiatrie und Neurologie [Psychiatry and Neurology Association] in Vienna, and, in particular, the Vienna Psychoanalytic Society, as well as the addresses to the B'nai-B'rith, the late declaration on the BBC, etc.

up, especially at auctions. However, it already seems likely that the inclusion of the entire body of letters could easily cause the number of volumes to run into three figures. It would therefore probably be utopian to demand anything approaching the complete reproduction of this part of the Freudian heritage. Apart from the indispensable correspondences,[12] we shall probably have to content ourselves with the reproduction of a selection. And this selection, however questionable, can be made only on the basis of as full a knowledge as possible of the entire surviving corpus of letters.[13] Owing to the obscurity of the situation at present, the letters are substantially left out of account in this sketch. The latter, for its part, does not even cover all fields of the oeuvre but only a few selected provinces—predominantly those that emerged into the light of day during my study of the manuscripts.[14]

Before discussing suggestions for the future editorial presentation of specific individual works or groups of works, I should like to put forward some general considerations. The principle is widely upheld among editorial theorists today that all textual stages of a work must be accorded equal status. However, Freud was an author whose object for almost all his writings, beyond the various phases of the genesis of a text, was the final stage of the printed version; he set great store by this final stage and no doubt wanted to have his name associated with it alone. The rigorous application of the principle of equal status of textual stages would therefore be inconsistent with this preference of the author. Without sharing the skepticism about a historical-critical edition expressed at that time by Anna Freud, I should like to quote a passage, which also has implications for the future, from a letter she wrote to me on 10 March 1968—that is, when we were considering the creation of such an edition for the first time:[15] "I know, of course, that a

---

[12]These would, however, then surely include not only the Fluss, Silberstein, Martha Bernays, Fliess, Abraham, Andreas-Salomé, Binswanger, Ferenczi, Jones, Jung, Pfister, and Arnold Zweig documents, but also the Bleuler, Bonaparte, Brill, Eitingon, Federn, Hitschmann, Mack Brunswick, Rank, Reik, and Riviere collections as well as the correspondences with members of the family.

[13]Having regard to the preeminent importance of the letters for an understanding of the oeuvre and the reconstruction of its genesis, however, it would appear desirable for all the letter sources disclosed in the context of the preparation of a new edition to be kept available in electronic databases, where possible in reliable transcriptions of the complete text—along the lines, for example, of the computerization of Musil's literary remains (cf. Wagner, 1990). But a minimum requirement would be to expand the "Konkordanz der Freud-Briefe" [concordance of Freud letters] (cf. Fichtner, 1989), established by Gerhard Fichtner at Tübingen University's Institute of the History of Medicine, which continuously records mainly the published letters from and to Freud, and to supplement it with brief summaries of their content.

[14]For this reason, the matter of the preanalytic works will be discussed by way of summary only in the final chapter, in the context of our conjectures on the results and influence of a new Freud edition.

[15]See above, p. 54ff.

'critical edition' calls for a comparison of the later printed versions with the manuscripts; but I should like to warn of the possible consequences that could easily ensue from excessive zeal in this connection. In the case of an author who writes so much by hand, as my father did throughout his life, it is naturally inevitable that there will be mistakes and slips of the pen. My father countered this situation by correcting the galley proofs with extreme care, so as to eradicate all such inaccuracies. Furthermore, he was never the only one to read them; either Dr. Rank or a member of the family (in later years myself) went through the galleys at the same time and compared them with his own corrections. It is therefore my opinion that in almost all cases the first printed version is a better guide to the correct text than the handwritten manuscript, and that all this work would be undone again by going back from the first printed version to the MS."

Even lacking this personal advice, the editors of a future critical edition would as a rule, presumably of their own accord, constitute the texts of the works from the printed versions—not necessarily from the first editions, but rather from the last editions supervised by the author—that is, from those revised new editions whose text Freud demonstrably intended to be in effect the final state of the relevant work, having supervised it right down to the stage of galley proof correction. By constituting the text in this way, the editors would strictly avoid the presentation of composite forms, contaminated textual patchworks put together arbitrarily by themselves, for instance by the tacit incorporation of elements from prior versions. On the other hand, such a procedure would in no way preclude the unrestricted application of an editorial method allowing for the dynamics of textual revision because, by flexibly matching the form of the apparatus of variants to each individual writing, the editors could reconstruct all stages of the genesis and alteration of the text and disclose them to the reader.

James Strachey and his assistants had begun to explore some of these transformations in their work on the *Standard Edition*. With a few exceptions, however, their research was confined to comparison of the successive editions that appeared during Freud's lifetime—that is, to determination of the print variants. In other words, they were concerned almost exclusively with the late phase in the textual dynamics. The editors of a future critical edition in the original language would have to resume this process of recovery of the print variants and refine it further. Their main task in the matter of establishment of the variant apparatus would surely be to explore—substantially for the first time—the manuscript variants. Only the systematic study of all the surviving manuscripts and their comparison with the first editions would make it possible fully to reveal the early phases of the textual dynamics, from the making of the very first notes to correction of the galleys, thereby allowing comprehensive documentation of the history of the text. A by no means negligible aspect of this process would be the disclosure of what are known as the paralipomena, independent texts that cannot be classified as textual versions of a particular work, to which they can be related not syntactically but only in accordance with criteria of content—initial schemata, subject lists, key words, contents summaries, excerpts, and so on. Many of the quotations presented in a different context in part II of this book will perhaps have already convinced the reader that Freud's letters and sheets of notes, in effect representing surfaces for tentative thinking and trial formulation, contain such paralipomena in abundance. The reproduction of as many as possible of such epistolary paralipomena[16] in the new edition could, moreover, compensate at least in part for the fact that it will no doubt be impossible to include the entire corpus of letters.

As also described in part II, Freud's fair copies make up the bulk of the surviving autographs. At least at first sight, their text in most cases shows no more than comparatively minor differences from the relevant first editions. For this reason, the complete reproduction of all the fair copies in transcription or even as facsimiles accompanied by letter-by-letter transcriptions would seem extravagant and would inflate the edition unnecessarily because it would not afford a commensurate gain in knowledge. However, the forgoing of complete reproduction of the fair copies would not mean that the manuscript variants surviving in them would be withheld from the reader—because clarifying, structuring, title, and emotive variants of importance could be reproduced in lists of variants and in textual notes, with detailed descriptions covering their dating, location, and material. Even without complete reproduction of the relevant fair copy, it should be possible in this way to illustrate to the reader, for example, the stratified structure of the "Wolf Man" case history.[17]

In the case of very extensive variants, such as the passage deleted by Eitingon and Jones from the 1927 "Postscript" to *The Question of Lay Analysis*,[18] individual fair copies could, of course, be reproduced in full— preferably in letter-by-letter transcriptions and faithfully reflecting the graphic layout of the original, to give the reader of the new edition at least a few examples whereby he can acquaint himself with the structure of Freud's

[16]I shall mention just two of those already published. Both are contained in the correspondence with Sándor Ferenczi: a telling summary of the essay "The Theme of the Three Caskets" in a letter of 23 June 1912 (1992g, p. 387) and a sketch of the "Overview of the Transference Neuroses," communicated to his friend on 12 July 1915 (to which there is a first reference in Jones, 1957, p. 208).

[17]See above, p. 161ff.

[18]Above, p. 177ff.

fair copies, their spelling, punctuation, correction marks, and so on. The stylistic-rhetorical variant category could be illustrated by specimens in the same way because these variants are too numerous and usually also too incidental to be recorded comprehensively in variant lists.

Unlike the situation with fair copies, which exist in large numbers and are mostly characterized by their close relationship to the relevant first editions, complete reproduction of the rare surviving testimonies to earlier textual stages—that is, of all drafts and first versions—would appear desirable and advisable. In the present state of our knowledge, this would mean specifically the following.

Besides the edited wording of the section "Our Attitude towards Death" from the essay "Thoughts for the Times on War and Death," dating from 1915, the new edition would present the text of the lecture "Wir und der Tod" ["Death and Ourselves"] delivered by Freud to the "Wien" Lodge of the Jewish B'nai B'rith, and the reader could in addition study the draft of this lecture in extenso.[19] The draft of the lost twelfth metapsychological essay, "Overview of the Transference Neuroses," set down in the same year, would also be reproduced as a matter of course because no fully written-out version, published by the author, of this last essay from the great metapsychological series has been preserved; the draft would probably feature both in a faithful transcription and as emended text.

The unique opportunity to document almost completely the dynamic process of the genesis of one of the main works of theory would certainly not be passed over: in the case of *The Ego and the Id*, a possible approach might be to reproduce not only the authorized published text, most likely constituted from the first edition, but also the original wording of both the draft and the fair copy. The "Demonological Neurosis" study could be made available not only in the textual form intended by Freud for publication: all the surviving passages of the draft would presumably also be included as well as the paralipomena, in particular from the notes.[20]

With regard to the reproduction of the first version of *Beyond the Pleasure Principle*, a synoptic presentation or at least line or paragraph correlation marks would make it easier for the reader to compare the definitive text, once again no doubt to be constituted from the first edition, passage for passage with the earlier version. In the case of this central opus too, it would be fascinating to provide, to the extent possible, complete documentation of the textual history: first version, fair copy, first edition together with all later print variants, and paralipomena.[21]

[19]Cf. above, p. 132ff.
[20]Cf. above, p. 117f. and p. 134ff.
[21]Above, p. 183ff.

Conversely, a consistently synoptic presentation of the versions of the Moses book would be out of the question because, in setting down the text ultimately released for publication, the author subjected the "historical novel" on the man Moses—that is, the first version—to thorough revision, modifying the text in both its microstructures and its macrostructures.[22] Hardly one stone remained in place in this process, so that parallel scrutiny of the two versions is precluded. At most the marking of thematic complexes might be worth considering, provided that readability was not thereby excessively impaired. Owing to the enigmatic character of the study of Moses and its conjectured autobiographical and self-analytic dimension of depth, only the presentation of the entire surviving material could be deemed an editorial approach relatively free of interpretation. At the same time, the reader should easily be able to identify which parts of the preserved material were intended by the author for publication and which are to be regarded as private documents. Once again, for the sake of authenticity, the manuscripts should preferably be reproduced in a transcription faithful to the original. The list of variants could show the extent of the differences between the first editions of the first two Moses essays, published in succession in the journal *Imago* in 1937, and the preprint of part of the third essay which appeared in the *Internationale Zeitschrift für Psychoanalyse und Imago* in 1939, on the one hand, and the text of the eventual Moses book, on the other. The differences are too slight to justify the complete reproduction of all the printed versions.

That concludes my suggestions on how to take account of the drafts and first versions. A place should also be found in the new edition for the small number of texts Freud wrote down presumably with the intention of publication, but which were not then published, manifestly for external reasons.[23] This applies in particular to the 1935 postscript for a planned new American edition of the essay on lay analysis and to the additional notes composed for it. With the aim of avoiding contaminated composite forms, these texts should not be tacitly integrated with the original text of the essay *The Question of Lay Analysis* together with the 1927 postscript but should be appended to the hitherto familiar text as a supplement in its own right. Certain overlaps between the opening passages of the 1927 "Nachwort" and the 1935 "Nachschrift" in any case strongly suggest that Freud did not intend to include a translation of the earlier postscript in the new American edition and that he therefore wanted to communicate some elements of what he had added for the German-speaking reader in 1927 to the American public in the shorter, 1935 postscript.

[22]Above, p. 191ff.
[23]Cf. above, the chapter "Unpublished Material."

The most delicate problems of deciphering, dating, structuring, and commenting will surely be encountered by the future editors in their work on the body of notes from the manuscripts. As described in detail in chapter 6, this is also the only part of the oeuvre which, however marginal, is still largely unknown and unexplored. The general principle will no doubt be to order the texts chronologically and in the configurations of the writing materials used, the analysis of which, beyond all clues from their content, may well help to date their genesis. A presentation of this kind would, in particular, enable the reader to acquaint himself with the specific structure of the body of notes and with its diversity of content and form.

Especially variable and inventive editorial techniques would be needed for the achievement of a second objective, which will presumably sometimes run counter to the first, namely, that of revealing the filiations between thematically defined segments of the notes and specific published works. Short, clearly delineated passages of the notations that can be directly assigned to a particular writing and whose absence would not detract from the overall impression of the character of the body of notes could perhaps be presented in the context of the work concerned, so to speak as a part of the paralipomena. An example might be the schematic outline of the structure and theses of the book on jokes.[24] Conversely, where only isolated points of contact with an individual work are identifiable comparatively vaguely in the compact textual mass of the notations, it would be appropriate not to extract the relevant passages from the body of notes but instead to resort only to editorial cross-references—from the note to the work, and from the work to the note—to draw the reader's attention to such correlations. An example of this approach would be the many notations on dreams that reappear, modified to a greater or lesser extent, in the first edition and in the successive revisions of *The Interpretation of Dreams*. Finally, there may be a small number of notes that prove indispensable both to perception of the structure of the body of notes and to understanding the genesis of a given individual work; these could well be reproduced in both contexts. The notes on *Totem and Taboo* are an example.[25]

The recommendation for the future presentation of the writings published after Freud's death in the posthumous-works volume of the *Gesammelte Werke* in 1941[26] is unequivocal: these texts should be edited authentically in the *precise* form they had reached at the end of the process of their genesis—that is, from the manuscripts. In the case of the "Preliminary Report" on the subject of telepathy, dating from 1921, this would mean that

[24]Above, p. 113ff.
[25]Above, p. 117ff.
[26]Cf. above, chapter 11, "Posthumous Publications."

it should be reproduced under its manuscript title and completely un-abridged, followed by the "Postscript," also in the original wording. The *Abriss der Psychoanalyse* [*An Outline of Psycho-Analysis*] might be an-other candidate for facsimile reproduction. This outstanding late work should at any rate be offered exactly as worded in the manuscript, and its rude, sketchy structure should remain conspicuous. This would admittedly make the text harder to read, causing the reader occasionally to stop in his tracks or resort to fruitless guesswork. Yet we should gain something of which we have so far been deprived: a further example of the short series of preserved draft texts. However, because some passages are indeed abbrevi-ated to the point of incomprehensibility, the addition of a quotable emended version would be advisable, subject to declaration and verifiability of the method of completion.

At the end of this loose sequence of suggestions on possible approaches to the editing, for a future critical edition of Freud, of texts such as those whose manuscripts I have described more or less fully in part II of this book, I should like to express a special wish, which may sound like an extravagant demand: in my opinion, it would be part of the very essence of a new edition to present, in the case of the *Traumdeutung* [*The Interpretation of Dreams*] and of the *Drei Abhandlungen zur Sexualtheorie* [*Three Essays on the Theory of Sexuality*], not only the text of the last editions supervised by the author but also the Deuticke first editions of each. After all, it is appropriate to stress again that not a single handwritten line of these primal texts has been preserved. Unless the reader is confronted in the here and now with the first edition as such, he can have no visual or conceptual impression of the actual appearance of the more radical earliest versions of these two texts of genius dating from 1900 and 1905, respectively, which substantially forced a change of paradigm in the understanding of the psyche—and this remains true even if the text in its final authorized version is provided with an indication of all the print variants, dated as accurately as possible, and reproduces all the passages deleted as edition followed edition. This con-cluding suggestion is in fact basically no more than a restatement, in some-what expanded form, of an idea that Freud himself tried out once in the *Gesammelte Schriften*, with his *Traumdeutung*.[27]

Some of the suggestions I shall now put forward on the character of the editorial commentary have been adumbrated in my remarks on the editor's attitude and on editorial principles. There will no doubt be a consensus on

[27]See above, p. 32. It is common practice in other major critical editions to duplicate the reproduction of the principal works, presenting the text of *both* the first edition *and* the last edition supervised by the author.

the fundamental principle to be observed in the formulation of the editorial introductions and prefatory notes, the textual and factual annotations, the appendixes, glossaries, and indexes, and so on: namely, to help the reader understand the works and place them in their context and to do so unobtrusively—that is, without patronizing him or flooding him with excessive material. There is no need to go into detail here on the aids that could facilitate surface-level understanding today and tomorrow—explaining names mentioned by the author but now forgotten; supplying bibliographic references for literature cited; verifying quotations; unraveling allusions that it was still possible to reconstruct in the post-Freud generation;[28] justifying the conjectures introduced; and so forth. What is relevant here is rather the editorial system of coordinates for anchoring at least the longer texts. Three coordinates appear indispensable for this purpose: those relative to biography, to the oeuvre itself, and to the history of ideas.

The reader would be aided in placing an individual Freudian text in its *biographical* context if he were to find information in the editorial commentary on such questions as the following: Were there external incentives for the writing of the work, such as an invitation to contribute to an anthology, to participate in a Festschrift, or to compose an encyclopedia article? Did novel observations and insights during Freud's clinical work, in his reading, or in the exploration of cultural and collective phenomena call for reorientations of theory and concepts? What was the discussion context from which the text concerned issued; did specific colleagues influence its content or form or both?[29] Was its genesis occasioned by specific political and institutional trends? Here is an example of this last case: the Sigmund Freud Collection includes comprehensive documentation of the contacts and correspondences that preceded the writing of the epistolary dialogue with Albert Einstein, "Why War?", at the beginning of the 1930s. Its evaluation may well permit a more detailed description of the biographical circumstances of its genesis than that given by James Strachey in his 1964 "Editor's Note" on this text.[30]

Particularly in the case of the hitherto unpublished texts and passages described in part II, the reader of a future edition is likely to be dependent on a degree of biographical assistance from the editors. This is so, for example,

---

[28]Plainly as part of a deliberate strategy of disguise, however, Freud in *The Interpretation of Dreams* sometimes used allusions that were probably not very easy to understand even for contemporary readers; allowance will have to be made for this fact. Anyone who wished to understand the profound layers of the dreams given as examples, especially those of the author, was no doubt *intended* to take some trouble to do so. (Cf. Grubrich-Simitis, 1971, p. 329.)

[29]Some examples of the exercise of such influence are given in part II of this book (cf. p. 143, p. 165, p. 169, p. 177ff., and p. 207).

[30]Strachey, 1964*a*, p. 197f.

in connection with Jung's disloyal behavior, which Freud describes in one of the suppressed passages in the posthumously published "Preliminary Report":[31] not only does the Freud-Jung correspondence refer repeatedly to this patient of Freud's, even before Jung's attempt to entice her away from him, but the reader can also study therein the comparatively gentle ripples caused by this event at the time of its occurrence.[32]

The biographical coordinate plane would also certainly include the reproduction of Freud's own comments on his texts, as recorded during the period of their genesis and afterward, especially in his letters: complaints about the toil of writing the relevant work, doubts concerning the validity of the results, exclamations of joy on the progress of the manuscript, and so on. However, it would also take account of concrete evaluations of the text concerned: it is well known that Freud's personal judgments in this regard were more frequently adverse than favorable. For instance, in a letter to Max Eitingon dated 8 September 1932, he calls the epistolary dialogue with Einstein mentioned above "the tedious and sterile so-called discussion with Einstein";[33] while *An Autobiographical Study* was dismissed in a letter to Sándor Ferenczi of 6 August 1924 as "a new infusion of the old tea." And in a letter to his daughter Anna of 13 April 1922, Freud bluntly calls his essay "Dreams and Telepathy" "a potboiler." Again, on completing the correction of the page proofs of *The Ego and the Id*, he takes dismal stock of the fruits of an entire phase of his work in another letter to Ferenczi, dated 17 April 1923: "It seems to me that the curve has turned steeply downwards since 'Beyond.' That work was still full of ideas and well written, Group Psychology borders on the banal, and this 'Id' is positively unclear, artificially assembled and loathsome in its diction. [. . .] Apart from the fundamental idea of the 'id' and the aperçu of the genesis of morality, everything about this book really displeases me." Freud's opinions were inclined to fluctuate violently, particularly during the gestation of certain of his writings.[34] Only a very small number of works were spared this self-deprecation: the study of Leonardo, on the occasion of whose second edition he wrote to Ferenczi on 13 February 1919, "certainly the only pretty thing I have ever written"; and above all *The Interpretation of Dreams*, about which predominantly satisfied comments have survived from almost every phase of his life: as late as 1931, Freud wrote in the preface to the third English edition of his magnum opus: "It contains, even according to my

[31]See above, p. 209ff.

[32]1974*a*; cf. in particular Freud's letters of 31 December 1911, 10 January and 29 February 1912, and Jung's letter of 2 January 1912.

[33]Quoted in Jones, 1957, p. 187.

[34]Cf., for example, above, p. 124f., concerning *Totem and Taboo*.

present-day judgment, the most valuable of all the discoveries it has been my good fortune to make. Insight such as this falls to one's lot but once in a lifetime."[35]

In line with the restraint in matters of interpretation and exegesis recommended in the section on the editor's attitude, the editorial commentary should be confined to the presentation of documentable information; it should not offer, for example, psychoanalytic interpretations of Freud's comments on his own work. The following example from the correspondence with Ferenczi may be adduced to illustrate how easily one can go wrong or at least be misled into misplacing the emphasis in the interpretation of a particular choice of words. It concerns an interpretation given by Ferenczi of Freud's title formulation "Der Untergang des Ödipuskomplexes" ["The Dissolution of the Oedipus Complex"].[36] This essay was mentioned in the chapter on the variants, and the reader is asked to consider the following against this background.[37] Freud had informed Ferenczi that his short study constituted an expansion of some trains of thought from the third chapter of *The Ego and the Id* and that it also contained a critique of Otto Rank's theory of the trauma of birth,[38] to which he had, he said, more and more objections. In a letter of 24 March 1924, Ferenczi defended Rank's position, claiming that the latter did not on any account wish to reduce the causation of neurosis to the trauma aspect and to replace Freud's psychoanalytic theory by his own etiological hypothesis. In addition, Ferenczi accused Freud of adopting an emotional and contradictory attitude toward the new theorem: "But the very title 'Untergang des Ödipuskomplexes' [after the title of Spengler's book perhaps?][39] is tinged with affect. Yet I am convinced that there is no reason for an affective reaction: nowhere do I see 'Untergang' [downfall], but everywhere only evidence of the bio-psychological *Unterlage* [substrate] for your immortal discoveries." Freud corrected this emphasis by return mail on 26 March: "Incidentally, I believe that you have analytically misunderstood the downfall of the Oedipus complex. I did not mean that the Oedipus complex meets its downfall in Rank's doctrine of the birth trauma; my little essay on it would be perfectly viable even if Rank had not written his book. It deals with the fact

[35]In 1900*a*, p. xxxii.

[36][*Translator's note*: A complication arises for the English-speaking reader here because Strachey's rendering of the word "Untergang" ("dissolution") is not the literal translation, "decline." The German word can also mean "downfall" or "extinction" and is used, too, for the setting of the sun. See also note 39 below.]

[37]Cf. above, p. 170f.

[38]In the published text of the essay, however, Freud mentions Rank's theory only very briefly at the end, considering it premature to subject it to critical examination at this point.

[39]Ferenczi's square brackets. [*Translator's note*: The reference is to Spengler's *Der Untergang des Abendlandes*, translated into English as *The Decline of the West*.]

that the Oedipus complex is normally not simply repressed, but is actually demolished, canceled out (by identification and superego formation), and that its mere repression gives rise to the pathogenic disposition. [. . .] You may be right in saying that the affectively tinged title points to an impulse in me which has to do with the birth trauma. But that is a secondary analytic meaning [. . .]." As it happens, with this last sentence Freud was making a kind concession to Ferenczi's interpretative zeal, for he had in reality coined the phrase "Untergang des Ödipuskomplexes" completely independently of Rank and had already used it in exactly the sense mentioned in the letter in *The Ego and the Id*,[40]—that is to say, before the book *Das Trauma der Geburt* [*The Trauma of Birth*] had appeared.

Precisely on the biographical coordinate plane, where interpretation and speculation are so tempting, the editorial commentary should be strictly descriptive, indeed documentary, in character; its subject should be not the internal, intimate biographical factors, but those that are in effect least personal, the external and objectivizable aspects. Another quasi-biographical interpretive dimension that has recently made its appearance in Freud research would be completely beyond its scope: that of unconscious transferences by the reader onto a text or author or, as the case may be, transferences in which a text or author tacitly invites the reader to indulge.[41]

The *oeuvre*-related coordinate plane is less problematic than the biographical one and, against the background of the foregoing remarks on editorial principles, can be summarized concisely. The editorial commentary should make it easy for the reader to place an individual writing in the context of the entire oeuvre, and it should do so in two respects. First of all, appropriate editorial information could clearly illustrate the individual history of the relevant text, thereby supplementing the notes, drafts, paralipomena, and lists of variants also reproduced. Second, a network of cross-references, which would, of course, have to cover the early writings too, should fix its position relative to other Freud works or, as appropriate, to the total oeuvre. This would also reveal thematic strands extending over decades as well as conceptual and terminological continuities or, indeed, discontinuities. The concealed architecture of material spanning the oeuvre as a whole and the ingenious multiple utilization of clinical illustrations, discussed in part II on the basis of a few examples only, would, when illuminated by the editorial commentary, emerge in compact and concrete form in the new edition.

---

[40]1923*b*, p. 300 and p. 301 in the *Studienausgabe* [p. 32 and p. 34 in *S. E.* 19, where the word "dissolution" is used]. James Strachey had already drawn attention to this occurrence of the phrase (1961*b*, p. 173).

[41]Cf. Mahony, 1987, pp. 185–88. See also note 16 in the introduction, above.

In James Strachey's editorial commentary for the *Standard Edition*, the oeuvre-related coordinate plane was the one to which he contributed most significantly. For this he deserves all the more credit in that there was no such thing in his day as a Freud electronic database or Freud concordance: Strachey in fact drew on his own stupendous familiarity with the oeuvre, acquired over decades of study, for his innumerable correlations. And indeed, in her obituary of Strachey, Anna Freud emphasized his outstanding competence as a commentator: "It is the reader's impression that the translator's preoccupation with the original text and its rendering led him to see logical sequences and historical connections which otherwise would have gone unnoticed and which, in many instances, were probably unknown to Freud himself."[42] The fabric of these correlations could surely be woven still more densely and be extended if not only the early work but the entire body of letters were taken into account. Although Strachey was in contact with Ernest Jones, who had been granted unrestricted access by the heirs to the correspondences while preparing his biography of Freud, with a few exceptions he himself did not work with these sources.

It will be obvious from the few extracts mentioned in the chapter on the notes that, for example, reconstruction of the history of the genesis of *Totem and Taboo* would remain incomplete without a consideration of the numerous traces of this process in the Freud-Ferenczi correspondence. The same no doubt applies to the references contained in the chapter "Posthumous Publications" to germs of the "Preliminary Report," alias "Psycho-Analysis and Telepathy," also featuring in the Freud-Ferenczi correspondence. I shall give just one more example of the inexhaustibility of the letters when it is a matter of tracking down preliminary and parallel formulations of a particular idea, on the one hand, and concealed work filiations, on the other. In the chapter on the variants, I mentioned a passage from Freud's introduction to the anthology *Zur Psychoanalyse der Kriegsneurosen* [The Psycho-Analysis of the War Neuroses].[43] It concerns the author's attempt to bring the concept of "traumatic neurosis" into contact with that of "transference neurosis"; in other words, it deals with that fundamental theoretical problem that has now been touched upon several times. In a letter written to Ernest Jones on 18 February 1919, in which he comments on Jones's contribution to the anthology, Freud formulates the theses enunciated in his preface directly in the context of his critique and at the same time weaves in a sketch of his second theory of anxiety, which was published in full only in 1926, in *Inhibitions, Symptoms and Anxiety*: "Later on, it seems you are losing the contact with the item of the 'Traumatische Neurose' [traumatic

[42]1969, p. 132.
[43]Cf. above, p. 160.

neurosis], and what you say on the relation to narcisstic anxiety is excellent, hits the point, but it is too short and may not impress sufficiently the reader. Let me propose to you the following formula: first consider the case of the traumatic neurosis of peace. It is a narcisstic affection like dem[entia] pr[aecox] etc.. Mechanism may be guessed. Angst [anxiety] is a protection against shock (Schreck). Now the condition of the tr[aumatische] N[eurose] seems to be that the soul had not time to recurr to this protection and is taken by the trauma unprepared. Its 'Reizschutz' ['protective shield against stimuli'] is overrun, the principal and primary function of keeping off excessive quantities of 'Reiz' [stimulus] frustrated. Then narc[isstic] lib[ido] is given out in shape of the signs of 'Angst.' This is the mechanism of every case of primary repression, a traumatic neurosis thus to be found at the bottom of every case of Übertrag[un]gsneurose [transference neurosis]."⁴⁴

Finally, let us turn to the third coordinate of the editorial commentary, that of the *history of ideas*. Editorial information of this kind should facilitate the reader's task of placing Freud's oeuvre—individual observations, thoughts, concepts, theories, methods of argument, logical techniques, stylistic characteristics, and so forth—in the relevant sign contexts, both contemporary and handed down from the past. The term "history of ideas" is used here in a comprehensive sense—that is to say, including, of course, the natural sciences.⁴⁵ We had already intended to emphasize this coordinate plane of the history of ideas in that failed first attempt to create a historical-critical edition in the 1960s;⁴⁶ for Strachey had paid relatively little heed to it, compared with the wealth of his contributions to the second dimension in particular. By so orienting his commentary, he may have been conforming to an inclination of the author—as with the decision to exclude almost the entire preanalytic early works from the *Standard Edition*.

To be sure, Freud himself affirmed: "Psychoanalysis [. . .] did not drop from the skies ready-made. It had its starting-point in older ideas, which it developed further; it sprang from earlier suggestions, which it elaborated."⁴⁷ It is indeed undeniable that, in his writings, he abundantly documents and illustrates his vast reading and its enormous range, which left untouched virtually no textual field between belles lettres and hard natural science. However, apart from a few heartfelt expressions of thanks, especially toward his great teachers, quotation of this kind gives the impression rather of the dutiful observance of academic rules. There are indications

---

⁴⁴1993*e*, p. 334 [in English in original].

⁴⁵For the importance of precisely this tradition in the history of the provenance of psychoanalysis, see the remarks in the concluding chapter 15.

⁴⁶See above, p. 54.

⁴⁷1924*f*, p. 191.

that Freud the innovator was not particularly interested in his intellectual forebears and neighbors. Even where he explicitly reconstructs the history of psychoanalysis, he focuses attention primarily on the point at which he broke with tradition—that is, the emphasis is on discontinuity rather than continuity. Conversely, what remained more or less unmentioned was that, not least precisely in the preparation of this break—for instance, in the invention of the instruments that were ultimately to afford him access to the unconscious inner world—he probably assimilated and utilized myriads of hints from others by way of analogy and borrowing of metaphors. In the 1890s in particular, he may, in his urgent questing, and also in his private reading, have preconsciously looked out for the kind of authors with whom he could feel a kinship and by whose textual gestures and thought configurations he could allow himself to be inspired.

As an example, we may recall the notation "Quotations & analogies" mentioned in the chapter on the notes: "For the proper attitude to the work of interpretation: Burckhardt. Hist. Greek Civilization p 5, intense effort is actually least likely to secure the desired result here; quietly attentive listening with steady diligence takes one further."[48] If we read the "Introduction" from which this quotation is taken,[49] we do indeed encounter a plethora of further analogies to positions and conceptions typical of Freud: Burckhardt's critique of academic practice in his discipline; his demand for a fundamentally new classification of fields and methods in the study of the history of civilization; the assertion that it is not external events that are the most important facts to be investigated but modes of thought and perception, living forces, both constructive and destructive—in a word, "the innermost soul of past humanity."[50] For Burckhardt, research on the history of civilization throve principally on what was communicated "unintentionally and disinterestedly, indeed involuntarily and *unconsciously*, by sources and monuments."[51] The recurrent was more important than the unique. Finally, he warned against perceptual illusions, and in particular the danger of overlooking much "that was of consistent importance,"[52] instead holding isolated chance instances to be significant and characteristic. Such mistaken appreciations could be offset only by continued reading and rereading of the sources. This is followed by the quotation noted by Freud, which sounds like an embryonic formulation of the concept of "evenly suspended attention." Again, Burckhardt's complaint about the difficulty of portraying

---

[48]See above, p. 100f.
[49]Burckhardt, 1962 [1898], p. 6.
[50]Ibid., p. 5.
[51]Ibid. (My emphasis.)
[52]Ibid., p. 6.

facts from the history of civilization—that discourse was "always merely successive, reporting gradually, whereas the things themselves were a largely simultaneous, tremendous unity"[53]—is reminiscent of Freud's formulation, quoted earlier, about the aporias of describing psychic structure.[54]

Drawing the reader's attention to as many as possible of these scattered affinities would be the aim of the editorial commentary on the third coordinate plane, that of the history of ideas. Without in any way detracting from the revolutionary character of Freud's originality, such a reconstruction of influences from the history of ideas—that is, of the sources in the fields of neurology, evolutionary biology, linguistics, the history of civilization, philosophy, theology, literature, and others—would permit an even wider and deeper understanding of the genesis of the oeuvre. It is hardly necessary to mention that commentaries on the history of ideas should refer only to texts composed by Freud's contemporaries or written before his time. Only these would be relevant to the genetic aspect. The editor's subject is textual history, not the history of the subsequent impact of an author's work. The literature after Freud, and in particular the entire later development of psychoanalysis as a science, would thus as a rule not be considered, if only on grounds of volume and owing to the inevitability of subjective assessments when the oeuvre is confronted with present-day research. Conversely, recently published contributions to the biography of Freud or the historiography of psychoanalysis could certainly be used as sources in the drafting of commentaries concerning the dimension of the history of ideas.

As with the biographical and oeuvre-related coordinate planes, the principle would again apply, on that of the history of ideas, that the editorial commentary should include only what can be deduced directly from Freud's wording; interpretation, by contrast, should be kept to a minimum. The documentation of intellectual affinities—of both structure and content—in this sense might not uncommonly call for extensive digressions; in order not to hold up the flow and detract from the pleasure of reading, they should preferably be presented in the form of appendixes. Many references on the level of the history of ideas could in any case presumably be no more than bibliographic pointers, signposts to the reader to works by other authors to consult if he wishes to become fully aware of the extent to which Freud was embedded in the European context of ideas.

As to the injunction to the editor not to intrude excessively with his own voice, brevity and conciseness should be the watchwords for all three coordinate planes. After all, the editorial commentary of a new critical edition should aspire neither to anticipate nor to usurp future Freud research. It

[53]Ibid., p. 7.
[54]Cf. above, p. 127f.

need not do any more than, as stated in the epigraph at the beginning of this book, reliably anchor the individual writings and guarantee them a maximum of presence by strengthening their material aspects.

That sounds simple. Yet the information ultimately communicated in the editorial commentaries would be the quintessence of a prolonged, onerous, and painstaking research process. Its many preparatory stages would include the systematic sifting of documents and sources of every conceivable provenance—always with the aim of securing traces of the development of Freud's thought and oeuvre meticulously and as completely as possible. The following is only a selection of the relevant investigative spheres to which the editors would have to devote themselves: the thousands upon thousands of Freud's published and unpublished letters together with the addressees' replies and their own correspondences with others, where these are likely to be pertinent to the object of the research; the entire minutes of the Vienna Psychoanalytic Society;[55] the surviving parts of Freud's extensive library with their many marginalia and markings, preserved mainly at the Freud Museum in London and the New York State Psychiatric Institute; memories of contemporaries, colleagues, patients, family members, and so on; and the sound parts of the gigantic secondary literature on Freud.

Constitution of the text and systematic investigation of the manuscript and print variants would, in the preparatory phase, call in addition for complete transcription of the manuscripts and their collation with the first editions as well as comparison of all editions published during the author's lifetime and study of his personal copies—in other words, an all-embracing process of checking. In this connection, it goes without saying that one of the fundamental aspects of the editors' task would be to peruse the numerous psychoanalytic archives that now exist—that is, not only the Sigmund Freud Collection in Washington.[56]

Although concrete questions of an institutional framework for the work on a future critical edition of Freud, its funding and staffing as well as the planning of the individual phases of the project are beyond the scope of the present sketch, these brief indications will nevertheless perhaps convey to the reader some impression of the order of magnitude of the enterprise.[57] It cannot, of course, be implemented by an individual or a publishing house. It would instead require an institution that would assure it the freedom and

---

[55]Cf. above, p. 69f.

[56]Some other relevant archives, such as that of the New York Leo Baeck Institute, would also need to be consulted.

[57]As stated, one of the objections raised by the assessor of the Deutsche Forschungsgemeinschaft at the time of Alexander Mitscherlich's application for a subsidy for a historical-critical edition of Freud was that it drastically underestimated the time and personnel requirements (cf. above, p. 58); in hindsight, the objection was perfectly justified.

resources without which such wide-ranging research processes cannot be undertaken and which, moreover, would provide it with at least a modicum of independence from biographical vicissitudes. Although James Strachey could feel that he had the support not only of his own small group of close collaborators but also of the Institute of Psycho-Analysis in London and of the American Psychoanalytic Association, he complained, on completion of the *Standard Edition*, that the decisive handicap to his work was that "it has been without the background of any established academic machine ready to provide either personnel or accommodation."[58]

An academic apparatus of this kind would certainly be indispensable for the creation of any new critical edition of Freud in the original language. Even if some of the most important editorial projects of recent times, such as the Nietzsche and Hölderlin editions, were begun solely on the initiative of enthusiastic, inspired editors and venturesome publishers, a certain institutionalization and recourse to sponsoring foundations proved to be unavoidable even in these cases as the work proceeded. In order to find the appropriate structure for the Freud project, information will have to be obtained on the forms of organization—even if they are found to be not directly transferable—which have proved successful with other editions—that is, on models such as a link, supported by major foundations, with one of the academies of sciences or the university world.[59]

If only because of the enormous scale of the work involved in the disclosure of the letters, it would surely be necessary to set up from the beginning an operations center for the preparatory phase of this fundamental Freud research—say, in association with one of the chairs of psychoanalysis or psychoanalytic university institutes or alternatively, in a second attempt,[60] at the Sigmund Freud-Institut in Frankfurt. Those in charge of the project, who would certainly seek forms of international and interdisciplinary cooperation from the beginning, would then have to be assured of complete independence. A crucial goal of the preparatory phase would be the establishment of a dedicated team, which would obviously have to be led by at least one psychoanalytically trained Freud researcher of undisputed competence and one editorial theorist thoroughly conversant with the craft of philology. As to the question central to the success of the project, concerning the type of person who would probably have a particular talent for such work, a number of hints can be found in the passage at the beginning of this chapter, on the attitude of the editor toward the texts entrusted to him.

[58]Strachey, 1966*a*, p. xviii.
[59]Cf. Brenner, 1987; Pöggeler, 1987.
[60]Cf. above, p. 57.

In conclusion, however, attention is drawn to some further special difficulties and obstacles. As already indicated several times, certain sections of the Sigmund Freud Collection, including notebooks and many individual letters as well as correspondences, are still restricted and will in some cases remain so until well into the next century. As in the 1960s,[61] a fundamental prerequisite for the creation of a new Freud edition, even if initially confined to the works themselves, would surely prove to be that the editors were granted full access at an early date, subject to the strict observance of certain obligatory conditions, for instance concerning information on patients. With regard to this question of access, too, cooperation would probably be if anything hampered by the fact that most of the material left behind after Freud's death is preserved in an archive that has no permanent links with an academic institution or foundation[62]—unlike other archives, which, being appropriately equipped, consider that they themselves have the competence to promote editions of the works of their authors and which initiate and cosponsor such editions; in more favorable constellations of this kind, the research center and the archive are institutionally linked.[63] Finally, restrictions and delays could result for a number of years from the fact that Freud's works and letters will remain under copyright protection in Germany until the year 2009. New publications, especially of the letters, thus remain subject to the control of the family.

The remarks of some critics who complain of the absence of a critical complete edition of Freud occasionally betray impatience, as if they were ignoring these specific difficulties and were closing their eyes to the usual time requirements of critical editing, and indeed to the fact that it is by no means unusual for papers in archives to be restricted for moderate or even long periods of time. What future editors of Freud could gain from an acquaintance with other editorial projects, apart from the honing of their methodological consciousness, would be serenity in regard to the aspect of time. To be sure, there are examples of historical-critical editions planned relatively soon after the death of the relevant author and implemented comparatively quickly. These, however, are the exception rather than the rule. To gain an idea of the extended chronology that is the normal fate of critical complete editions, one need only consider the example of the history of the Leibniz edition—which is not, of course, to say that we must resign

[61]Cf. above, p. 58f.

[62]After retiring as director of the Sigmund Freud Archives, however, K. R. Eissler founded the Freud Literary Heritage Foundation, which now assists in the preparation of critical editions of Freud's letters.

[63]An example of a living scientific center of this kind, established around another literary estate rescued from the Nazis, is the Husserl Archive at the University of Louvain, with its various branches in the United States, Germany, and France. Cf. IJsseling, 1987.

ourselves to similar, centuries-long waiting times before the new Freud edition comes into being. Although the demand for full publication also of the extensive literary remains was first voiced shortly after the death of Leibniz in 1716, the Akademie-Ausgabe is still far from completion. A century after the decision to initiate the Akademie-Ausgabe of Kant in 1894, this, too, remains unfinished. As to the two innovators who wounded the narcissism of man, to whom Freud liked to compare himself:[64] it was not before 1944—some four hundred years after his death—that preparations for a complete edition of Copernicus were set in train, but they soon foundered and were not resumed until the 1970s; while to this day there is no great historical-critical edition of Darwin. Many other important authors could be mentioned whose ideas have been and still are influential although the texts in which they are recorded are not yet available in standard historical-critical editions. They include, for example, Georg Christoph Lichtenberg, who was highly esteemed by Freud.

Another, of course, as described in detail in part I, is Freud himself. Only gradually are we approaching the point when the securing and documentation of the surviving material can be deemed substantially complete, full access to the archives is beginning to be afforded, the texts are emerging from the family's sphere of influence, and the author is increasingly becoming a figure of history. Only now are all the elements falling into place for the transition to the fourth phase of the editorial history—that is, for the beginning of work on a large-scale critical edition.

[64]For example, in 1917a, pp. 139–41.

15 CONJECTURES: ON RESULTS AND EFFECTS

What might ultimately emerge from such editorial work in the fourth phase of the history of the editions? And what effects would it be legitimate to expect or to hope for from a new large-scale critical edition? Approaching the end of this book, we can at best conjecture on these matters.

To remain faithful to the principle *Back to Freud's Texts*, let these conjectures once again be centered on the work. Following our initial exploration of the landscape of the manuscripts, it can be predicted with some certainty that the overall form of the oeuvre, as it presents itself to the reader today, toward the end of the third stage of its editorial history, will not change radically, any more than will the image of the author himself. We shall not come face-to-face with a completely different Freud. To hold out a sensational prospect—such as the discovery of a hitherto unknown major work or the exposure as a rank forgery of a text included in the canon for decades—would constitute misleading dramatization. And anyone who expects scandal is in for disappointment. In the case of the founder of psychoanalysis, there will be nothing comparable to the dissolution of *The Will to Power*, that arbitrary compilation by the administrators of Nietzsche's literary estate, which was so influential in the political popularization of his philosophy. Anna Freud and Ernst Freud were of a different caliber from Elisabeth Förster-Nietzsche and Peter Gast.

So there will be no shattering of the tectonics of the oeuvre, and yet we may prepare ourselves for significant elaboration and differentiation of the microstructures in every direction. Myriads of individual finds that may be expected to accrue from the fundamental research associated with the preparation of the edition indicate that the effort will be worthwhile—for the material described in part II of this book at any rate suggests that our image of the author and his work could thereby gain substantially in perspective. Certain textual areas are likely to emerge from obscurity and become fully visible for the very first time, particularly, as it were, in the peripheral zones: the earliest phases of the creative process—the notes—and the earliest publications—the so-called preanalytic writings—on the one hand, and the late works, on the other.

The editing of the *body of notes*, as yet substantially concealed and unexplored, would cast light on the earliest stage of Freud's working process to be fixed in writing. As unofficial, private documents, the notes certainly make up a category of works in their own right; the particular material constitution of these texts, their semantic and syntactic structure as well as their thematic diversity were described in some detail in part II of this book. The reader would in effect be confronted for the first time with the *raw material of the oeuvre*. Precisely because these notes present Freud's scientific colloquy with himself, unsmoothed and unpolished, they record the toilsomeness of his approach and its basis in empirical observation more concretely than do the printed writings. After all, he wrote the latter with courteous consideration for the reader, whom as a rule he wished to spare excessive effort; in consequence, their obvious rightness and elegance usually give the impression that the information imparted in them must have been easy to establish. The notes, by contrast, show us Freud the researcher, struggling by the sweat of his brow to describe mental phenomena in a new way, strenuously hoarding dream texts, forcing himself to take infinite pains over his observations as well as goading himself on to theoretical audacity, self-critically subjecting his concepts, theories, and works to ongoing revision.

Again, it is only these handwritten traces that can fully reveal to us that the revolutionary innovations introduced by Freud in the traditional doctor-patient relationship—having the patient speak, listening to him, speaking to him, and being utterly persuaded, on the basis of a profound faith in the power of words, that the patient has something to say about the nature of his suffering—were strokes of genius not only in terms of therapy but also in the strategy of research. As the notes make even clearer to us, his most important partners in the process of discovery were his analysands, not his pupils and colleagues, except those who were his training analysands. The editing of all the surviving note manuscripts will supplement the documentable reconstruction of Freud's creative process with the earliest dimension of the interlocking of observation and intuition and may well come to represent a paradigm for interest in research on creativity in general.

Although Freud's *preanalytic writings* have been mentioned repeatedly in this book, they have not been treated in a section of their own, unlike, for instance, the notes. This is because the currently accessible parts of the Sigmund Freud Collection, as described in the chapter "Vicissitudes of the Manuscripts," contain hardly any surviving manuscript documentation from his early period—nothing, in fact, but the texts once attached to the letters to Wilhelm Fliess, including the "Project" and a photocopy of the unpublished, undated "Kritische Einleitung in die Nervenpathologie" ["Critical Introduction to Neuropathology"], whereas there is no trace of the manuscript of, say, the study on aphasia or the important monographs on child neurology. Because this aspect of the oeuvre is not represented in the landscape of the manuscripts, it was impossible for it to feature comprehensively in the second part of this book or indeed in the previous chapter, with its suggestions on principles for a new Freud edition, which is in turn based almost exclusively on the material of part II.

As already described in detail in the account of the history of the editions, Freud, once he had founded psychoanalysis, resolutely placed his early work beyond the pale, as if he no longer wished to count it a part of his oeuvre. The effects of his ban have persisted. The editors of the *Gesammelte Werke*, published in London after his death, and also James Strachey, editor of the *Standard Edition*, acquiesced in it. Although attention has been drawn in the Freud secondary literature to the importance of the early writings, starting with isolated articles in the 1950s[1] and continuing more recently in a growing number of solid contributions, there is still a latent tendency to imitate the author's defensive movement as a reflex action. Let this not be the case here. In the prominent position of the final chapter, I should like to point the reader toward this region of the oeuvre—for its editorial disclosure may be expected to exert a particularly lasting influence, even if so few manuscripts have been preserved. It therefore seems not inappropriate for this digression to constitute the focal point of this chapter.

A detailed examination of the reasons for Freud's negative attitude is beyond the scope of this discussion. A number of elements may have been involved: an aversion to the experiences of his pioneering days, the pain of which remained with him throughout his life, when he had wanted to commend his new methods of access to the understanding of the psyche and the neuroses to his academic colleagues, who had committed themselves exclusively to the appreciation of anatomical, physical, and chemical factors, and had met predominantly with rejection, contempt, or indifference; a sense of injury at the fact that he, himself raised in the positivism of the nineteenth century, had finally had to give up his original ambition of succeeding during his lifetime in accommodating the organic substrate within the science of unconscious mental life; and perhaps also his profound identification with the biblical Moses, which would after all have favored the imago of a sudden, transition-free inception of his teachings. However, the fact of cutting himself off so abruptly from his own scientific past no doubt also, and in particular, served the purposes of a highly effective ca-

---

[1]See above, p. 55. For an even earlier appreciation, cf. Brun, 1936. A fresh survey was given by Solms in 1991.

thectic strategy, presumably adopted on the preconscious level: not to look back but to concentrate all his forces on the continuation and promotion of psychoanalysis—that is, on what could be achieved in the present and immediate future.

These reasons no longer hold good. It is time to integrate the whole of Freud's early work into the oeuvre. Indeed, as a first step, a change in nomenclature would be appropriate. The word "preanalytic" cannot but sound pejorative, as if everything published by Freud before psychoanalysis came into being was not worth mentioning because it was as it were blind when compared with his real work. This is a view that in no way does justice to the status of Freud's early publications, by which alone, as historians of science have long since confirmed quite independently of psychoanalysis, he would have made his mark in the history of neurology even if nothing more had issued from his pen thereafter. After all, even the young author was already Sigmund Freud.

It is unclear when and how the word "preanalytic" came into general use. Where Freud happens to mention his early publications in his writings, he does not, at any rate, seem to have used this term. Where it occurs at all, it almost always denotes times and disciplines in which an understanding of the psyche was still completely lacking and does not characterize his early work.[2] If the part of the oeuvre hitherto described as "preanalytic" were to be called simply "early writings" in a future critical edition of Freud, the split that has hitherto existed would be overcome—for the paper "On the Psychical Mechanism of Hysterical Phenomena" or the essay "The Neuro-Psychoses of Defense"[3] as well as other works would then surely have to be counted among the early writings.[4] In retrospect, this bipartition, which was introduced by the author and retained after his death, would in any case presumably appear artificial, as it would be found on closer scrutiny that Freud was already on the path toward psychoanalysis in many of his ostensibly purely neurological writings.[5]

We can illustrate this by a single example, the study on aphasia already

[2]Not so in a letter of 23 February 1937 to Smith Ely Jelliffe, in which he does use it in this sense. An English translation of this letter has been published (1983a, p. 272).

[3]1893h and 1894a.

[4]The designation "Neuroscientific Works" proposed by Mark Solms for the English edition, no doubt chosen mainly to distinguish the contents from those of Strachey's *Standard Edition of the Complete Psychological Works*, does admittedly stress the independent significance of these texts but maintains the differentiation from the psychoanalytic oeuvre.

[5]At the end of the letter to Jelliffe quoted above, which incidentally contained Freud's response to a manuscript that Jelliffe had sent him entitled "Sigmund Freud as a Neurologist," he added that this article on his early writings, which had now grown so remote from him, might have some influence on those who "still like to believe that I pulled psychoanalysis out of my hat."

discussed more fully in the context of the history of the editions. In the view of Mark Solms and Michael Saling,[6] Freud so to speak laid the theoretical foundations of psychoanalysis in this monograph, from which, significantly, he never distanced himself and to whose subject he even occasionally referred in his subsequent psychoanalytic writings;[7] it was in fact his first major investigation of mental processes. In these authors' opinion, it is not, as is generally assumed, the "Project for a Scientific Psychology" of 1895 that forms the link between his neurological and psychoanalytic concerns, but the classic monograph on speech disorders, dating from 1891. Here, they maintain, he broke definitively with established neurology, in particular with the conception of the brain advanced by his teacher Theodor Meynert, and, by his espousal of the dynamic-evolutionistic doctrines of the English neurologist John Hughlings Jackson, who was still underrated at the time, forged ahead decisively with the construction of his own lifework, psychoanalysis.

Jackson had derived a physiological theory of complex mental processes from the treatment of his patients. Its elements include: the principle that physical and psychic processes should be conceptualized separately; a model of the mental apparatus incorporating different hierarchical levels of functioning—both primitive and more highly structured ones, of phylogenetically earlier and later origin, respectively—so that what he called functional retrogressions from a higher to a lower level become theoretically conceivable; as well as a kind of theory of meaning suggesting that seemingly nonsensical utterances by aphasic patients can be decoded as meaningful communications if transposed into a traumatic past context.

Although this cannot be considered in detail here,[8] anyone familiar with psychoanalysis will have already noticed affinities of several kinds among these few points—for example, with the concept of regression, with the topographical model, with the early trauma view of the genesis of hysteria and the associated method of treatment—that is to say, with the very foundations of Freud's etiological theory.[9] Solms and Saling summarize the literally fundamental importance of Freud's encounter with Jackson's ideas and the topic of aphasia for the development of psychoanalysis in the fol-

[6]Solms and Saling, 1986.

[7]Cf. Ingeborg Meyer-Palmedo's editorial annotations for the new edition of the book on aphasia.

[8]In addition to Solms and Saling, cf. Forrester, 1980, and Leuschner, 1992.

[9]Wolfgang Leuschner (ibid.) has shown that a number of psychoanalytic concepts—e.g., word-presentation/thing-presentation—have their direct roots in the aphasia context and that, because Freud transposed them almost unaltered into his psychoanalytic arguments, they seem to us today to be hard to understand, arbitrary, and obscure. In his view, they can be clarified only if newly illuminated from the perspective of their provenance.

lowing terms: "Jackson's theory [. . .] made it possible to see dreams and the ideation of the mentally ill, as *normal and lawful, lower level functioning*," and: "This notion that dreams were 'positive symptoms,' the result of topographic regression, had its origins in 'On aphasia,' and it resulted in Freud's monumental 'The interpretation of dreams.'"[10]

Integration of the whole of the hitherto scattered early work into the oeuvre for all to see would most powerfully flesh out the figure of Freud as a scientist and writer.[11] It is already apparent how much these texts from the first twenty years of his working life could enrich the entire second and third coordinate planes of the editorial commentary of a future critical edition. They would not only throw light on the historical roots of psychoanalysis in the ideas of the humanities and the social sciences, but also bring out the full extent of the natural-science sources, so to speak the "Parnassus" and the "School of Athens" of that "citizen of the civilized world,"[12] Freud—the inspiration derived not only from Jacob Burckhardt but also from John Hughlings Jackson.

At the same time, strong emphasis would be placed on the twofold character of psychoanalysis, as, in effect, a "hermeneutic empirical science,"[13] which has been described most consistently by Alfred Lorenzer. This twofold character corresponds to the dual relationship of man to nature and sociality, to the bodiliness of the social and the sociality of the body. Freud tried indefatigably to conceptualize it in his metapsychology and thereby to mark the special position of psychoanalysis—a position that is as much a source of tension as it is productive—in relation to physiology and the neurosciences on the one hand and to psychology and sociology on the other. To the extent that the early writings emerged from the twilight into which their author plunged them, they would surely not only inject new life into the metapsychology debate but perhaps also resolve the barren dilemma of whether Freud was a neurophysiologist in disguise or a poet

[10]Solms and Saling, 1986, p. 406. Heinz G. Schott (1981) has made another connection between an early neurological work, the monograph *Die infantile Cerebrallähmung* [Infantile Cerebral Palsy] (1897a), and *The Interpretation of Dreams*, highlighting conceptual analogies, for instance, between a neural mechanism of suppression that is weakened in the genesis of cerebral palsy and a psychic mechanism of suppression that is suspended in dream formation: "the more highly developed system in each case (consciousness and the cerebral cortex respectively) normally suppresses that which is more primitive (the unconscious and the spinal marrow respectively). The symptoms (the dream and the neurological manifestations respectively) arise because the suppressing system is no longer capable of performing its function and of keeping the suppressed one in check" (p. 103).

[11]This may well already be achieved by the edition of the neuroscientific works now being prepared by Mark Solms (cf. above, note 36, chapter 3). The results of his work could subsequently be integrated into a critical edition of the oeuvre as a whole.

[12]1915b, p. 277.

[13]Lorenzer, 1984, p. 149ff.

bound by the shackles of science. What would instead appear would be the figure of an investigator who focused his attention precisely on the "marriage of subjective experience and bodily sensation"[14] and whose true modernity will probably not come to be fully recognized until some time in the future.

Solms and Saling have shown how advanced the neurology outlined in Freud's study on aphasia actually was—decades ahead of his time. This text would have to be taken as the basis for the development of ideas on any future cooperation between psychoanalysis and the neurosciences, a link that, in their view, has been broken almost entirely. Indeed, conceptions bridging the gap between the psychic and the somatic realms have burgeoned precisely in recent times: for instance, brain research has now discovered that the process of postnatal brain growth, the linkage of different cerebral centers as a neuronal prerequisite for receptivity to certain cognitive fields, is controlled partly by interaction with the environment—that is, not least by object relations.[15] Research projects of this kind, which evade the body-mind antagonism, are usually implemented through interdisciplinary collaboration. Yet precisely psychoanalysis seems to be involved hardly at all in this work, although its unique experience with unconscious mental life and its insights into the structure and scope of the early developmental processes would surely predestine it at least to ask productive questions. The hope would be that by making Freud's early work visible—that is, by providing a concrete reminder of the extent to which the founder of psychoanalysis was indeed *not* inclined "to leave the psychology hanging in the air without an organic basis"[16]—the new edition could stimulate curiosity in respect of such interdisciplinary collaboration. However, it would be naïve to assume that such cooperation could in any way enrich or facilitate understanding in the here and now of specific individual subjectivity in the analytic situation.

The other peripheral zone—at the opposite end of the chronology of the oeuvre—in which a new critical edition could more clearly bring out much

[14]Ibid., p. 162.

[15]Cf. the review by Singer, 1990*a*; for a more detailed account, cf., for example, Singer, 1990*b*.

[16]1985*c*, p. 326. The quotation is taken from a letter to Fliess dated 22 September 1898. Even in old age, Freud, in a confidently materialistic vein, albeit in a different context, repeated: "We know that the mechanisms of the psychoses are in essence no different from those of the neuroses, but we do not have at our disposal the quantitative stimulation necessary for changing them. The hope of the future here lies in organic chemistry or the access to it through endocrinology. This future is still far distant, but one should study analytically every case of psychosis because this knowledge will one day guide the chemical therapy." (Letter to Marie Bonaparte dated 15 January 1930, quoted in Jones, 1957, p. 480.)

that has hitherto been barely discernible comprises the *late writings*. This area of Freud's work, like the notes, was discussed comprehensively in part II of this book. Once again, therefore, a few sentences will suffice. In the previous chapter I recommended that these texts be presented authentically in the form in which Freud bequeathed them to us. This applies in particular to the entire surviving Moses material and to the manuscript of the *Abriss* [*Outline*]. In other words, nothing should be completed or retouched; the shaky, fragmentary character of these writings should be seen not as a sign of failure or clumsiness, but as a communication sui generis. Only then would the reader be able to perceive the uniqueness and greatness of this work of old age *as* a work of old age: its enigmatic and unfathomable aspects, its origins in a desperate, late process of self-exploration, but also the detached grace of the aged writer even in the last flickerings of his life. The Moses documents would then in turn surely appear even more clearly as a category of work in their own right, one that today is still beyond our ken: as the epitome of a life, as an autobiographical metaphor, as a wish-fulfilling daydream, but also as a dismal prophecy of a looming loss of "intellectuality" and of an unstoppable increase in collective seducibility—at the time, these were forebodings of the phenomena of the Nazi period, but, on a different plane of reality, they seem to be assuming new relevance in our contemporary situation.

As to the gain in perspective that may be expected to accrue to our image of the mighty *central area* of the oeuvre, let us briefly focus again on some salient passages from the description given in part II. In the new edition, careful analysis of the manuscript would more clearly reveal the stratified structure of the "Wolf Man" case history and at the same time facilitate the reconstruction of a crucial stage in the evolution of Freud's theories. The same would apply to the presentation for the first time of the two versions of *Beyond the Pleasure Principle*. On the one hand, more light would be thrown on the genesis of the death-drive hypothesis; while, on the other, the link represented by the phenomenon and concept of the "compulsion to repeat" would more tellingly bring out affinities with, for example, "The 'Uncanny,'" an essay that Freud had begun years earlier and then put aside, reintroducing it into his current creative process at approximately the same time as *Beyond*; here, then, we have another diphasic genesis, although to the best of our knowledge so far nothing of its first stage has survived in manuscript form. The dynamics of textual development could also be demonstrated for a third major work by presenting both the draft and the definitive version of *The Ego and the Id*. The nature of the gain in perspective becomes comprehensible if we imagine the incorporation not only of a number of other drafts but also, for example, of the texts that were deliberately suppressed or that remained unpublished for external, mainly chance reasons, of the paralipomena, the letter references, and the lists of variants: a textual structure hitherto perceived as static, frozen in a single plane, will then be endowed with an additional spatial dimension, so that in certain cases we can look right through it, back to the tentative beginnings of its formulation, and see for ourselves how each successive version emerges from its predecessor.

The principal result of a new edition would surely be to document the *textual history of the entire oeuvre* as comprehensively as possible and to make it transparent. Just as Freud placed the whole of his early work beyond the pale, so he also consistently expunged the immediate prior stages of the long sequence of works with which he wished his name to be permanently associated—even though this past, in which the work, to quote Starobinski's fine essay for the last time, "was not yet what it would become," nevertheless "nourishes and sustains" the definitive text, so that its ultimate being will in effect be "revealed differentially by the distance separating its final state from the series of states which go before it."[17]

The reconstruction of this past, as far as the surviving documents permit, would not only allow the profile of the oeuvre to emerge more graphically but also emphatically promote the understanding of psychoanalysis—to be more precise, of the specific variability and softness of its concepts. In a letter dated 20 November 1912, the Zurich psychiatrist Eugen Bleuler, while engaged in the preparatory work for an introductory lecture on Freud's psychoanalysis,[18] put the following critique to him: "Your psychological concepts are provisional ones, created in accordance with your instantaneous experiences; you are prepared to modify them at every moment following new experiences, sometimes perhaps without being very conscious of the fact; they thus have no definite boundaries. That is virtually a *conditio sine qua non* for the discoverer; but for the mere parrot, faced with the task of divining the reasons for the change, it presents an insuperable difficulty. It is, for instance, all well and good if you define the concept of libido as that part of our striving which is direct or transformed sexuality; but when you speak elsewhere in the same terms of the connoisseur's appreciation of a painting, the ingestion of food by an infant, sucking, etc., the pupil is unable to accommodate these things within the definition. Your regression is a chameleon, the sole permanent characteristic of which can be derived only from your own psychological ideas, and so on. Your theory of

---

[17]1974, p. 170.
[18]Bleuler, 1913.

sexuality was bound to remain incomprehensible to me until you told me how you arrived at it. In a word, all your concepts are describable almost solely in terms of their developmental history, and they continue to develop. This means that they can be comprehended only by someone who has in his head their entire history, only a tiny fraction of which exists in print." Far from justifying himself, let alone apologizing, Freud wrote in his answering letter of 1 December 1912 that he regarded this characterization "as a great compliment." Only such a mobile, open way of forming concepts "from provisionalities" made it possible, he said, "to mate up with the progressive discovery of the Ucs."[19] So, if the edition were to bring the *unprinted* part of the conceptual history into the light of day, one of the resulting advantages would be an enrichment of the psychoanalytic dictionaries based on the texts sent by Freud to the printer.[20]

In the previous chapter I outlined the important role that would fall to the editorial commentary in illuminating the history of the text: the editors could make explicit the hidden continuities of the oeuvre—for example, thematic strands extending over decades, the complex histories of certain concepts, the architecture of material spanning the work as a whole as well as the way Freud's thought was embedded in the European context of ideas. One of the benefits here would be the gradual clarification of how Freud worked, from the first observations and jottings, via their expansion into fully formulated texts, to the planning of an effective publication policy. Moreover, we should see all this as process. And to the extent that motion is the hallmark of life, the outcome would indeed be in the nature of a *vivifying effect*. I became aware of this effect even as I worked on the manuscripts— as if the confrontation with them were helping to loosen up the statuesque character of the oeuvre. The countless snapshots from the history of its genesis afforded by the study of the notes, drafts, fair copies, variants, galley proofs, and so on make it even plainer how Freud unremittingly pursued his travels as an investigator, thinker, and writer throughout his life.

One of the more far-reaching effects of the new edition might be to bring out for the first time the full extent of this mobility of the founder of psychoanalysis. It is precisely the revelation of the early stages of Freud's creative process that would once again focus attention on the effectiveness of the psychoanalytic method in the investigation of human subjectivity, as a method still unmatched by any other, as in the past in the context of its discovery. This might inspire today's psychoanalysts in a number of re-

[19]Translated from a transcription of Freud's letter and a copy of Bleuler's typewritten letter, for which I am indebted to Professor Manfred Bleuler.

[20]In particular, the classic work by Jean Laplanche and J.-B. Pontalis, *The Language of Psycho-Analysis* (1973).

spects, not least in regard to the *future* of their science, reinforcing their trust in the modernity of Freud's thought and in its potential for development and serving as a counterpoint to the recent crescendo of self-historicization.

As to the function of a historical-critical edition, therefore, the situation toward the end of the century would no doubt differ from that which prevailed in the 1960s, as described in part I of this book.[21] Such an edition might in those days indeed have transported the texts prematurely into the realms of classical perfection, even before they had come to be received in the German-speaking world as vital, contemporary documents, following the interruption in the history of their influence brought about by the Nazi regime. Today, by contrast, after a phase of intensive, productive discussion of the work, especially in the 1960s and 1970s, public interest in Freud, while not extinguished, has, as described in the introduction, been transposed more and more onto his person, as if people were reluctant—as a new kind of resistance—to engage in the demanding and strenuous confrontation with the texts themselves, preferring to believe that their inherent driving force toward further development was spent. By narrating the history of the genesis of the work and exposing hitherto concealed layers of meaning, the new edition could give rise to completely *new ways of reading* and inspire an approach directed toward the future, even perhaps contributing to a genuine Freud renaissance based on his oeuvre. It would not be the first time that a historical-critical edition has had a catalytic effect of this kind.

This, however, is speculation. Another, more specific effect can surely be predicted with greater certainty: if Freud's texts were to appear in a historical-critical edition in the "beloved mother tongue,"[22] this would provide a more reliable foundation for all future efforts to translate the oeuvre more appropriately into other languages.

For all the uncertainty attaching to most of the conjectures put forward in this chapter, with its prevailing hypothetical air, they nevertheless appear to justify the conclusion that it would be worthwhile to embark in the foreseeable future on preparations for a large-scale critical edition. In the words of the epigraph to this last part of the book: "An ideal, no doubt. But an ideal which can and must be realized."[23] However, is there any probability of its being achieved? It is surely more likely that it will not—because the project would literally lie athwart the current of the times.

In a nutshell, the situation is as follows. With the ending of the East-West conflict and the bankruptcy of totalitarian state socialism, the univer-

[21]See above, in chapter 3.
[22]1915*b*, p. 278.
[23]1927*a*, p. 252.

salistic ideas of the Enlightenment, to which Freud owed allegiance, have been indiscriminately discredited. The rise of a new nationalism and particularism has eroded tolerance of anything that is alien or different. Freud's image of the "citizen of the civilized world," whose passing with the barbarism of the First World War he lamented,[24] is once again hardly in vogue. Yet he himself is one of the outstanding protagonists of this precious European tradition, and his oeuvre is one of the culminating points of the German-language Enlightenment.

The charge of a "lack of affinity with the ideas of the Enlightenment"[25] has justifiably been leveled at the Germans in the past. This country in particular cannot therefore be expected to spring to the defense of that cultural heritage. Furthermore, the unification process has encouraged a mentality of drawing a line under the past; people would like to set aside the Nazi period and its consequences and move on at last to today's agenda. Even worse, the repudiation of the crimes of the Hitler regime that prevailed for decades is now manifestly no longer as unconditional as it once was. In view of the present sudden right-wing extremist regression, it must be placed on record that, as long as the *Gesammelte Werke*, which originated in London during the Second World War, remain the most comprehensive German-language edition, the author Sigmund Freud has not truly returned from exile. He once gave a young Jew the following piece of advice "as the precipitate of a long life": "Do not impose yourself on the Germans."[26] Would this still, or again, be justified today?

But the project for a new Freud edition would lie athwart the current of the times in regard to the situation of psychoanalysis as a therapeutic procedure too. Although there is today hardly any school of psychotherapy, regardless of its name, that has not appropriated Freud's discoveries and concepts, however much diluted or reinterpreted, psychoanalysis proper is often discriminated against as being too extravagant and too slow; the importance it assigns to language and internalization is held to brand it as obsolete. We may merely note in passing that this criticism, which slavishly aligns itself with our age's insistence on acceleration, seeks to divert attention from the ineluctable slow pace of the processes of psychic growth. At any rate, it is hardly likely to be possible to arouse enthusiasm in this camp for the equally extravagant and slow project of a historical-critical edition of Freud. The defiant initiative would have to come from the psychoanalytic

[24]1915*b*, p. 277.

[25]Plessner, 1959 [1935], p. 85.

[26]Letter of 4 July 1923 to Erich Leyens (1979*e*, p. 74), who had appealed to Freud when the writer Hans Blüher, although having formerly praised Freud's scientific achievement publicly, disputed the entitlement of Jews to deem themselves part of the German youth movement.

community itself, perhaps with the support of philologists and literary scholars, who in any case often have more feeling for Freud's texts than the exponents of the profession.

Does this mean that the ideal of an edition of this kind will prove to be no more feasible than that of psychoanalytic academies? After all, the epigraph mentioned above actually refers to such dedicated teaching institutions, which, as Freud demanded, were to impart to candidates everything they would subsequently really need for their complicated work, but which in the event never came into being. The question cannot be answered. But why should we not, in blithe melancholy, deem the improbable possible? As Freud once surmised in a letter to Ludwig Binswanger, he did ultimately set in train something "which will exercise people constantly," something whose loss we simply cannot afford to countenance—notwithstanding the warning about the future which he immediately added in the same letter of 28 May 1911 and which retains all its validity today: "There is in truth nothing for which man's organization qualifies him less than an occupation with psychoanalysis."[27]

Yet, besides its subject matter which provokes such resistance, Freud's seditious oeuvre also has qualities that can directly prepossess one in its favor: those of breadth and beauty. To bring out a historical-critical edition of his work would be to nurture one of the greatest exemplars of German-language prose. In an epoch that seems to be gradually distancing itself from the written mode of expression, this would at the same time constitute commendable advocacy of the unlimited and incomparable subtlety that is the hallmark of the written word.

[27]1992*a*, p. 80.

Appendix: List of Freud Titles

As stated in the introduction, this list contains in alphabetical order (disregarding only definite and indefinite articles) the titles of Freud works or editions of his letters that are mentioned in this book, sometimes without bibliographic references. The abbreviated forms occasionally used in the text are also included. The years given refer to the full Freud entries in the bibliography.

Additions to the Interpretation of Dreams	1911*a*
Address to the Members of the B'nai B'rith	1926*j*
American lectures	1910*a*
Analysis of a Phobia in a Five-Year-Old Boy	1909*b*
Analysis Terminable and Interminable	1937*c*
"Anna O." (case history by J. Breuer)	in 1895*d*
Aphasia: book/monograph/study	1891*b*
An Autobiographical Study	1925*d*
Beyond/Beyond the Pleasure Principle	1920*g*
Boyhood letter to Emil Fluss	1941*i*
Boyhood letters to Eduard Silberstein	1989*a*
Character and Anal Erotism	1908*b*
Charcot: Obituary	1893*f*
Charcot: Translation	1886*f*
"A Child is Being Beaten"	1919*e*
Child neurology: monographs/papers	1891*a*, 1893*b*, 1897*a*
A Childhood Recollection from *Dichtung und Wahrheit*	1917*b*
Chronology	1989*m*
Civilization and its Discontents	1930*a*
"Civilized" Sexual Morality and Modern Nervous Illness	1908*d*
Cocaine papers	1884*e*, 1885*a*, 1885*b*, 1885*e*, 1885*f*, 1887*d*
Constructions in Analysis	1937*d*
Contributions to the Psychology of Love	1910*h*, 1912*d*, 1918*a*
Correspondence with Karl Abraham	1965*a*
Correspondence with Lou Andreas-Salomé	1966*a*

BIBLIOGRAPHY

LIST OF ABBREVIATIONS

Collected Papers: Sigmund Freud, *Collected Papers* (5 volumes). Vols. 1, 2, 4 under the direction of Joan Riviere; vol. 3 translated and with commentaries by Alix Strachey and James Strachey; vol. 5 edited and with commentaries by James Strachey. Vol. 1: International Psychoanalytic Press, New York, London, Vienna, 1924; vols. 2–5: The Hogarth Press and The Institute of Psycho-Analysis, London 1924–50.

Erg.: Unnumbered additional volume (*Ergänzungsband*) to the *Studienausgabe: Schriften zur Behandlungstechnik*. S. Fischer Verlag, Frankfurt am Main 1975.

Gesammelte Schriften / G. S.: Sigmund Freud, *Gesammelte Schriften* (12 volumes). Vols. 1, 2, 3, 6, 9, 11 edited by Anna Freud and A. J. Storfer; vols. 4, 5, 7, 8, 10 edited by Anna Freud, Otto Rank, and A. J. Storfer; vol. 12 edited by Anna Freud and Robert Wälder. Internationaler Psychoanalytischer Verlag, Vienna 1924–34.

Gesammelte Werke / G. W.: Sigmund Freud, *Gesammelte Werke* (18 volumes and an unnumbered supplementary volume). Vols. 1–8, 10–14, 16, 17 edited by Anna Freud, Edward Bibring, Willi Hoffer, Ernst Kris, Otto Isakower; vols. 9, 15 edited by Anna Freud, Edward Bibring, Ernst Kris; vol. 18 (general index, compiled by Lilla Veszy-Wagner) edited by Anna Freud and Willi Hoffer; supplementary volume edited and with commentaries by Angela Richards with the collaboration of Ilse Grubrich-Simitis. Vols. 1–17: Imago Publishing Co., Ltd., London 1940–52 (since 1960 S. Fischer Verlag, Frankfurt am Main); vol. 18: S. Fischer Verlag, Frankfurt am Main 1968; supplementary volume: S. Fischer Verlag, Frankfurt am Main 1987.

Nachtr.: Unnumbered supplementary volume (*Nachtragsband*) to the *Gesammelte Werke: Texte aus den Jahren 1885 bis 1938*. S. Fischer Verlag, Frankfurt am Main 1987.

Standard Edition / S. E.: *The Standard Edition of the Complete Psychological Works of Sigmund Freud* (24 volumes). Vols. 1–23 edited by James Strachey in collaboration with Anna Freud, Alix Strachey, and Alan Tyson, assisted by Angela Richards; vol. 24 (Indexes and Bibliography) compiled by Angela Richards. The Hogarth Press and The Institute of Psycho-Analysis, London 1953–74.

Studienausgabe / S. A.: Sigmund Freud, *Studienausgabe* (10 volumes and an unnumbered additional volume). Vols. 1–10 edited by Alexander Mitscherlich, Angela Richards, and James Strachey; additional volume edited by Alexander

Mitscherlich, Angela Richards, James Strachey, and Ilse Grubrich-Simitis. S. Fischer Verlag, Frankfurt am Main 1969–75.

Werkausgabe: Sigmund Freud, *Werkausgabe in zwei Bänden*, edited and with commentaries by Anna Freud and Ilse Grubrich-Simitis. Vol. 1: *Elemente der Psychoanalyse*; vol. 2: *Anwendungen der Psychoanalyse*. S. Fischer Verlag, Frankfurt am Main 1978.

The italicized letters following the years in the Freud entries relate to the *Freud-Bibliographie mit Werkkonkordanz*, compiled by Ingeborg Meyer-Palmedo and Gerhard Fichtner (Frankfurt am Main: S. Fischer 1989), and its as yet unpublished continuation. All Freud works contained in the *Studienausgabe* are cited in accordance with that edition in the case of the German versions; English translations are also included, where applicable from the *Standard Edition*.

For authors other than Freud, all entries normally give the English-language reference only, where one exists, or the original-language reference where no English version has been identified.

Abraham, K. (1969, 1971) *Psychoanalytische Studien*. 2 vols. Ed. J. Cremerius. Frankfurt am Main: S. Fischer. [The contents of the volumes of Abraham's works in English do not correspond to those of the German volumes.]

Benjamin, W. (1969 [1935/36]) "The Work of Art in the Age of Mechanical Reproduction." In: *Illuminations*. Ed. H. Arendt. Trans. H. Zohn. New York: Schocken Books.

———. (1980) *Gesammelte Schriften*, werkausgabe, vol. 6. Ed. R. Tiedemann and H. Schweppenhäuser. Frankfurt am Main: Suhrkamp.

Bermann Fischer, G. (1967) *Bedroht—bewahrt. Weg eines Verlegers*. Frankfurt am Main: S. Fischer.

Bettelheim, B. (1983) *Freud and Man's Soul*. New York: Alfred A. Knopf.

Bleuler, E. (1913) "Kritik der Freudschen Theorie." *Allgemeine Zeitschrift für Psychiatrie und psychisch-gerichtliche Medizin*, vol. 70, pp. 665–718.

Bonaparte, M. (1937): see Freud, S. (1939*b*).

———. (1956) "John Rodker (1894–1955)." *Revue Française de Psychanalyse*, vol. 20, pp. 587–89.

Bourguignon, A., P. Cotet, J. Laplanche, and F. Robert (1989) *Traduire Freud*. Paris: Presses Universitaires de France.

Brandt, L. W. (1961) "Some Notes on English Freudian Terminology." *Journal of the American Psychoanalytic Association*, vol. 9, pp. 331–39.

———. (1966) "Process or Structure." *Psychoanalytic Review*, vol. 53, pp. 50–54.

Brenner, G. (1987) "Akademienprogramm—Die Lage der Editionen nach der Überleitung." In: Jaeschke, W., et al. (1987), pp. 39–49.

Brun, R. (1936) "Sigmund Freuds Leistungen auf dem Gebiete der organischen Neurologie." *Schweizer Archiv für Neurologie und Psychiatrie*, vol. 37, pp. 200–07.

Burckhardt, J. (1962 [1898]) *Griechische Kulturgeschichte* (first volume). *Gesammelte Werke*, vol. 5. Darmstadt: Wissenschaftliche Buchgesellschaft.

Coles, R. (1992) *Anna Freud: The Dream of Psychoanalysis*. Reading, Mass.: Addison-Wesley.

Derrida, J. (1980) *La carte postale: de Socrate à Freud et au-delà*. Paris: Flammarion.

Dräger, K. (1971) "Einige Bemerkungen zu den Zeitumständen und zum Schicksal der Psychoanalyse und der Psychotherapie in Deutschland zwischen 1933 und 1949." In: *Psychoanalyse in Berlin: Beiträge zur Geschichte, Theorie und Praxis.* 50-Jahr-Gedenkfeier des Berliner Psychoanalytischen Instituts (Karl Abraham-Institut). Meisenheim: Anton Hain, pp. 40–49.

Eissler, K. R. (1980) "Report on the Sigmund Freud Archives." *International Journal of Psycho-Analysis*, vol. 61, p. 104f.

Erdheim, M. (1991) "Einleitung" zu Freud, S., *Totem und Tabu*. Frankfurt am Main: Fischer Taschenbuch Verlag, pp. 7–42.

Ferenczi, S. (1920*a*) Referat über: "Dr. Julius Schaxel, *Abhandlungen zur theoretischen Biologie.*" *Internationale Zeitschrift für Psychoanalyse*, vol. 6, pp. 82–84.

———. (1920*b*) Referat über: "Lipschütz, A.: Die Pubertätsdrüse und ihre Wirkungen." *Internationale Zeitschrift für Psychoanalyse*, vol. 6, pp. 84–89.

———. (1927) "Introduction" to: Freud, S., *The Problem of Lay-Analyses*. New York: Brentano's Publisher, pp. 11–21.

———. (1927, 1938) *Bausteine der Psychoanalyse*. Vols. 1 and 2: 1927; vols. 3 and 4: 1938. Leipzig, Vienna: Internationaler Psychoanalytischer Verlag. [The contents of the volumes of Ferenczi's works in English do not correspond to those of the German volumes.]

———. (1970, 1972) *Schriften zur Psychoanalyse*. 2 vols. Ed. M. Balint. Frankfurt am Main: S. Fischer. [The contents of the volumes of Ferenczi's works in English do not correspond to those of the German volumes.]

Ferenczi, S., and O. Rank (1925) *The Development of Psycho-Analysis*, trans. Caroline Newton. New York: Nervous and Mental Diseases Series, No. 40. [Reprinted 1956 by Dover Publications, New York, in one volume with S. Ferenczi, *Sex in Psycho-Analysis*.]

Fichtner, G. (1987) "Unbekannte Arbeiten von Freud—Schätze im Keller." *Medizinhistorisches Journal*, vol. 22, pp. 246–62.

———. (1989) "Freuds Briefe als historische Quelle." *Psyche*, vol. 43, pp. 803–29.

Flaubert, G., and I. Turgenev (1985) *A Friendship in Letters: The Complete Correspondence*. Ed. and trans. B. Beaumont. London: Athlone Press.

Forrester, J. (1980) *Language and the Origins of Psychoanalysis*. London: Macmillan.

Freud, A. (1946) *The Psycho-Analytic Treatment of Children: Technical Lectures and Essays*. Parts I (1926) and II (1927) trans. N. Procter-Gregg; Part III (1945). London: Imago.

———. (1976 [1936]) *The Ego and the Mechanisms of Defense*. London: The Hogarth Press and The Institute of Psycho-Analysis.

———. (1952 [1951]) "Vorwort der Herausgeber." In: Freud, S., *Gesammelte Werke*. Vol. 1, London: Imago, pp. v–vii.

———. (1969) "Obituary James Strachey, 1887–1967." *International Journal of Psycho-Analysis*, vol. 50, p. 131f.

Freud, A., and Th. Bergmann (1972) *Kranke Kinder: Ein psychoanalytischer Beitrag zu ihrem Verständnis*. Frankfurt am Main: S. Fischer.

Freud, A., and D. Burlingham (1942) *Young Children in War-Time*. London: Allen and Unwin.

———. (1943) *Infants without Families*. London: Allen and Unwin.

Freud, E., L. Freud, and I. Grubrich-Simitis (ed.) (1978) *Sigmund Freud: His Life in Pictures and Words*. New York/London: Harcourt Brace Jovanovich.

Freud, M. (1937) Bericht über die geschäftliche Entwicklung des Internationalen Psychoanalytischen Verlags. In: *Internationale Zeitschrift für Psychoanalyse*, vol. 23, pp. 188–91.

Freud, S. (1879a) "Notiz über eine Methode zur anatomischen Präparation des Nervensystems." *Zentralblatt für die medizinischen Wissenschaften*, vol. 17, p. 468f.

———. (1884e) "Über Coca." *Zentralblatt für die gesamte Therapie*, vol. 2, pp. 289–314. [Reprint Vienna: Moritz Perles 1885, with addenda, see (1885f).]
[*Trans.*: "On Coca." In *The Cocaine Papers*. Ed. A. Donoghue and J. Hillman. Vienna and Zurich: Dunguin Press, 1963.]

———. (1885a) "Beitrag zur Kenntniss der Cocawirkung." *Wiener Medizinische Wochenschrift*, vol. 35, cols. 129–133.
[*Trans.*: "Contribution to the Knowledge of the Effect of Cocaine." In *The Cocaine Papers*. Ed. A. Donoghue and J. Hillman. Vienna and Zurich: Dunguin Press, 1963.]

———. (1885b) "Über die Allgemeinwirkung des Cocaïns." *Zeitschrift für Therapie*, vol. 3, pp. 49–51.
[*Trans.*: "On the General Effect of Cocaine." In *The Cocaine Papers*. Ed. A. Donoghue and J. Hillman. Vienna and Zurich: Dunguin Press, 1963.]

———. (1885e) "Gutachten über das Parke-Cocaïn." In: Guttmacher, H., "Über die verschiedenen Cocaïn-Präparate und deren Wirkung." *Wiener Medizinische Presse*, vol. 26, col. 1036.
[*Trans.*: "Opinion on Parke's Cocaine." In *The Cocaine Papers*. Ed. A. Donoghue and J. Hillman. Vienna and Zurich: Dunguin Press, 1963.]

———. (1885f) "Nachträge" [zur Arbeit "Über Coca"]. In: Reprint of (1884e), Vienna: Moritz Perles 1885, p. 25f.
[*Trans.*: Addenda to "Über Coca." Included in (1884e).]

———. (1886d) "Beobachtung einer hochgradigen Hemianästhesie bei einem hysterischen Manne." *G. W.*, Nachtr., pp. 54–64.
[*Trans.*: "Observation of a Severe Case of Hemi-Anesthesia in a Hysterical Male." *S. E.*, vol. 1, pp. 25–31.]

———. (1886f) Translation with Preface and Footnotes of: Charcot, J.-M., *Leçons sur les maladies du système nerveux*, vol. 3, Paris 1887, under the title *Neue Vorlesungen über die Krankheiten des Nervensystems insbesondere über Hysterie*. Leipzig and Vienna: Toeplitz & Deuticke.
[*Trans.*: Preface to the Translation of Charcot's *Lectures on the Diseases of the Nervous System*. *S. E.*, vol. 1, p. 21f. (preface only).]

———. (1887d) "Bemerkungen über Cocaïnsucht und Cocaïnfurcht, mit Beziehung auf einen Vortrag W. A. Hammonds." *Wiener Medizinische Wochenschrift*, vol. 37, cols. 929–32.
[*Trans.*: "Craving for and Fear of Cocaine." In *The Cocaine Papers*. Ed. A. Donoghue and J. Hillman. Vienna and Zurich: Dunguin Press, 1963.]

———. (1888–89a) Translation with Preface and Notes of: Bernheim, H., *De la suggestion et de ses applications à la thérapeutique*, Paris 1886, under the title *Die Suggestion und ihre Heilwirkung*. Part 1. Leipzig and Vienna: Franz Deuticke.
[*Trans.*: Preface to the Translation of Bernheim's *Suggestion*. *S. E.*, vol. 1, pp. 75–85. (Preface and one footnote only.)]

———. (1889*a*) Review of: Forel, A., *Der Hypnotismus. G. W.*, Nachtr., pp. 125–39.
[*Trans.*: Review of August Forel's *Hypnotism. S. E.*, vol. 1, pp. 91–102.]

———. (1890*a*) "Psychische Behandlung (Seelenbehandlung)." *S. A.*, Erg., pp. 13–35.
[*Trans.*: "Psychical (or Mental) Treatment." *S. E.*, vol. 7, pp. 283–302.]

———. (1891*a*) (With O. Rie) *Klinische Studie über die halbseitige Cerebrallähmung der Kinder.* Vienna: Moritz Perles (*Beiträge zur Kinderheilkunde*, Heft 3, ed. M. Kassowitz).

———. (1891*b*) *Zur Auffassung der Aphasien: Eine kritische Studie.* Vienna: Franz Deuticke. (New edition Frankfurt am Main: Fischer Taschenbuch Verlag 1992.)
[*Trans.*: *On Aphasia: A Critical Study.* Ed. E. Stengel. London: Imago Publishing Co. Ltd, 1953. Also *S. E.*, vol. 14, pp. 206–15 (part only).]

———. (1891*d*) "Hypnose." In: Bum, A. (ed.), *Therapeutisches Lexikon. G. W.*, Nachtr., pp. 141–50.
[*Trans.*: "Hypnosis." *S. E.*, vol. 1, pp. 105–14.]

———. (1892*a*) Translation of: Bernheim, H., *Hypnotisme, suggestion et psychothérapie, études nouvelles*, Paris 1891, under the title *Neue Studien über Hypnotismus, Suggestion und Psychotherapie*. Leipzig and Vienna: Deuticke.

———. (1892–94*a*) Translation with Preface and Footnotes of: Charcot, J.-M., *Leçons du mardi à la Salpêtrière (1887–8)*, Paris 1888, under the title *Poliklinische Vorträge*. Vol. 1. Leipzig, Vienna: Deuticke.
[*Trans.*: Preface and Footnotes to the Translation of Charcot's *Tuesday Lectures. S. E.*, vol. 1, pp. 133–36 (preface); pp. 137–43 (extracts from footnotes).]

———. (1893*a*) (With J. Breuer) "Über den psychischen Mechanismus hysterischer Phänomene: Vorläufige Mitteilung." *G. W.*, vol. 1, pp. 81–98.
[*Trans.*: On the Psychical Mechanism of Hysterical Phenomena: Preliminary Communication." *S. E.*, vol. 2, pp. 3–17.]

———. (1893*b*) *Zur Kenntniss der cerebralen Diplegien des Kindesalters (im Anschluss an die Little'sche Krankheit).* Vienna: Franz Deuticke (*Beiträge zur Kinderheilkunde*, ed. M. Kassowitz, N. F., Heft 3).

———. (1893*c*) "Quelques considérations pour une étude comparative des paralysies motrices organiques et hystériques." *G. W.*, vol. 1, pp. 39–55.
[*Trans.*: "Some Points for a Comparative Study of Organic and Hysterical Motor Paralyses." *S. E.*, vol. 1, pp. 160–72.]

———. (1893*f*) "Charcot †." *G. W.*, vol. 1, pp. 21–35.
[*Trans.*: "Charcot." *S. E.*, vol. 3, pp. 11–23.]

———. (1893*h*) "Über den psychischen Mechanismus hysterischer Phänomene" (Lecture). *S. A.*, vol. 6, pp. 9–24.
[*Trans.*: Lecture "On the Psychical Mechanism of Hysterical Phenomena." *S. E.*, vol. 3, pp. 27–39.

———. (1894*a*) "Die Abwehr-Neuropsychosen: Versuch einer psychologischen Theorie der acquirierten Hysterie, vieler Phobien und Zwangsvorstellungen und gewisser halluzinatorischer Psychosen." *G. W.*, vol. 1, pp. 59–74.
[*Trans.*: "The Neuro-Psychoses of Defense." *S. E.*, vol. 3, pp. 45–61.]

———. (1895*c* [1894]) "Obsessions et phobies: Leur mécanisme psychique et leur étiologie." *G. W.*, vol. 1, pp. 345–53.
[*Trans.*: "Obsessions and Phobias." *S. E.*, vol. 3, pp. 74–84.]

————. (1895d [1893–95]) (With J. Breuer) *Studien über Hysterie*. Freud's contributions in: G. W., vol. 1, pp. 75–312; Breuer's contributions in: G. W., Nachtr., pp. 217–310.
[*Trans.*: *Studies on Hysteria*. S. E., vol. 2. Including Breuer's contributions.]
————. (1896a) "L'hérédité et l'étiologie des névroses." G. W., vol. 1, pp. 407–22.
[*Trans.*: "Heredity and the Etiology of the Neuroses." S. E., vol. 3, pp. 143–56.]
————. (1896b) "Weitere Bemerkungen über die Abwehr-Neuropsychosen." G. W., vol. 1, pp. 379–403.
[*Trans.*: "Further Remarks on the Neuro-Psychoses of Defense." S. E., vol. 3, pp. 162–85.]
————. (1897a) *Die infantile Cerebrallähmung*. Teil II, Abt. II, in: Nothnagel, H. (ed.), *Specielle Pathologie und Therapie*, vol. 9. Vienna: Alfred Hölder.
————. (1897b) *Inhaltsangaben der wissenschaftlichen Arbeiten des Privatdozenten Dr. Sigm. Freud (1877–1897)*. G. W., vol. 1, pp. 461–88.
[*Trans.*: *Abstracts of the Scientific Writings of Dr. Sigm. Freud (1877–1897)*. S. E., vol. 3, pp. 227–57.]
————. (1898b) "Zum psychischen Mechanismus der Vergesslichkeit." G. W., vol. 1, pp. 519–27.
[*Trans.*: "The Psychical Mechanism of Forgetfulness." S. E., vol. 3, pp. 289–97.]
————. (1900a) *Die Traumdeutung*. S. A., vol. 2.
[*Trans.*: *The Interpretation of Dreams*. S. E., vol. 4–5.]
————. (1901a) *Über den Traum*. G. W., vol. 2/3, pp. 643–700.
[*Trans.*: *On Dreams*. S. E., vol. 5, pp. 633–86.]
————. (1901b) *Zur Psychopathologie des Alltagslebens (Über Vergessen, Versprechen, Vergreifen, Aberglaube und Irrtum)*. G. W., vol. 4.
[*Trans.*: *The Psychopathology of Everyday Life*. S. E., vol. 6.]
————. (1905c) *Der Witz und seine Beziehung zum Unbewussten*. S. A., vol. 4, pp. 9–219.
[*Trans.*: *Jokes and their Relation to the Unconscious*. S. E., vol. 8.]
————. (1905d) *Drei Abhandlungen zur Sexualtheorie*. S. A., vol. 5, pp. 37–145.
[*Trans.*: *Three Essays on the Theory of Sexuality*. S. E., vol. 7, pp. 135–243.]
————. (1905e [1901]) "Bruchstück einer Hysterie-Analyse" ['Dora']. S. A., vol. 6, pp. 83–186.
[*Trans.*: "Fragment of an Analysis of a Case of Hysteria." S. E., vol. 7, pp. 7–122.]
————. (1906b) Preface to: Freud, S., *Sammlung kleiner Schriften zur Neurosenlehre aus den Jahren 1893–1906*. G. W., vol. 1, p. 557f.
[*Trans.*: Preface to Freud's Shorter Writings 1893–1906. S. E., vol. 3, p. 5f.
————. (1907a [1906]) *Der Wahn und die Träume in W. Jensens "Gradiva."* S. A., vol. 10, pp. 9–83.
[*Trans.*: *Delusions and Dreams in Jensen's "Gradiva."* S. E., vol. 9, pp. 7–93.]
————. (1907e) "Anzeige" [der *Schriften zur angewandten Seelenkunde*]. G. W., Nachtr., p. 695f.
[*Trans.*: Prospectus for *Schriften zur angewandten Seelenkunde*. S. E., vol. 9, p. 248f.]
————. (1908b) "Charakter und Analerotik." S. A., vol. 7, pp. 23–30.
[*Trans.*: "Character and Anal Erotism." S. E., vol. 9, pp. 169–75.]
————. (1908c) "Über infantile Sexualtheorien." S. A., vol. 5, pp. 169–84.
[*Trans.*: "On the Sexual Theories of Children." S. E., vol. 9, pp. 209–26.]

————. (1908*d*) "Die 'kulturelle' Sexualmoral und die moderne Nervosität." *S. A.*, vol. 9, pp. 9–32.
[*Trans.*: " 'Civilized' Sexual Morality and Modern Nervous Illness." *S. E.*, vol. 9, pp. 181–204.]
————. (1908*e* [1907]) "Der Dichter und das Phantasieren." *S. A.*, vol. 10, pp. 169–79.
[*Trans.*: "Creative Writers and Day-Dreaming." *S. E.*, vol. 9, pp. 143–53.]
————. (1909*a* [1908]) "Allgemeines über den hysterischen Anfall." *S. A.*, vol. 6, pp. 197–203.
[*Trans.*: "Some General Remarks on Hysterical Attacks." *S. E.*, vol. 9, pp. 229–34.]
————. (1909*b*) "Analyse der Phobie eines fünfjährigen Knaben" ['Kleiner Hans']. *S. A.*, vol. 8, pp. 9–122.
[*Trans.*: "Analysis of a Phobia in a Five-Year-Old Boy" ('Little Hans'). *S. E.*, vol. 10, pp. 5–147.]
————. (1909*d*) "Bemerkungen über einen Fall von Zwangsneurose" ['Rattenmann']. *S. A.*, vol. 7, pp. 31–103.
[*Trans.*: "Notes upon a Case of Obsessional Neurosis" ('Rat Man'). *S. E.*, vol. 10, pp. 155–249.]
————. (1910*a* [1909]) *Über Psychoanalyse. G. W.*, vol. 8, pp. 1–60.
[*Trans.*: "Five Lectures on Psycho-Analysis." *S. E.*, vol. 11, pp. 7–55.]
————. (1910*c*) *Eine Kindheitserinnerung des Leonardo da Vinci. S. A.*, vol. 10, pp. 87–159.
[*Trans.*: *Leonardo da Vinci and a Memory of his Childhood. S. E.*, vol. 11, pp. 63–137.]
————. (1910*h*) "Über einen besonderen Typus der Objektwahl beim Manne" ("Beiträge zur Psychologie des Liebeslebens" I). *S. A.*, vol. 5, pp. 185–95.
[*Trans.*: "A Special Type of Choice of Object made by Men." *S. E.*, vol. 11, pp. 165–75.]
————. (1910*i*) "Die psychogene Sehstörung in psychoanalytischer Auffassung." *S. A.*, vol. 6, pp. 205–13.
[*Trans.*: "The Psycho-Analytic View of Psychogenic Disturbance of Vision." *S. E.*, vol. 11, pp. 211–18.]
————. (1910*k*) "Über 'wilde' Psychoanalyse." *S. A.*, Erg., pp. 133–41.
[*Trans.*: " 'Wild' Psycho-Analysis." *S. E.*, vol. 11, pp. 221–27.
————. (1911*a*) "Nachträge zur Traumdeutung." *G. W.*, Nachtr., pp. 604–11.
[*Trans.*: "Additions to the Interpretation of Dreams." Wholly incorporated in *The Interpretation of Dreams. S. E.*, vol. 5, pp. 360–66, 408f.]
————. (1911*b*) "Formulierungen über die zwei Prinzipien des psychischen Geschehens." *S. A.*, vol. 3, pp. 13–24.
[*Trans.*: "Formulations on the Two Principles of Mental Functioning." *S. E.*, vol. 12, pp. 218–26.]
————. (1911*c* [1910]) "Psychoanalytische Bemerkungen über einen autobiographisch beschriebenen Fall von Paranoia (Dementia paranoides)" [Schreber]. *S. A.*, vol. 7, pp. 133–200.
[*Trans.*: "Psycho-Analytic Notes on an Autobiographical Account of a Case of Paranoia (Dementia Paranoides). *S. E.*, vol. 12, pp. 9–79.]
————. (1911*e*) "Die Handhabung der Traumdeutung in der Psychoanalyse." *S. A.*, Erg., pp. 149–56.

[*Trans.*: "The Handling of Dream-Interpretation in Psycho-Analysis." *S. E.*, vol. 12, pp. 91–96.]

———. (1911*f*) " 'Gross ist die Diana der Epheser'." *G. W.*, vol. 8, pp. 360f.
[*Trans.*: " 'Great is Diana of the Ephesians.' " *S. E.*, vol. 12, pp. 342–44.]

———. (1912*b*) "Zur Dynamik der Übertragung." *S. A.*, Erg., pp. 157–68.
[*Trans.*: "The Dynamics of Transference." *S. E.*, vol. 12, pp. 99–108.]

———. (1912*c*) "Über neurotische Erkrankungstypen." *S. A.*, vol. 6, pp. 215–26.
[*Trans.*: "Types of Onset of Neurosis." *S. E.*, vol. 12, pp. 231–38.]

———. (1912*d*) "Über die allgemeinste Erniedrigung des Liebeslebens" ("Beiträge zur Psychologie des Liebeslebens" II). *S. A.*, vol. 5, pp. 197–209.
[*Trans.*: "On the Universal Tendency to Debasement in the Sphere of Love." *S. E.*, vol. 11, pp. 179–90.]

———. (1912*e*) "Ratschläge für den Arzt bei der psychoanalytischen Behandlung." *S. A.*, Erg., pp. 169–80.
[*Trans.*: "Recommendations to Physicians Practicing Psycho-Analysis." *S. E.*, vol. 12, pp. 111–20.]

———. (1912*g*) "Einige Bemerkungen über den Begriff des Unbewussten in der Psychoanalyse." *S. A.*, vol. 3, pp. 25–36.
[*Trans.*: "A Note on the Unconscious in Psycho-Analysis" (in English). *S. E.*, vol. 12, pp. 260–66.]

———. (1912–13*a*) *Totem und Tabu. S. A.*, vol. 9, pp. 287–444.
[*Trans.*: *Totem and Taboo. S. E.*, vol. 13, pp. vii, xiiif., 1–161.]

———. (1913*a*) "Ein Traum als Beweismittel." *G. W.*, vol. 10, pp. 12–22.
[*Trans.*: "An Evidential Dream." *S. E.*, vol. 12, pp. 269–77.]

———. (1913*c*) "Zur Einleitung der Behandlung" ("Weitere Ratschläge zur Technik der Psychoanalyse," I). *S. A.*, Erg., pp. 181–203.
[*Trans.*: "On Beginning the Treatment (Further Recommendations on the Technique of Psycho-Analysis, I)." *S. E.*, vol. 12, pp. 123–44.]

———. (1913*d*) "Märchenstoffe in Träumen." *G. W.*, vol. 10, pp. 2–9.
[*Trans.*: "The Occurrence in Dreams of Material from Fairy-Tales." *S. E.*, vol. 12, pp. 281–87.]

———. (1913*f*) "Das Motiv der Kästchenwahl." *S. A.*, vol. 10, pp. 181–93. Complete facsimile edition with transcription, ed. I. Grubrich-Simitis, with an afterword by H. Politzer. Frankfurt am Main: S. Fischer 1977.
[*Trans.*: "The Theme of the Three Caskets." *S. E.*, vol. 12, pp. 291–301.]

———. (1913*g*) "Zwei Kinderlügen." *S. A.*, vol. 5, pp. 229–34.
[*Trans.*: "Two Lies Told by Children." *S. E.*, vol. 12, pp. 305–09.]

———. (1913*h*) "Erfahrungen und Beispiele aus der analytischen Praxis." *G. W.*, Nachtr., pp. 614–19.
[*Trans.*: "Observations and Examples from Analytic Practice." *S. E.*, vol. 13, pp. 193–98. Also partly included in *The Interpretation of Dreams, S. E.*, vol. 4, p. 232, and *S. E.*, vol. 5, pp. 354, 356, 409f., 431.]

———. (1913*i*) "Die Disposition zur Zwangsneurose: Ein Beitrag zum Problem der Neurosenwahl." *S. A.*, vol. 7, pp. 105–17.
[*Trans.*: "The Disposition to Obsessional Neurosis." *S. E.*, vol. 12, pp. 317–26.]

———. (1914*a*) "Über fausse reconnaissance ('déjà raconté') während der psychoanalytischen Arbeit." *S. A.*, Erg., pp. 231–38.

[*Trans.*: "Fausse Reconnaissance ('déjà raconté') in Psycho-Analytic Treatment." *S. E.*, vol. 13, pp. 201–07.]

———. (1914*b*) "Der Moses des Michelangelo." *S. A.*, vol. 10, pp. 195–220.

[*Trans.*: "The Moses of Michelangelo." *S. E.*, vol. 13, pp. 211–36.]

———. (1914*c*) "Zur Einführung des Narzissmus." *S. A.*, vol. 3, pp. 37–68.

[*Trans.*: "On Narcissism: An Introduction." *S. E.*, vol. 14, pp. 73–102.]

———. (1914*d*) "Zur Geschichte der psychoanalytischen Bewegung." *G. W.*, vol. 10, pp. 43–113.

[*Trans.*: "On the History of the Psycho-Analytic Movement." *S. E.*, vol. 14, pp. 7–66.]

———. (1914*f*) "Zur Psychologie des Gymnasiasten." *S. A.*, vol. 4, pp. 235–40.

[*Trans.*: "Some Reflections on Schoolboy Psychology." *S. E.*, vol. 13, pp. 241–44.]

———. (1914*g*) "Erinnern, Wiederholen und Durcharbeiten" ("Weitere Ratschläge zur Technik der Psychoanalyse", II). *S. A.*, Erg., pp. 205–15.

[*Trans.*: "Remembering, Repeating and Working-Through (Further Recommendations on the Technique of Psycho-Analysis, II)." *S. E.*, vol. 12, pp. 147–56.]

———. (1915*a* [1914]) "Bemerkungen über die Übertragungsliebe" ("Weitere Ratschläge zur Technik der Psychoanalyse", III). *S. A.*, Erg., pp. 217–30.

[*Trans.*: "Observations on Transference-Love (Further Recommendations on the Technique of Psycho-Analysis, III)." *S. E.*, vol. 12, pp. 159–71.]

———. (1915*b*) "Zeitgemässes über Krieg und Tod." *S. A.*, vol. 9, pp. 33–60.

[*Trans.*: "Thoughts for the Times on War and Death." *S. E.*, vol. 14, pp. 275–300.]

———. (1915*c*) "Triebe und Triebschicksale." *S. A.*, vol. 3, pp. 75–102.

[*Trans.*: "Instincts and their Vicissitudes." *S. E.*, vol. 14, pp. 117–40.]

———. (1915*d*) "Die Verdrängung." *S. A.*, vol. 3, pp. 103–18.

[*Trans.*: "Repression." *S. E.*, vol. 14, pp. 146–58.]

———. (1915*e*) "Das Unbewusste." *S. A.*, vol. 3, pp. 119–62.

[*Trans.*: "The Unconscious." *S. E.*, vol. 14, pp. 166–204.]

———. (1915*g* [1914]) Letter to Dr. Frederik van Eeden. *G. W.*, Nachtr., p. 697f.

[*Trans.*: *S. E.*, vol. 14, p. 301f.]

———. (1915*i*) "Wir und der Tod." *Zweimonats-Bericht für die Mitglieder der österr. israel. Humanitätsvereine B'nai B'rith*, vol. 18, No. 1, pp. 41–51.

———. (1916*a* [1915]) "Vergänglichkeit." *S. A.*, vol. 10, pp. 223–27.

[*Trans.*: "On Transience." *S. E.*, vol. 14, pp. 305–07.]

———. (1916*d*) "Einige Charaktertypen aus der psychoanalytischen Arbeit." *S. A.*, vol. 10, pp. 229–53.

[*Trans.*: "Some Character Types Met with in Psycho-Analytic Work." *S. E.*, vol. 14, pp. 311–33.]

———. (1916–17*a* [1915–17]) *Vorlesungen zur Einführung in die Psychoanalyse.* *S. A.*, vol. 1, pp.33–445.

[*Trans.*: *Introductory Lectures on Psycho-Analysis. S. E.*, vols. 15–16.]

———. (1916–17*e*) "Über Triebumsetzungen, insbesondere der Analerotik." *S. A.*, vol. 7, pp. 123–31.

[*Trans.*: "On Transformations of Instinct as Exemplified in Anal Erotism." *S. E.*, vol. 17, pp. 127–33.]

———. (1916–17*f* [1915]) "Metapsychologische Ergänzung zur Traumlehre." *S. A.*, vol. 3, pp. 175–91.

[*Trans.*: "A Metapsychological Supplement to the Theory of Dreams." *S. E.*, vol. 14, pp. 222–35.]

———. (1916–17g [1915]) "Trauer und Melancholie." *S. A.*, vol. 3, pp. 193–212.

[*Trans.*: "Mourning and Melancholia." *S. E.*, vol. 14, pp. 243–58.]

———. (1917a [1916]) "Eine Schwierigkeit der Psychoanalyse." *G. W.*, vol. 12, pp. 3–12.

[*Trans.*: "A Difficulty in the Path of Psycho-Analysis." *S. E.*, vol. 17, pp. 137–44.]

———. (1917b) "Eine Kindheitserinnerung aus *Dichtung und Wahrheit.*" *S. A.*, vol. 10, pp. 255–66.

[*Trans.*: "A Childhood Recollection from *Dichtung und Wahrheit.*" *S. E.*, vol. 17, pp. 147–56.]

———. (1918a [1917]) "Das Tabu der Virginität" ("Beiträge zur Psychologie des Liebeslebens" III). *S. A.*, vol. 5, pp. 211–28.

[*Trans.*: "The Taboo of Virginity." *S. E.*, vol. 11, pp. 193–208.]

———. (1918b [1914]) "Aus der Geschichte einer infantilen Neurose" ['Wolfsmann']. *S. A.*, vol. 8, pp. 125–231.

[*Trans.*: "From the History of an Infantile Neurosis" ('Wolf Man'). *S. E.*, vol. 17, pp. 7–122.]

———. (1919a [1918]) "Wege der psychoanalytischen Therapie." *S. A.*, Erg., pp. 239–49.

[*Trans.*: "Lines of Advance in Psycho-Analytic Therapy." *S. E.*, vol. 17, pp. 159–68.]

———. (1919c) "Internationaler psychoanalytischer Verlag und Preiszuteilungen für psychoanalytische Arbeiten." *G. W.*, vol. 12, pp. 333–36.

[*Trans.*: "A Note on Psycho-Analytic Publications and Prizes." *S. E.*, vol. 17, pp. 267–69.]

———. (1919d) "Einleitung" zu: *Zur Psychoanalyse der Kriegsneurosen. G. W.*, vol. 12, pp. 321–24.

[*Trans.*: Introduction to *Psycho-Analysis and the War Neuroses. S. E.*, vol. 17, pp. 207–10.]

———. (1919e) " 'Ein Kind wird geschlagen': Beitrag zur Kenntnis der Entstehung sexueller Perversionen." *S. A.*, vol. 7, pp. 229–54.

[*Trans.*: " 'A Child is Being Beaten.' " *S. E.*, vol. 17, pp. 179–204.]

———. (1919h) "Das Unheimliche." *S. A.*, vol. 4, pp. 241–74.

[*Trans.*: "The 'Uncanny.' " *S. E.*, vol. 17, pp. 219–56.]

———. (1920a) "Über die Psychogenese eines Falles von weiblicher Homosexualität." *S. A.*, vol. 7, pp. 255–81.

[*Trans.*: "The Psychogenesis of a Case of Female Homosexuality." *S. E.*, vol. 18, pp. 147–72.]

———. (1920g) *Jenseits des Lustprinzips. S. A.*, vol. 3, pp. 213–72.

[*Trans.*: *Beyond the Pleasure Principle. S. E.*, vol. 18, pp. 7–64.]

———. (1921c) *Massenpsychologie und Ich-Analyse. S. A.*, vol. 9, pp. 61–134.

[*Trans.*: *Group Psychology and the Analysis of the Ego. S. E.*, vol. 18, pp. 69–143.]

———. (1922a) "Traum und Telepathie." *G. W.*, vol. 13, pp. 165–91.

[*Trans.*: "Dreams and Telepathy." *S. E.*, vol. 18, pp. 197–220.]

———. (1922b [1921]) "Über einige neurotische Mechanismen bei Eifersucht, Paranoia und Homosexualität." *S. A.*, vol. 7, pp. 217–28.

[*Trans.*: "Some Neurotic Mechanisms in Jealousy, Paranoia and Homosexuality." *S. E.*, vol. 18, pp. 223–32.]

————. (1922c) "Nachschrift zur Analyse des kleinen Hans" (1909b). S. A., vol. 8, p. 123.
[Trans.: "Postscript to the 'Analysis of a Phobia in a Five-Year-Old Boy.'" S. E., vol. 10, p. 148f.]
————. (1923b) Das Ich und das Es. S. A., vol. 3, pp. 273–325.
[Trans.: The Ego and the Id. S. E., vol. 19, pp. 12–59.]
————. (1923c [1922]) "Bemerkungen zur Theorie und Praxis der Traumdeutung." S. A., Erg., pp. 257–70.
[Trans.: "Remarks on the Theory and Practice of Dream-Interpretation." S. E., vol. 19, pp. 109–21.]
————. (1923d [1922]) "Eine Teufelsneurose im siebzehnten Jahrhundert." S. A., vol. 7, pp. 283–319.
[Trans.: "A Seventeenth-Century Demonological Neurosis." S. E., vol. 19, pp. 72–105.]
————. (1923e) "Die infantile Genitalorganisation (Eine Einschaltung in die Sexualtheorie)." S. A., vol. 5, pp. 235–41.
[Trans.: "The Infantile Genital Organization." S. E., vol. 19, pp. 141–45.]
————. (1924d) "Der Untergang des Ödipuskomplexes." S. A., vol. 5, pp. 243–51.
[Trans.: "The Dissolution of the Oedipus Complex." S. E., vol. 19, pp. 173–79.]
————. (1924e) "Der Realitätsverlust bei Neurose und Psychose." S. A., vol. 3, pp. 355–61.
[Trans.: "The Loss of Reality in Neurosis and Psychosis." S. E., vol. 19, pp. 183–87.]
————. (1924f [1923]) "Kurzer Abriss der Psychoanalyse." G. W., vol. 13, pp. 405–27.
[Trans.: "A Short Account of Psycho-Analysis." S. E., vol. 19, pp. 191–209.]
————. (1924g [1923]) Letter to Fritz Wittels (dated 18 December 1923). G. W., Nachtr., pp. 754–58 [including list of corrections (1987a)].
[Trans.: Letter to Wittels (extracts). S. E., vol. 19, pp. 286–88.]
————. (1925a [1924]) "Notiz über den 'Wunderblock.'" S. A., vol. 3, pp. 363–69.
[Trans.: "A Note upon the 'Mystic Writing-Pad.'" S. E., vol. 19, pp. 227–32.]
————. (1925d [1924]) "Selbstdarstellung." G. W., vol. 14, pp. 31–96. (Complete in: Freud, S., "Selbstdarstellung". Ed. and with an introduction by I. Grubrich-Simitis. Frankfurt am Main: Fischer Taschenbuch Verlag 1971.)
[Trans.: An Autobiographical Study. S. E., vol. 20, pp. 7–70.]
————. (1925h) "Die Verneinung." S. A., vol. 3, pp. 371–77.
[Trans.: "Negation." S. E., vol. 19, pp. 235–39.]
————. (1925i) "Einige Nachträge zum Ganzen der Traumdeutung." G. W., vol. 1, pp. 561–73.
[Trans.: "Some Additional Notes on Dream-Interpretation as a Whole." S. E., vol. 19, pp. 127–38.]
————. (1926c) Bemerkung zu E. Pickworth Farrow's "Eine Kindheitserinnerung aus dem 6. Lebensmonat." G. W., vol. 14, p. 568.
[Trans.: Prefatory Note to a Paper by E. Pickworth Farrow. S. E., vol. 20, p. 280.]
————. (1926d [1925]) Hemmung, Symptom und Angst. S. A., vol. 6, pp. 227–308.
[Trans.: Inhibitions, Symptoms and Anxiety. S. E., vol. 20, pp. 87–172.]
————. (1926e) Die Frage der Laienanalyse: Unterredungen mit einem Unparteiischen. S. A., Erg., pp. 271–341.
[Trans.: The Question of Lay Analysis. S. E., vol. 20, pp. 183–250.]

———. (1926*f*) "Psycho-Analysis: Freudian School" (Article, in English, in *Encyclopaedia Britannica*). *S. E.*, vol. 20, pp. 263–70.

———. (1926*j*) Ansprache an die Mitglieder des Vereins B'nai B'rith. *G. W.*, vol. 17, pp. 51–53.

[*Trans.*: Address to the Members of the *B'nai B'rith. S. E.*, vol. 20, p. 273f.]

———. (1927*a*) "Nachwort zur *Frage der Laienanalyse.*" *S. A.*, Erg., pp. 342–49.

[*Trans.*: "Postscript to *The Question of Lay Analysis.*" *S. E.*, vol. 20, pp. 251–58.]

———. (1927*c*) *Die Zukunft einer Illusion. S. A.*, vol. 9, pp. 135–89.

[*Trans.*: *The Future of an Illusion. S. E.*, vol. 21, pp. 5–56.]

———. (1927*d*) "Der Humor." *S. A.*, vol. 4, pp. 275–82.

[*Trans.*: "Humor." *S. E.*, vol. 21, pp. 161–66.]

———. (1927*e*) "Fetischismus." *S. A.*, vol. 3, pp. 379–88.

[*Trans.*: "Fetishism." *S. E.*, vol. 21, pp. 152–57.]

———. (1928*a*) "Ein religiöses Erlebnis." *G. W.*, vol. 14, pp. 393–96.

[*Trans.*: "A Religious Experience." *S. E.*, vol. 21, pp. 169–72.]

———. (1928*b* [1927]) "Dostojewski und die Vatertötung." *S. A.*, vol. 10, pp. 267–86.

[*Trans.*: "Dostoevsky and Parricide." *S. E.*, vol. 21, pp. 177–94.]

———. (1929*a*) "Ernest Jones zum 50. Geburtstag." *G. W.*, vol. 14, p. 554f.

[*Trans.*: "Dr. Ernest Jones (on his 50th Birthday)." *S. E.*, vol. 21, p. 249f.]

———. (1930*a* [1929]) *Das Unbehagen in der Kultur. S. A.*, vol. 9, pp. 191–270.

[*Trans.*: *Civilization and its Discontents. S. E.*, vol. 21, pp. 64–145.]

———. (1930*b*) "Vorwort" zu: *Zehn Jahre Berliner Psychoanalytisches Institut (Poliklinik und Lehranstalt).* Ed. Deutsche Psychoanalytische Gesellschaft. Leipzig, Vienna, Zurich: Internationaler Psychoanalytischer Verlag. *G. W.*, vol. 14, p. 572.

[*Trans.*: Preface to *Zehn Jahre Berliner Psychoanalytisches Institut. S. E.*, vol. 21, p. 257.]

———. (1930*c*) "Geleitwort" zu: *The Medical Review of Reviews*, vol. 36, Sonderheft "Psychopathology." *G. W.*, vol. 14, p. 570f.

[*Trans.*: Introduction to the Special Psychopathology Number of *The Medical Review of Reviews. S. E.*, vol. 21, p. 254f.]

———. (1931*a*) "Über libidinöse Typen." *S. A.*, vol. 5, pp. 267–72.

[*Trans.*: "Libidinal Types." *S. E.*, vol. 21, pp. 217–20.]

———. (1931*b*) "Über die weibliche Sexualität." *S. A.*, vol. 5, pp. 273–92.

[*Trans.*: "Female Sexuality." *S. E.*, vol. 21, pp. 225–43.]

———. (1932*b* [1931]) "Geleitwort" zu: Nunberg, H., *Allgemeine Neurosenlehre auf psychoanalytischer Grundlage.* Bern: Huber. *G. W.*, vol. 16, p. 273.

[*Trans.*: Preface to Hermann Nunberg's *Allgemeine Neurosenlehre auf psychoanalytischer Grundlage. S. E.*, vol. 21, p. 258.]

———. (1933*a* [1932]) *Neue Folge der Vorlesungen zur Einführung in die Psychoanalyse. S. A.*, vol. 1, pp. 447–608.

[*Trans.*: *New Introductory Lectures on Psycho-Analysis. S. E.*, vol. 22, pp. 5–182.]

———. (1933*b* [1932]) "Warum Krieg?" *S. A.*, vol. 9, pp. 271–86.

[*Trans.*: "Why War?" *S. E.*, vol. 22, pp. 203–15.]

———. (1933*c*) "Sándor Ferenczi †." *G. W.*, vol. 16, pp. 267–69.

[*Trans.*: "Sándor Ferenczi." *S. E.*, vol. 22, pp. 227–29.]

———. (1935a) "Nachschrift 1935" [zur 'Selbstdarstellung']. G. W., vol. 16, pp. 31–34.

[Trans.: Postscript (1935) to An Autobiographical Study. S. E., vol. 20, pp. 71–74.]

———. (1935b) "Die Feinheit einer Fehlhandlung." G. W., vol. 16, pp. 37–39.

[Trans.: "The Subtleties of a Faulty Action." S. E., vol. 22, pp. 233–35.]

———. (1935c) Thomas Mann zum 60. Geburtstag [letter, April 1935]. G. W., vol. 16, p. 249.

[Trans.: "Thomas Mann on his Sixtieth Birthday." S. E., vol. 22, p. 255.]

———. (1937a) "Lou Andreas-Salomé †." G. W., vol. 16, p. 270.

[Trans.: "Lou Andreas-Salomé." S. E., vol. 23, p. 297f.]

———. (1937b) "Moses, ein Ägypter." First essay of Der Mann Moses und die monotheistische Religion (1939a). S. A., vol. 9, pp. 459–67.

[Trans.: "Moses an Egyptian." Essay I of Moses and Monotheism (1939a). S. E., vol. 23, pp. 7–16.]

———. (1937c) "Die endliche und die unendliche Analyse." S. A., Erg., pp. 351–92.

[Trans.: "Analysis Terminable and Interminable." S. E., vol. 23, pp. 216–53.]

———. (1937d) "Konstruktionen in der Analyse." S. A., Erg., pp. 393–406.

[Trans.: "Constructions in Analysis." S. E., vol. 23, pp. 257–69.]

———. (1937e) "Wenn Moses ein Ägypter war . . . " Second essay of Der Mann Moses und die monotheistische Religion (1939a). S. A., vol. 9, pp. 468–502.

[Trans.: "If Moses was an Egyptian . . . " Essay II of Moses and Monotheism (1939a). S. E., vol. 23, pp. 17–53.]

———. (1938c) Letter to the Editor of Time and Tide [in English]. S. E., vol. 23, p. 301.]

———. (1939a [1934–38]) Der Mann Moses und die monotheistische Religion: Drei Abhandlungen. S. A., vol. 9, pp. 455–581.

[Trans.: Moses and Monotheism. S. E., vol. 23, pp. 7–137.]

———. (1939b) (With A. Freud) Translation of: Bonaparte, M., Topsy, Chow-Chow au Poil d'Or, Paris 1937, under the title Topsy. Der goldhaarige Chow. Amsterdam: Allert de Lange.

———. (1939e) "Vorbemerkung" [preliminary note on the publication of the first issue of the combined Internationale Zeitschrift für Psychoanalyse und Imago (London)]. Internationale Zeitschrift für Psychoanalyse und Imago, vol. 24, p. 1. Facsimile in: Freud, E., et al., 1978, p. 319.

———. (1940a [1938]) Abriss der Psychoanalyse. G. W., vol. 17, pp. 63–138; Nachtr., p. 749.

[Trans.: An Outline of Psycho-Analysis. S. E., vol. 23, pp. 144–207.]

———. (1940b [1938]) "Some Elementary Lessons in Psycho-Analysis." [Title in English; German text.] G. W., vol. 17, pp. 139–47.

[Trans.: "Some Elementary Lessons in Psycho-Analysis." S. E., vol. 23, pp. 281–86.]

———. (1940c [1922]) "Das Medusenhaupt." G. W., vol. 17, pp. 45–48.

[Trans.: "Medusa's Head." S. E., vol. 18, p. 273f.]

———. (1940d [1892]) (With J. Breuer) "Zur Theorie des hysterischen Anfalls." G. W., vol. 17, pp. 7–13.

[Trans.: "On the Theory of Hysterical Attacks." S. E., vol. 1, pp. 151–54.]

———. (1940e [1938]) "Die Ichspaltung im Abwehrvorgang." S. A., vol. 3, pp. 389–94.

[*Trans.*: "Splitting of the Ego in the Process of Defense." *S. E.*, vol. 23, pp. 275–78.]

———. (1941*c* [1899]) "Eine erfüllte Traumahnung." *G. W.*, vol. 17, pp. 19–23.
[*Trans.*: "A Premonitory Dream Fulfilled." *S. E.*, vol. 5, pp. 623–25.]

———. (1941*d* [1921]) "Psychoanalyse und Telepathie." *G. W.*, vol. 17, pp. 25–44.
[*Trans.*: "Psycho-Analysis and Telepathy." *S. E.*, vol. 18, pp. 177–93.]

———. (1941*f* [1938]) "Ergebnisse, Ideen, Probleme." *G. W.*, vol. 17, pp. 149–52.
[*Trans.*: "Findings, Ideas, Problems." *S. E.*, vol. 23, p. 299f.]

———. (1941*i* [1873]) "Ein Jugendbrief" [letter to Emil Fluss]. *Internationale Zeitschrift für Psychoanalyse und Imago*, vol. 26, pp. 5–8. [Also in (1969*a*).]

———. (1950*a* [1887–1902]) *Aus den Anfängen der Psychoanalyse, Briefe an Wilhelm Fliess, Abhandlungen und Notizen aus den Jahren 1887–1902*. Ed. M. Bonaparte, A. Freud, and E. Kris. London: Imago. [Includes "Entwurf einer Psychologie" of 1895.] New editions: see (1950*c*) and (1985*c*).
[*Trans.*: *The Origins of Psycho-Analysis*. (Partly, including "Project for a Scientific Psychology," in *S. E.*, vol. 1, pp. 177–387.]

———. (1950*c* [1895]) Entwurf einer Psychologie. *G. W.*, Nachtr., pp. 387–477 [here new 1987 transcription].

———. (1955*a* [1907–08]) Originalnotizen zu einem Fall von Zwangsneurose ['Rattenmann']. *G. W.*, Nachtr., pp. 509–569.
[*Trans.*: Original Record of the Case of Obsessional Neurosis (the "Rat Man"). *S. E.*, vol. 10, pp. 254f., 259–318.]

———. (1956*a* [1886]) "Bericht über meine mit Universitäts-Jubiläums-Reisestipendium unternommene Studienreise nach Paris and Berlin October 1885–Ende März 1886." *G. W.*, Nachtr., pp. 31–44.
[*Trans.*: "Report on my Studies in Paris and Berlin, on a Traveling Bursary Granted from the University Jubilee Fund, 1885–6." *S. E.*, vol. 1, pp. 5–15.]

———. (1960*a* [1873–1939]) *Briefe 1873–1939*. Ed. E. and L. Freud. Frankfurt am Main: S. Fischer. 2d, corrected and enlarged, edition 1968.
[*Trans.*: *Letters of Sigmund Freud 1873–1939*. Ed. Ernst L. Freud. Trans. T. and J. Stern. London: The Hogarth Press.]

———. (1963*a* [1909–39]) Sigmund Freud / Oskar Pfister, *Briefe 1909–1939*. Ed. E. L. Freud and H. Meng. Frankfurt am Main: S. Fischer. 2d edition 1980.
[*Trans.*: *Psycho-Analysis and Faith. The Letters of Sigmund Freud and Oskar Pfister*. Ed. H. Meng and E. L. Freud. Trans. E. Mosbacher. London: The Hogarth Press and The Institute of Psycho-Analysis 1963.]

———. (1965*a* [1907–26]) Sigmund Freud / Karl Abraham, *Briefe 1907–1926*. Ed. H. C. Abraham and E. L. Freud. Frankfurt am Main: S. Fischer. 2d, corrected, edition 1980.
[*Trans.*: *A Psycho-Analytic Dialogue: The Letters of Sigmund Freud and Karl Abraham 1907–1926*. Ed. H. C. Abraham and E. L. Freud. Trans. B. Marsh and H. C. Abraham. London: The Hogarth Press and The Institute of Psycho-Analysis 1965.]

———. (1965*b* [1919–29]) Briefe an Edward L. Bernays. In: Bernays, E. L., *Biographie einer Idee. Die Hohe Schule der PR. Lebenserinnerungen*. Düsseldorf, Vienna: Econ 1967.
[*Trans.*: Letters to Edward L. Bernays. In: Bernays, E. L., *Biography of an Idea: Memoirs of Public Relations Counsel Edward L. Bernays*, pp. 254–75. New York: Simon and Schuster 1965.]

———. (1966a [1912–36]) Sigmund Freud / Lou Andreas-Salomé, *Briefwechsel.* Ed. E. Pfeiffer. Frankfurt am Main: S. Fischer. 2d, revised, edition 1980.

[*Trans.*: Sigmund Freud and Lou Andreas-Salomé: *Letters.* Ed. E. Pfeiffer. Trans. W. and E. Robson Scott. London: The Hogarth Press and The Institute of Psycho-Analysis 1972.]

———. (1966b [1938]) Introduction to: Freud, S., and W. C. Bullitt, *Thomas Woodrow Wilson, Twenty-eighth President of the United States: A Psychological Study.* London, New York: Weidenfeld & Nicolson 1967. [German: *G. W.,* Nachtr., pp. 686–92.]

———. (1968a [1927–39]) Sigmund Freud / Arnold Zweig, *Briefwechsel.* Ed. E. L. Freud. Frankfurt am Main: S. Fischer. 3d edition 1980.

[*Trans.*: *The Letters of Sigmund Freud and Arnold Zweig.* Ed. E. L. Freud. Trans. W. and E. Robson Scott. New York: New York University Press 1970.]

———. (1969a [1872–74]) Sieben Briefe und zwei Postkarten an Emil Fluss. Reprinted in: Freud, S., *"Selbstdarstellung;" Schriften zur Geschichte der Psychoanalyse.* Ed. and with an introduction by I. Grubrich-Simitis. Frankfurt am Main: Fischer Taschenbuch Verlag 1971, pp. 107–23. [Includes (1941i).]

[*Trans.*: Seven Letters and two Postcards to Emil Fluss. In "Some Early Unpublished Letters of Freud." *International Journal of Psycho-Analysis,* vol. 50, p. 419ff.]

———. (1970a [1919–36]) Sigmund Freud / Edoardo Weiss, *Briefe zur psychoanalytischen Praxis.* Ed. M. Grotjahn. Frankfurt am Main: S. Fischer 1973, pp. 38–92.

———. (1970b [1917–34]) Briefe an Georg Groddeck. In: Groddeck, G., *Der Mensch und sein Es.* Ed. M. Honegger. Wiesbaden: Limes. (Reprinted in: S. Freud / G. Groddeck, *Briefe über das Es.* Ed. M. Honegger. Frankfurt am Main: Fischer Taschenbuch Verlag 1988, pp. 7–92.)

———. (1971a [1909–16]) Letters to James Jackson Putnam. In: Hale, N. G., Jr. (ed.), *James Jackson Putnam and Psychoanalysis: Letters between Putnam and Sigmund Freud, Ernest Jones, William James, Sándor Ferenczi, and Morton Prince, 1877–1917.* Cambridge: Harvard University Press, pp. 351–79.

———. (1974a [1906–13]) Sigmund Freud / C. G. Jung, *Briefwechsel.* Ed. W. McGuire and W. Sauerländer. Frankfurt am Main: S. Fischer.

[*Trans.*: *The Freud / Jung Letters: The Correspondence between Sigmund Freud and C. G. Jung.* Ed. W. McGuire. Trans. R. Manheim and R. F. C. Hull. Princeton: Princeton University Press 1974.]

———. (1976m [1929–39]) "Kürzeste Chronik" [part facsimile, part reproduction]. In: Freud, E., et al. (1976), pp. 270, 281, 288, 336, 337. [Complete in: *The Diary of Sigmund Freud 1929–1939: A Record of the Final Decade.* Translated and with a commentary and introduction by M. Molnar. London: The Hogarth Press 1992, pp. 266–70. All facsimiles between pages 3 and 40.]

———. (1979e [1923, 1936]) Postcard and two letters to Erich Leyens. In: Grubel, F., "Zeitgenosse Sigmund Freud." *Jahrbuch der Psychoanalyse,* vol. 11, pp. 73–80; the actual documents are on p. 74f.

———. (1979j [1934]) "Der Mann Moses: Ein historischer Roman" [First version of (1939a)]. Introductory passage in: Bori, P. C., "Una pagina inedita di Freud [etc.]," *Rivista di storia contemporanea,* vol. 8, p. 7f.

———. (1983a [1921–39]) Letters and postcards to Smith Ely Jelliffe. In: Burnham, J. C., *Jelliffe: American Psychoanalyst and Physician.* Part 2: *Jelliffe's Correspon-*

dence with Sigmund Freud and C. G. Jung. Ed. W. McGuire. Chicago and London: University of Chicago Press, pp. 206–79.

———. (1983g [undated]) "Kritische Einleitung in die Nervenpathologie" [manuscript]. Partial reproductions and facsimile of a drawing in: J. A. *Stargardt Katalog 628*, No. 485.

———. (1985a [1915]) "Übersicht der Übertragungsneurosen." In: Freud, S., *Übersicht der Übertragungsneurosen: Ein bisher unbekanntes Manuskript.* Edited and with an essay by I. Grubrich-Simitis. Frankfurt am Main: S. Fischer.
[*Trans.*: *A Phylogenetic Fantasy: Overview of the Transference Neuroses.* Edited and with an essay by I. Grubrich-Simitis. Trans. A. Hoffer and P. T. Hoffer. Cambridge and London: Harvard University Press 1987.]

———. (1985c [1887–1904]) *Briefe an Wilhelm Fliess 1887–1904.* Ungekürzte Ausgabe. (Edition first published in English translation.) Ed. J. M. Masson. German version (1986) coedited by M. Schröter, transcribed G. Fichtner. Frankfurt am Main: S. Fischer.
[*Trans.*: *The Complete Letters of Sigmund Freud to Wilhelm Fliess 1887–1904.* Trans. and ed. J. M. Masson. Cambridge: Belknap Press of Harvard University Press 1985.]

———. (1987a [1923]) List of corrections accompanying the letter to Fritz Wittels of 18 December 1923. [Letter itself under (1924g).] G. W., Nachtr., pp. 756–58.

———. (1987c [1908–38]) Briefe an Stefan Zweig. In: Zweig, S., *Briefwechsel mit Hermann Bahr, Sigmund Freud, Rainer Maria Rilke und Arthur Schnitzler.* Ed. J. B. Berlin, H.-U. Lindken and D. A. Prater. Frankfurt am Main: S. Fischer, pp. 163–221.

———. (1988g [1929–37]) Four letters to Thomas Mann. In: Mann, T., *Briefwechsel mit Autoren.* Ed. H. Wysling. Frankfurt am Main: S. Fischer, pp. 183f., 186–91.

———. (1989a [1871–81, 1910]) *Jugendbriefe an Eduard Silberstein 1871–1881.* Ed. W. Boehlich. Frankfurt am Main: S. Fischer.
[*Trans.*: *The Letters of Sigmund Freud to Eduard Silberstein 1871–1881.* Ed. W. Boehlich. Trans. A. J. Pomerans. Cambridge and London: Harvard University Press, 1990.]

———. (1989f [after 1902]) "Meine individuelle Traumcharakteristik (Typische Träume)" [manuscript]. Part facsimile and part reproduction in: *Christie, Manson & Woods Cat.* 21 June 1989, No. 132.

———. (1989m [year not stated]) "Chronologie" [chronology of publications]. Facsimiles of the first two pages in: Grubrich-Simitis, I., (1989), p. 776f.

———. (1990q [1938]) Will of 28 July 1938. In: Roazen, P., "Freud's Last Will," *Journal of the American Academy of Psychoanalysis,* vol. 18, pp. 386–91.

———. (1992a [1908–38]) Sigmund Freud / Ludwig Binswanger, *Briefwechsel 1908–1938.* Ed. G. Fichtner. Frankfurt am Main: S. Fischer.

———. (1992g [1908–14]) Sigmund Freud / Sándor Ferenczi, *Briefwechsel,* vol. I/1 1908–1911, vol. I/2 1912–1914. Ed. E. Brabant, E. Falzeder, and P. Giampieri-Deutsch. Vienna, Cologne, Weimar: Böhlau Verlag 1993. Letters first published in French by Calmann-Lévy, Paris, in 1992.
[*Trans.*: *The Correspondence of Sigmund Freud and Sándor Ferenczi,* vol. I, 1908–1914. Cambridge and London: Harvard University Press 1993.]

———. (1993e) *The Complete Correspondence of Sigmund Freud and Ernest Jones,*

1908-1939. Ed. R. A. Paskauskas. Introduction by R. Steiner. Cambridge and London: Harvard University Press 1993.

Freud anthologies:

———. (1906) *Sammlung kleiner Schriften zur Neurosenlehre aus den Jahren 1893-1906.* Vienna, Leipzig: Deuticke.

———. (1909) *Sammlung kleiner Schriften zur Neurosenlehre.* Zweite Folge [2d series]. Vienna, Leipzig: Deuticke.

———. (1913) *Sammlung kleiner Schriften zur Neurosenlehre.* Dritte Folge [3d series]. Vienna, Leipzig: Deuticke.

———. (1918) *Sammlung kleiner Schriften zur Neurosenlehre.* Vierte Folge [4th series]. Leipzig, Vienna: Heller.

———. (1922) *Sammlung kleiner Schriften zur Neurosenlehre.* Fünfte Folge [5th series]. Leipzig, Vienna, Zurich: Internationaler Psychoanalytischer Verlag.

———. (1924) *Psychoanalytische Studien an Werken der Dichtung und Kunst.* Vienna, Leipzig: Internationaler Psychoanalytischer Verlag.

———. (1924) *Zur Technik der Psychoanalyse und zur Metapsychologie.* Vienna, Leipzig: Internationaler Psychoanalytischer Verlag.

———. (1925) *Kleine Beiträge zur Traumlehre.* Vienna, Leipzig: Internationaler Psychoanalytischer Verlag.

———. (1926) *Studien zur Psychoanalyse der Neurosen aus den Jahren 1913-1925.* Vienna, Leipzig: Internationaler Psychoanalytischer Verlag.

———. (1931) *Schriften zur Neurosenlehre und zur psychoanalytischen Technik (1913-1926).* Vienna, Leipzig: Internationaler Psychoanalytischer Verlag.

———. (1931) *Kleine Schriften zur Sexualtheorie und zur Traumlehre.* Vienna, Leipzig: Internationaler Psychoanalytischer Verlag.

———. (1931) *Theoretische Schriften (1911-1925).* Vienna, Leipzig: Internationaler Psychoanalytischer Verlag.

———. (1932) *Vier psychoanalytische Krankengeschichten.* Vienna, Leipzig: Internationaler Psychoanalytischer Verlag.

Gardiner, M. (ed.) (1971) *The Wolf-Man.* New York: Basic Books.

———. (1983) *Code Name "Mary": Memoirs of an American Woman in the Austrian Underground.* New Haven and London: Yale University Press.

Gathelier, F.-M. (1991) "Die Veröffentlichung von Freuds 'Gesammelten Werken' in französischer Sprache: Gespräch mit Jean Laplanche." *Psyche,* vol. 45, pp. 700-12.

Gay, P. (1988) *Freud: A Life for Our Time.* New York, London: W. W. Norton.

Geiger, L. (1869) *Der Ursprung der Sprache.* Stuttgart: Cotta'sche Buchhandlung.

Gilman, S. L. (1991) "Reading Freud in English: Problems, Paradoxes, and a Solution." *International Review of Psycho-Analysis,* vol. 18, pp. 331-44.

Gressmann, H. (1913) *Mose und seine Zeit: Ein Kommentar zu den Mose-Sagen.* Göttingen: Vandenhoeck & Ruprecht.

Grubrich-Simitis, I. (1971) "Sigmund Freuds Lebensgeschichte und die Anfänge der Psychoanalyse." *Neue Rundschau,* vol. 82, pp. 311-33.

———. (1977) "Notizen zum Manuskript." In: Freud, S., *Das Motiv der Kästchenwahl.* Facsimile edition 1977, Frankfurt am Main: S. Fischer, pp. 39-46.

———. (1978): see Freud, E., L. Freud, and I. Grubrich-Simitis (ed.) (1978).

———. (1981) "Extreme Traumatization as Cumulative Trauma; Psychoanalytic Investigations of the Effects of Concentration Camp Experiences on Survivors and Their Children." In: *The Psychoanalytic Study of the Child*, vol. 36, pp. 415–50.

———. (1986*a*) "Reflections on Sigmund Freud's Relationship to the German Language and to Some German-Speaking Authors of the Enlightenment." *International Journal of Psycho-Analysis*, vol. 67, pp. 287–94.

———. (1986*b*) "Six Letters of Sigmund Freud and Sándor Ferenczi on the Interrelationship of Psychoanalytic Theory and Technique." *International Review of Psycho-Analysis*, vol. 13, part 3, pp. 259–77.

———. (1987*a*) "Metapsychology and Metabiology." In: Freud, S. (1985*a*), English edition pp. 73–107.

———. (1987*b*) "Introduction" to: Freud, S., *Gesammelte Werke*. Nachtragsband. Frankfurt am Main: S. Fischer, pp. 15–28.

———. (1988) "Trauma or Drive—Drive and Trauma; A Reading of Sigmund Freud's Phylogenetic Fantasy of 1915." In: *The Psychoanalytic Study of the Child*, vol. 43, pp. 3–32.

———. (1989) "Zur Geschichte der deutschsprachigen Freud-Ausgaben." *Psyche*, vol. 43, pp. 773–802 and 889–917.

———. (1991) *Freuds Moses-Studie als Tagtraum: Ein biographischer Essay*. Die Sigmund-Freud-Vorlesungen, vol. 3. Weinheim: Verlag Internationale Psychoanalyse. Revised edition 1994, Frankfurt am Main: Fischer Taschenbuch Verlag.

———. (1995) " 'No Greater, Richer, More Mysterious Subject [. . .] than the Life of the Mind.' An Early Exchange of Letters between Freud and Einstein." *International Journal of Psycho-Analysis*, vol. 76, part 1, pp. 115–22.

Grunberger, B. (1980) "From the 'Active Technique' to the 'Confusion of Tongues:' On Ferenczi's Deviation." In: *Psychoanalysis in France*, ed. S. Lebovici and D. Widlöcher, pp. 127–52. New York: International Universities Press.

Habermas, J. (1987) *Knowledge and Human Interests*. Trans. J. J. Shapiro. Cambridge and Oxford: Polity Press and Blackwell Publishers.

Hall, M. G. (1988) "The Fate of the Internationaler Psychoanalytischer Verlag." In: Timms, E., and N. Segal (ed.), *Freud in Exile*. New Haven and London: Yale University Press, pp. 90–105.

Husserl, E. (1984 [1906]) Personal notes from 25 September 1906, reproduced as Beilage B IX (pp. 442–47) in: Husserl, E., *Einleitung in die Logik und Erkenntnistheorie: Vorlesungen 1906/07* (Ges. W., vol. XXIV). Ed. U. Melle. Dordrecht/Boston/Lancaster: Martinus Nijhoff.

IJsseling, S. (1987) "Das Husserl-Archiv in Leuven und die Husserl-Ausgabe." In: Jaeschke, W., et al. (1987), pp. 137–46.

Jacobs, W. G. (1987) "Textüberlieferung und historisch-kritische Edition—Typen von Editionen." In: Jaeschke, W., et al. (1987), pp. 21–26.

Jaeschke, W., W. G. Jacobs, H. Krings, and H. Schepers (ed.) (1987) *Buchstabe und Geist: Zur Überlieferung und Edition philosophischer Texte*. Hamburg: Felix Meiner.

Jelliffe, S. E. (1937) "Sigmund Freud as a Neurologist." *Journal of Nervous and Mental Disease*, vol. 85, pp. 696–711.

Jensen, W. (1903) *Gradiva: Ein pompejanisches Phantasiestück*. Dresden and Leipzig: Carl Reissner.

Jones, E. (1950 [1947]) "Foreword" to: Freud, S., *The Question of Lay Analysis: An Introduction to Psychoanalysis*. New York: Norton 1950, p. 5f.

————. (1953) *Sigmund Freud: Life and Work*, vol. I. London: The Hogarth Press.

————. (1955) *Sigmund Freud: Life and Work*, vol. II. London: The Hogarth Press.

————. (1957) *Sigmund Freud: Life and Work*, vol. III. London: The Hogarth Press.

Kittler, W., and G. Neumann (1982) "Kafkas 'Drucke zu Lebzeiten'—Editorische Technik und hermeneutische Entscheidung." *Freiburger Universitätsblätter*, Heft 78, pp. 45–84.

Kroeber, A. L. (1920) "Totem and Taboo: An Ethnologic Psychoanalysis." *American Anthropologist*, vol. 22, pp. 48–55.

Laplanche, J., and J.-B. Pontalis (1973) *The Language of Psycho-Analysis*. Trans. D. Nicholson-Smith. London: The Hogarth Press. (Original: *Vocabulaire de la psychanalyse*. Paris: Presses Universitaires de France 1967.)

Leupold-Löwenthal, H. (1988) "Die Vertreibung der Familie Freud 1938." *Sigmund Freud House Bulletin*, vol. 12, pp. 1–11.

Leuschner, W. (1992) "Einleitung" zu Freud, S., *Zur Auffassung der Aphasien*. Frankfurt am Main: Fischer Taschenbuch Verlag, pp. 7–31.

Levine, I. (1923) *The Unconscious: An Introduction to Freudian Psychology*. London: L. Parsons. (German translation by Anna Freud entitled *Das Unbewusste*: Internationaler Psychoanalytischer Verlag, 1926.)

Lévi-Strauss, C., and Eribon, D. (1988) *De près et de loin*. Paris: Editions Odile Jacob.

Lloyd, W. W. (1863) *The Moses of Michael Angelo: A Study of Art, History and Legend*. London: Williams & N.

Lorenzer, A. (1984) *Intimität und soziales Leid: Archäologie der Psychoanalyse*. Frankfurt am Main: S. Fischer.

————. (1986) Review of Freud, S. (1985a). *Psyche*, vol. 40, pp. 1163–66.

Mahony, P. J. (1982) *Freud as a Writer*. New York: International Universities Press.

————. (1987) *Freud as a Writer*. Expanded edition. New Haven and London: Yale University Press.

Mann, T. (1936) "Freud and the Future." In: Mann, T., *Essays of Three Decades*. Trans. H. T. Lowe-Porter. New York: Alfred A. Knopf 1976.

————. (1978) *Tagebücher 1935–1936*. Ed. P. de Mendelssohn. Frankfurt am Main: S. Fischer.

Martens, G. (1971) "Textdynamik und Edition: Überlegungen zur Bedeutung und Darstellung variierender Textstufen." In: Martens, G., and H. Zeller (1971), pp. 165–201.

Martens, G., and H. Zeller (ed.) (1971) *Texte und Varianten: Probleme ihrer Edition und Interpretation*. Munich: C. H. Beck'sche Verlagsbuchhandlung.

Martin, E. D. (1920) *The Behaviour of Crowds*. New York: Harper.

Masson, J. M. (1984) *The Assault on Truth: Freud's Suppression of the Seduction Theory*. New York: Farrar, Straus and Giroux.

May-Tolzmann, U. (1991) "Zu den Anfängen des Narzissmus: Ellis—Näcke—Sadger—Freud." *Luzifer-Amor*, vol. 4, Heft 8, pp. 50–88.

McGuire, W. (1974) Introduction to: Freud, S. (1974a), pp. xiii–xxxvii [in the English edition].

Meyer-Palmedo, I. (ed.) (1975) *Sigmund Freud-Konkordanz und-Gesamtbibliographie*. Frankfurt am Main: S. Fischer. [For enlarged and revised new edition see Meyer-Palmedo, I., and G. Fichtner (1989).]

Meyer-Palmedo, I., and G. Fichtner (ed.) (1989) *Freud-Bibliographie mit Werk-*

konkordanz. Frankfurt am Main: S. Fischer. (Ongoing continuation as yet unpublished.)

Mitscherlich, A. (1954) "50 Jahre später. Einige Empfehlungen an den Leser." Foreword to paperback: Freud, S., *Zur Psychopathologie des Alltagslebens*. Frankfurt am Main: Fischer Bücherei, pp. 6–12.

———. (1960) "Nachwort" to large-format paperback edition of: Freud, S., *Das Unbewusste: Schriften zur Psychoanalyse*. Ed. A. Mitscherlich. Frankfurt am Main: S. Fischer, pp. 443–60.

———. (1961) "Nachwort. Freuds Sexualtheorie und die notwendige Aufklärung der Erwachsenen." In: Freud, S., *Drei Abhandlungen zur Sexualtheorie: Und verwandte Schriften*. Selection and afterword by A. Mitscherlich. Frankfurt am Main: Fischer Taschenbuch Verlag, pp. 191–201.

———. (1969) "Über mögliche Missverständnisse bei der Lektüre der Werke Sigmund Freuds." Introduction to: Freud, S., *Studienausgabe*. Vol. 1, pp. 19–25.

Mitscherlich, A., and F. Mielke (ed.) (1962) *The Death Doctors*. Trans. J. Cleugh. London: Elek Books. [Original German edition: *Medizin ohne Menschlichkeit*. Frankfurt am Main: Fischer Bücherei, 1960.]

Mitscherlich, A., and M. Mitscherlich (1975) *The Inability to Mourn: Principles of Collective Behavior*. Trans. B. R. Placzek; preface by Robert Jay Lifton. New York: Grove Press. [Original German edition: *Die Unfähigkeit zu trauern: Grundlagen kollektiven Verhaltens*. Munich: Piper.

Montinari, M. (1980) "Vorwort" in: Nietzsche, F., *Sämtliche Werke: Kritische Studienausgabe in 15 Bänden*. Ed. Montinari, M., and G. Colli. Munich, Berlin, New York: Deutscher Taschenbuch Verlag/Walter de Gruyter, vol. 14, pp. 7–17.

Muschg, W. (1975 [1930]) *Freud als Schriftsteller*. Munich: Kindler Taschenbücher.

Nitzschke, B. (1991) "Freuds Vortrag vor dem Israelitischen Humanitätsverein 'Wien' des Ordens B'nai B'rith: Wir und der Tod (1915)." *Psyche*, vol. 45, pp. 97–131.

Nunberg, H., and E. Federn (ed.) (1962, 1967, 1974, 1975) *Minutes of the Vienna Psychoanalytic Society*. Trans. M. Nunberg. 4 volumes. New York: International Universities Press.

Ornston, D. (1982) "Strachey's Influence: A Preliminary Report." *International Journal of Psycho-Analysis*, vol. 63, pp. 409–26.

Ornston, D. (ed.) (1992) *Translating Freud*. New Haven and London: Yale University Press.

Plessner, H. (1959 [1935]) *Die verspätete Nation*. In: idem, *Gesammelte Schriften*. Frankfurt am Main: Suhrkamp, vol. 6 (1982).

Pöggeler, O. (1987) "Die historisch-kritische Edition in der Wissenschaftsorganisation." In: Jaeschke, W., et al. (1987), pp. 27–37.

Ponge, F. (1942) *Le parti pris des choses*. Paris: Gallimard.

Rank, O. (1914) *The Myth of the Birth of the Hero: A Psychological Interpretation of Mythology*. Trans. F. Robbins and Smith Ely Jelliffe. Nervous and Mental Diseases Monograph Series No. 18. New York: Journal of Nervous and Mental Disease Publishing Co. [Original German-language edition: *Der Mythus von der Geburt des Helden: Versuch einer psychoanalytischen Mythendeutung*. Leipzig, Vienna : Deuticke, 1909.]

———. (1927) *Grundzüge einer genetischen Psychologie auf Grund der Psycho-*

analyse der Ichstruktur I. Leipzig, Vienna: Deuticke. [English abstract: "The Main Features of a Genetic Psychology (on a Basis of Psychoanalysis of the Ego Structure) Part I." *Archives of Psychoanalysis,* vol. I, part IV, July 1927. Stamford, Conn.: Psychoanalytic Institute.]

————. (1929) *The Trauma of Birth.* London: Paul, Trench, and Trübner. [Original German-language edition: *Das Trauma der Geburt und seine Bedeutung für die Psychoanalyse.* Leipzig, Vienna, Zurich: Internationaler Psychoanalytischer Verlag, 1924.]

Reichmayr, J. (1990) *Spurensuche in der Geschichte der Psychoanalyse.* Frankfurt am Main: Nexus.

Reik, T. (1949) *The Inner Experience of a Psychoanalyst.* London: Allen and Unwin.

————. (1956) *The Search Within.* New York: Grove Press.

Richards, A. (1969) "Erläuterungen zur Edition." In: Freud, S., *Studienausgabe.* vol. 1, pp. 27–32.

Roazen, P., and B. Swerdloff (ed.) (1995) *Heresy: Sandor Rado and the Psychoanalytic Movement.* Northvale, London: Jason Aronson.

Sattler, D. E. (1984) Introduction to vol. 4 (Oden I, ed. D. E. Sattler and M. Knaupp) of: Hölderlin, F., *Sämtliche Werke.* Ed. Sattler, D. E., and W. Groddeck. Frankfurt am Main: Roter Stern.

Saussure, F. de (1955 [1916]) *Cours de linguistique générale.* Ed. Bally, Ch., and A. Sechehaye. Paris: Payot.

Scheibe, S. (1971) "Zu einigen Grundprinzipien einer historisch-kritischen Ausgabe." In: Martens, G., and H. Zeller (1971), pp. 1–44.

Schepers, H. (1987) "Die Leibniz-Ausgabe." In: Jaeschke, W., et al. (1987), pp. 71–81.

Schönau, W. (1968) *Sigmund Freuds Prosa: Literarische Elemente seines Stils.* Stuttgart: J. B. Metzlersche Verlagsbuchhandlung.

Schott, H. G. (1981) "'Traumdeutung' und 'Infantile Cerebrallähmung': Überlegungen zu Freuds Theoriebildung." *Psyche,* vol. 35, pp. 97–110.

Schur, M. (1972) *Sigmund Freud: Living and Dying.* New York: International Universities Press.

Singer, W. (1990a) "Das Jahrzehnt des Gehirns." *Frankfurter Allgemeine Zeitung.* Heading 'Natur und Wissenschaft,' 27 December 1990, p. N1.

————. (1990b) "Hirnentwicklung und Umwelt." In: Singer, W. (ed.), *Gehirn und Kognition: Spektrum der Wissenschaft.* Heidelberg: Spektrum der Wissenschaft Verlagsges. m.b.H., pp. 50–65.

Solms, M. (1991) "An Introduction to the Neuroscientific Works of Sigmund Freud." Lecture delivered at the Centro Milanese di Psicoanalisi. (Manuscript.)

Solms, M., and M. Saling (1986) "On Psychoanalysis and Neuroscience: Freud's Attitude to the Localizationist Tradition." *International Journal of Psycho-Analysis,* vol. 67, pp. 397–416.

Spehlmann, R. (1953) *Sigmund Freuds neurologische Schriften: Eine Untersuchung zur Vorgeschichte der Psychoanalyse.* Berlin, Göttingen, Heidelberg: Springer.

Starobinski, J. (1974) "La littérature; Le texte et l'interprète." In: *Faire de l'histoire: Nouvelles approches.* Ed. J. Le Goff and P. Nora. Paris: Gallimard, pp. 168–82.

Steiner, R. (1991) "'To Explain our Point of View to English Readers in English Words.'" *International Review of Psycho-Analysis,* vol. 18, pp. 351–92.

Strachey, J. (1957) Editor's Note on Freud, S., "Footnote on Ewald Hering." In: *S. E.*, vol. 14, p. 205.

———. (1961*a*) Editor's footnote on Freud, S. (1932*b*). In: *S. E.*, vol. 21, p. 258, note 2.

———. (1961*b*) Editor's footnote on Freud, S. (1924*d*). In: *S. E.*, vol. 19, p. 173.

———. (1962) "Editor's Note" on Freud, S. (1895*c*). In: *S. E.*, vol. 3, pp. 71–73.

———. (1964*a*) "Editor's Note" on Freud, S. (1933*b*). In: *S. E.*, vol. 22, p. 197f.

———. (1964*b*) "Editor's Note" on Freud, S. (1940*a*). In: *S. E.*, vol. 23, pp. 141–43.

———. (1966*a*) "General Preface." *S. E.*, vol. 1, pp. xiii–xxii.

———. (1966*b*) Editor's footnote on the Letter to Wilhelm Fliess of 19 February 1899. In: *S. E.*, vol. 1, p. 278, note 5.

———. (1972) "Editor's Introduction" [to *The Interpretation of Dreams*]. In: *S. E.*, vol. 4, pp. xi–xx.)

Strachey, J., and A. Strachey (1986) *Bloomsbury / Freud: The Letters of James and Alix Strachey 1924–1925*. Ed. P. Meisel and W. Kendrick. London: Chatto & Windus.

Sylvester, D. (1985) *Interviews with Francis Bacon 1962–1979*. New and enlarged edition. London: Thames and Hudson.

Tyson, A., and J. Strachey (1956) "A Chronological Hand-List of Freud's Works." *International Journal of Psycho-Analysis*, vol. 37, pp. 19–33.

Vogel, P. (1953) "Eine erste, unbekannt gebliebene Darstellung der Hysterie von Sigmund Freud." *Psyche*, vol. 7, pp. 481–85.

———. (1954) "Zur Aphasielehre Sigmund Freuds." *Monatsschrift für Psychiatrie und Neurologie*, vol. 128, pp. 256–64.

Wagner, K. (1990) "Musil im Computer: Der ganze Dichter auf Diskette—Abschluss eines deutsch-österreichischen Modellprojekts." *Frankfurter Allgemeine Zeitung*, 15 June 1990.

Wallace, E. R. (1983) *Freud and Anthropology: A History and Reappraisal*. New York: International Universities Press.

Wilson, E. (1987) "Did Strachey Invent Freud?" *International Review of Psycho-Analysis*, vol. 14, pp. 299–315.

Winnicott, D. W. (1960) "Ego Distortion in Terms of True and False Self." In: idem, *The Maturational Processes and the Facilitating Environment: Studies in the Theory of Emotional Development*. London: The Hogarth Press 1972, pp. 140–52.

———. (1967) *Playing and Reality*. London: Tavistock Publications.

Wittels, F. (1924) *Sigmund Freud: Der Mann, die Lehre, die Schule*. Leipzig, Vienna, Zurich: Internationaler Psychoanalytischer Verlag.

Woesler, W. (ed.) (1987ff.) *editio. Internationales Jahrbuch für Editionswissenschaft*. Tübingen: Max Niemeyer.

Young-Bruehl, E. (1988) *Anna Freud: A Biography*. New York: Summit Books.

NAME INDEX

The index contains the names of persons and of figures from literature and mythology, as well as of institutions; patients' names or pseudonyms are included only for the principal case histories.

INDEX OF FREUD'S WRITINGS

The index contains the page references to Freud's published writings as well as to anthologies of his works selected by himself or under his supervision. Included also are major German and English editions of his works. The alphabetical order disregards definite and indefinite pronouns.